Explorations in Post-Secular Metaphysics

Explorations in
Post-Secular Metaphysics

Josef Bengtson
University of Southern Denmark

palgrave
macmillan

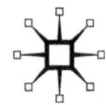

© Josef Bengtson 2016

All rights reserved. No reproduction, copy or transmission of this publication may be made without written permission.

No portion of this publication may be reproduced, copied or transmitted save with written permission or in accordance with the provisions of the Copyright, Designs and Patents Act 1988, or under the terms of any licence permitting limited copying issued by the Copyright Licensing Agency, Saffron House, 6–10 Kirby Street, London EC1N 8TS.

Any person who does any unauthorized act in relation to this publication may be liable to criminal prosecution and civil claims for damages.

The author has asserted his right to be identified as the author of this work in accordance with the Copyright, Designs and Patents Act 1988.

First published 2016 by
PALGRAVE MACMILLAN

Palgrave Macmillan in the UK is an imprint of Macmillan Publishers Limited, registered in England, company number 785998, of Houndmills, Basingstoke, Hampshire RG21 6XS.

Palgrave Macmillan in the US is a division of St Martin's Press LLC,
175 Fifth Avenue, New York, NY 10010.

Palgrave Macmillan is the global academic imprint of the above companies and has companies and representatives throughout the world.

Palgrave® and Macmillan® are registered trademarks in the United States, the United Kingdom, Europe and other countries.

ISBN: 978–1–137–55335–5

This book is printed on paper suitable for recycling and made from fully managed and sustained forest sources. Logging, pulping and manufacturing processes are expected to conform to the environmental regulations of the country of origin.

A catalogue record for this book is available from the British Library.

A catalog record for this book is available from the Library of Congress.

Contents

Preface   vi

Acknowledgments   viii

1 Introduction: Between Scientism and Fundamentalism   1

2 Whose Religion, Which Secular?   10
  2.1 Post-secularism   13
  2.2 Metaphysics   18
  2.3 Difference and metaphysics   23

3 Phenomenology and Overlapping Consensus   27
  3.1 Charles Taylor   27
  3.2 Ontology and difference   39
  3.3 Taylor's post-secularism in practice   46

4 Analogy and Corporatist Pluralism   53
  4.1 John Milbank   53
  4.2 Milbank's metaphysics   61
  4.3 Milbank's post-secularism in practice   68

5 Becoming and Rhizomatic Pluralism   75
  5.1 William Connolly   75
  5.2 William Connolly's ontology   86
  5.3 William Connolly's post-secularism in practice   93

6 Post-Secular Visions   103
  6.1 Different accounts of being: univocity vs. analogy   105
  6.2 Transcendence and immanence: an attempt at a typology   112
  6.3 Practical implications   117
  6.4 Three post-secular visions   142

7 Conclusion   151
  7.1 Transcending the secular   151
  7.2 A metaphysical post-secularity   155
  7.3 Differing accounts of difference   160

Notes   163

Bibliography   197

Index   209

Preface

This is a book about how we, despite our differences, might live peacefully together in pluralistic societies. It is at the same time a book about attempts to overcome the strict dualisms of nature/culture, transcendence/immanence, and religious/secular. The assumption that ties these two themes together concerns the centrality of metaphysics, and the inseparability of ethics and politics – that the way we construe the underlying structure of reality is deeply related to how we negotiate cultural and political differences. During much of modernity political philosophers have met with deep suspicion the assumption that metaphysics is a relevant subject to discuss in relation to politics. Instead it has been argued that conflicts and disagreement are best resolved if we disregard issues such as religion, worldview, and metaphysics and instead seek to be "rational." In critique of such a position, thinkers, such as the Canadian philosopher Charles Taylor, the British theologian John Milbank, and the American democracy theorist William E. Connolly, have all sought to deconstruct the notion of secularity as a universal and neutral position from which it is possible to relegate the religious to a "private sphere." The delimitation between "religion" and "secularity," and between the transcendent and the immanent, has in their view to do with metaphysics. But, it also has practical implications concerning the conditions under which we can live together peacefully. Accordingly, the reading of these three theorists will be focused on their accounts of metaphysics, as well as the political implications of these accounts in terms of pluralism. It will be suggested that Taylor, Milbank, and Connolly should be read as seeking to re-establish the link between metaphysics and political morality, or differently put, as seeking to establish an ontological dimension of the political.

Today, most liberal states are torn between attempts to accommodate different religions within floating limits of tolerance, and at the same time trying to uphold a sense of national identity. The traditionally liberal way to negotiate this dilemma has been, to put it bluntly, to address religion as a generic category, relegate it to the private sphere, and to make religion an object of tolerance. The idea of a strict separation between religion and the secular rests on the Kantian philosophy of an authoritative public morality based on a singular conception of reason. Underlying this Kantian distinction is the idea that universal moral norms can be generated out of human reason, abstracted from specific religious or metaphysical traditions. This Enlightenment notion of a secular reason disembodied from tradition has played a central role in shaping liberal democracy as well as for the idea of "religion" as a phenomenon of its own kind. However, the very concepts of "religion" and "the secular," not to mention "reason," have since been deconstructed and interpreted from genealogical or non-essentialist perspectives. These queries regarding the alleged neutrality and objectivity of the secular, paired with a renewed interest concerning the political aspects of religion, pose difficult questions regarding the relation between religion and secularity. For, if the "doctrine" of secularism that has governed public discourse in liberal democracies rests on disputed Enlightenment principles such as an autonomous, universal rationality, then, what alternatives are there for how to reconfigure the relationship between "religion" and "the secular"? And furthermore, what do these alternative narratives entail, both philosophically and in terms of a social vision for how we are to live together in increasingly diverse societies?

Framed in a different way, the central theme of this book concerns the question of what happens with the relation between "religion" and "secularity" when the Kantian idea of pure, or secular, reason is challenged, or different again, when the injunction to "bracket" references to transcendence is ignored. By comparing the thought of three post-secular theorists, I seek to bring out some of the complexities, risks, and possibilities related to the attempt to "transcend" the Kantian account of secular reason. In particular, alternative construals of the relationship between transcendence and immanence, as well as more practical aspects of how religious and political differences are to be negotiated without secular reason, will be explored.

Acknowledgments

Writing is a lonely process filled with ups and downs. This is why good advice and encouragement from friends and family are so important. I have been very lucky to experience that support can come in many forms: initiated academic advice by scholars, conversations with friends during dinners and late night runs, and love and care by family.

The topic of this book concerns the crossing of boundaries. My project has, in a similar way, involved the crossing of several boundaries – between subjects, institutions, and countries. As the interdisciplinary nature of this work aims to show, boundary crossing involves difficulties as well as new perspectives and possibilities. I here want to acknowledge my gratitude for the new perspectives given to me through discussions with people from other academic disciplines, from other universities, and at conferences in other countries. These experiences have been crucial for the development of my own thought.

First, my gratitude goes out to Olav Hammer at the University of Southern Denmark who made this project possible for me and has guided me with great patience. I am also particularly grateful to the institutions, and people who have allowed me to present my work to them and furthered it through their comments and concerns. I want to mention The Telos-Paul Piccone Institute in New York, The Centre of Theology and Philosophy in Nottingham, The University Centre Saint-Ignatius Antwerp (a special thanks to Professor José Casanova who gave important comments on my project during a rewarding summer school), The Department of Philosophy at UC Berkeley, Charles Taylor, John Milbank, and William Connolly. I also want to express my gratitude to Ola Sigurdson and Arne Rasmusson, for allowing me to attend research seminars in The Department of Literature, History of Ideas, and Religion, at the University of Gothenburg. I further wish to acknowledge and thank The Danish Council for Independent Research, Culture and Communication (Det Frie Forskningsråd, Kultur og Kommunikation), whose funding has made this project possible.

Special thanks go out to Henrik Friberg-Fernros, Lovisa Bergdahl, Andreas Nordlander, Peter Carlson, and Jonatan Bäckelie for their insightful comments and suggestions on my manuscript. I also want to thank Joel Halldorf for organizing theology seminars and stimulating academic conversations at Bjärka-Säby castle.

Finally, I want to thank my family. My parents, Åke & Gunnel Bengtson have supported me in so many ways during these years. My sisters' families and wonderful kids – you bring joy to my life! Finally, my wife Kris who has endured this strange time of our lives and has put up with my sometimes rather absent mind. Thank you for your encouragement, for proof reading, and vivid grammar discussions during those hot weeks in July. I love you!

1
Introduction: Between Scientism and Fundamentalism

Is the universe reducible to the merely material, or is there a transcendent dimension? And if there is transcendence, how does it relate to our mundane reality? These have been central questions for every civilization throughout human history, expressed and explored through poetry, literature, music, philosophy, and religions. But, how do we relate to the notion of transcendence in our own secular age? Central to the story of how the Western world became modern has been a certain narrative of how we got rid of transcendence and religion, and became both rational and secular in the process. A popular claim that has accompanied this narrative of secularization has been that citizens should disconnect their beliefs about metaphysics and religion from their dealings with politics and the public sphere. The political philosophy of John Rawls, Jürgen Habermas, and Robert Audi are influential examples of this perspective, suggesting that religion should be kept to a "private sphere," and that citizens who participate politically should adhere to a "communicative rationality" or "generally acceptable reasons," rather than reasons based on religious doctrine.[1]

However, in recent years it has become impossible to disregard the public presence, as well as the political impact, of religions in the Western world. This has been accounted for in terms of the "return of religion," or perhaps more correctly, by religion's "new visibility," suggesting that religious beliefs may have always existed, but are now visible in different ways.[2] The new visibility of religion has been studied in relation to fundamentalism and extremism, as well as politics, the public sphere, and liberal democracy. Furthermore, the resurgence of religion has also been noticed within philosophy, where the critique of Enlightenment account of reason in the guise of postmodern critical theory, according to the Italian philosopher Gianni Vattimo, has accomplished a "breakdown of the philosophical prohibition of religion."[3] Several politically radical thinkers in the continental tradition can be seen exemplifying Vattimo's claim through their engagement with theological themes. Without believing in, or belonging to, religion in any traditional sense, thinkers such as the Slovenian philosopher Slavoj Žižek, the French philosopher Alain Badiou, and the Italian philosopher Giorgio Agamben, have all analyzed religion, and in particular Christian theology, as a means to critique a neo-liberal or capitalist hegemony.[4] As a consequence of these engagements, new ways of approaching religion and the secular have emerged. Many of these accounts have sought to go beyond the concept of "religion" understood as merely personally held beliefs, inner feelings, and theoretical propositions, and have thus rejected earlier approaches as being essentialist, constructed, provincially Western, and post-colonial. Instead, more focus has been given to the lived, material, and political aspects of religion.[5] The secular, understood as a realm differentiated from "the religious," has in a similar way undergone a renewed scholarly scrutiny that has often been tied to the "legitimacy" and "autonomy" of modern reality.[6] Furthermore, the typical Enlightenment narrative, in which human history is understood as a straightforward progression from religion to reason and is thought to culminate in secular modernity, is today being increasingly challenged, for reasons I shall explore.

Some of these questions, concerning the social role of religions in relation to the secular state, were in 2001 addressed by the German philosopher Jürgen Habermas, in a speech later published under the title *Glauben und Wissen* (Faith and Knowledge).[7] Habermas, who has been one of the most influential theorists of secular modernity, initiated a discourse concerning "post-secular" societies in this speech, which has since gained widespread use and commentary.[8] But, what does it mean to say that a society is post-secular? By this question Habermas, as well as later engagements with this theme, is not primarily interested in empirical accounts of the demise of Enlightenment accounts of secularity, but rather in the social and political role of religions in relation to the secular state. The central questions thus concern how the relation between religion and politics, and between transcendence and immanence, should be construed in the wake of critiques towards the Enlightenment account of religion. In his engagement with these questions Habermas makes certain claims and delimitations regarding metaphysics, which will serve as a backdrop for my account of Taylor, Milbank, and Connolly. So, before proceeding, let's look closer at some more recent comments of Habermas' regarding the dilemma related to the notion of the post-secular.

"Two countervailing trends mark the intellectual tenor of the age – the spread of naturalistic worldviews and the growing political influence of religious orthodoxies."[9] That is how Jürgen Habermas opens his book *Between Naturalism and Religion* from 2005. In this book Habermas points out the paradoxical spread of naturalism and return of religion at the same time, and the challenge that this raises for liberal democracy. Habermas sets out, without dismissing either naturalism or religion, to find a path between what he perceives as the malaises of both "scientism" and "fundamentalism." I will here briefly explain the "gap" Habermas identifies between scientism and fundamentalist religion, since it is in relation to this gap that I will position the three different post-secular narratives that I intend to examine.

A central issue in Habermas' account of the post-secular concerns the distinction between belief and knowledge. He refuses to limit knowledge to the sum of statements that empirical science is able to verify. This, Habermas argues, results in a scientism that "misleads us into blurring the boundary between scientific knowledge which is relevant for understanding ourselves and our place in nature as a whole, on the one hand, and a synthetic naturalistic worldview constructed on this basis, on the other."[10] The problem with this form of scientism is, according to Habermas, that it operates within a narrow mindset, unaware of its own limits. Habermas exemplifies this "narrow-mindedness," or the unawareness of scientism's own underlying assumptions, with "the blurred distinction between secular reasons and statements that should count, and secular worldviews that should count just as little as religious doctrines." Habermas here refers to the American philosopher Nicholas Wolterstorff's claim that "Much, if not most of the time we will be able to spot religious reasons from a mile a way...Typically, however, comprehensive secular perspectives will go undetected."[11] In this way, Habermas seeks to point out elements of "belief," or metaphysics, in scientism. However, according to Habermas, religion, in its fundamentalist forms, is haunted by a similar blindness and "cannot be reconciled with the mentality that a sufficient proportion of citizens must share if a democratic polity is not to disintegrate."[12]

The dilemma that Habermas here identifies is closely related to the concept of the post-secular, a term by which Habermas denotes two things. First, on a sociological level, it signifies how in secularized societies "religion maintains a public influence and relevance, while the secularistic certainty that religion will disappear worldwide in the course of modernization is losing ground." But secondly, and more importantly for my project, it involves the question of what we should "reciprocally expect from one another in order to ensure that in firmly entrenched nation states, social relations remain civil despite the growth of a plurality of cultures and religious worldviews."[13] Habermas argues that "scientism," understood as a form of radical naturalism, is unable to provide the normative resources necessary to sustain a society: in the sense that it "devalues all types of statements that cannot be traced back to empirical observation, statements of laws, or causal explanations, hence moral, legal and evaluative statements no less than religious ones."[14] Habermas here fears that the "naturalization" of the human mind that has been brought about by advances in biogenetics and brain research "places our practical self-understanding as responsibly acting persons in question."[15] Habermas has in another essay described this dilemma in the sense that "pure practical reason can no longer be so confident in its ability to counteract a modernization spinning out of control armed solely with the insights of a theory of justice."[16] Habermas here points to how the secular state is faced with important ethical and political questions related to pluralism as well as science and capitalism – problems he argues a narrow account of reason fails to address. Accordingly, the post-secular dilemma, as defined by Habermas, concerns the constructive discussion of how diverse societies may live in peace despite inner cultural or religious differences, and furthermore, which resources and strategies might be employed in this process.

To problematize the relation between reason, religion and metaphysics, Habermas cites the German legal philosopher Ernst Wolfgang Böckenförde's question: "Does the free, secularized state exist on the basis of normative presuppositions that it itself cannot guarantee?."[17] This question is rooted in the assumption that democracy depends on moral stances that stem from pre-political sources such as religion. Here Habermas goes beyond the influential liberal political philosopher John Rawls in his willingness to allow both metaphysical naturalists (scientism) and representatives of religious traditions to speak in their own language in public. However, Habermas maintains a filter between the spheres of church and state – "a filter through which only 'translated', i.e., secular, contributions may pass from the confused din of voices in the public sphere into the formal agendas of state institutions."[18] In this sense Habermas claims agnostic neutrality in public discourse, free from metaphysical commitments of either a naturalistic or a religious kind. Instead, Habermas argues that the liberal state can satisfy its own need for legitimacy, independent of metaphysical or religious traditions.

Nevertheless, he claims that religions have cognitive and motivational aspects that are valuable for the virtues necessary to sustain a democracy.[19] It should here be pointed out that, while Habermas sometimes operates with a broad understanding of the term "religion," with the distinction between reason and revelation as its defining trait, it is more specifically Christianity that stands at the center of his engagements with religion.

Habermas' "solution" to the post-secular dilemma consists of seeking to affirm a neutral, secular ground of reasonable humanism. He expressly rejects two positions: first "the blinkered enlightenment which is unenlightened about itself and which denies religion any rational content" and a Hegelian view "in which religion represents an intellectual formation worthy of being recalled, but only in the form of a 'representational thinking' (*vorstellendes Denken*) which is subordinate to philosophy."[20] By the term "representational thinking" Habermas employs a Hegelian distinction between objective thought (where thought alone can reveal the true nature of things), and subjective thought. "Vorstellendes Denken," or "pictorial thought" is part of the objective thought that assumes that the object of our knowledge is easily accessible and can become subject to our mastery. In this sense representational thinking suggests a straightforward and easily available connection between words and things, or a sort of naive realism.[21] Accordingly, Habermas denies that religious imagery is able to provide insights that are untranslatable into rational language. Instead, he seeks to re-appropriate the Kantian distinction between discursive immanent reason on the one hand, and inexpressible faith on the other.

Habermas' rejection of both scientism and fundamentalism is grounded in his critique of metaphysics. Habermas rejects any attempts to ground philosophy or religion on supposedly absolute, universal, transcendent, or timeless principles – what he associates with the Western metaphysical tradition, along with what he argues is an exaggerated conception of reason.[22] It is metaphysics understood in this sense that he sees to be at the root of both religious fundamentalism and scientism. Instead, for Habermas, the "awareness that we live in a post-secular world is reflected philosophically in the form of post-metaphysical thought."[23] By "postmetaphysical" Habermas means, and here I risk oversimplification, a world of politics in which controversial religious and existential orientations, if not subjected to translation into a secular language, are kept from public discourse and political life. Differently put "respecting the precedence of secular reasons and the institutional translation requirement."[24] Habermas has accordingly characterized postmetaphysical thinking in terms of a re-articulation that, based on his account of a communicative rationality, emphasizes a linguistified and procedural account of reason.[25]

> Post-metaphysical thought draws, with no polemical intention, a strict line between faith and knowledge. But it rejects a narrow scientistic conception of reason and the exclusion of religious doctrines from the genealogy of reason. Post-metaphysical thought certainly refrains from passing ontological statements on the constitution of the whole of beings.[26]

Habermas' postmetaphysical position "between naturalism and religion" is an influential construal of the relation between reason, religion and metaphysics in Western democracies. However, it is not the only one. This was made clear by the now famous dialogue between Jürgen Habermas and Cardinal Joseph Ratzinger (later Pope Benedict XVI) in 2004.[27] Habermas, self-proclaimed "tone-deaf in the religious sphere," and Cardinal Ratzinger, both agreed that religion needs to be "purified and structured by reason," while at the same time, reason must also be "kept within proper limits."[28] The plea for limiting reason is connected with Habermas' critique of naturalism and his insistence on "detranscendentalization:" that is, reason must be situated within history and social reality.[29] By transcendental, or pure, reason Kant intended reason that "contains the origin of certain concepts and principles, which it derives neither from the senses nor from the understanding."[30] Against such an understanding Habermas seeks to account for "the transcendental tension between the ideal and the real," between the "'pure' and the 'situated' reason."[31] Differently put, Habermas seeks to balance between, on the one hand, an idealized, universal and detached account of reason, and on the other hand, a Hegelian account that emphasizes language and practice as embodied and historical dimensions of reason.[32] According to Habermas, Hegel accounted for a subject that was "always already linked to the world," and that, in contrast to Kant "finds itself already connected with an environment and functioning as part of it."[33] However, while seeking to modify Kant with Hegel, Habermas maintains a Kantian distinction between discursive reason, or rationality, and religious faith.[34] Habermas' "solution" to the dilemma of "valueless" science and fundamentalist religion lies in asserting the neutrality of discursive reason. Habermas posits that a certain universality of reason is available through the process of argumentation or deliberation; "a legitimacy-guaranteeing procedure that meets the same postmetaphysical, and hence world-view-neutral, standards of justification as rational morality."[35]

From one perspective, Habermas' dilemma is concerned with metaphysical questions about the proper relationship between the immanent and the transcendent, between faith and reason (*Glauben und Wissen*), or between philosophy and theology. From another perspective, however, his dilemma concerns something more practical: namely, the democratic and social challenges that stem from living in a society with a plurality of religions, and thus conceptions of human flourishing. However, where Habermas' brand of post-secularism has rejected metaphysics according to his postmetaphysical approach, I want to focus on thinkers who, within their work on religion and secularity, have actively engaged questions of metaphysics and the underlying structure of reality.

The reasons that I intend to focus my study around post-secular theorists, who have rejected the postmetaphysical approach taken by Habermas, are twofold. *First,* I intend to take seriously a specific philosophical critique against the very idea that any position can be referred to as postmetaphysical, given that any philosophical position conveys a set of fundamental assumptions that cannot be proven (and thus can be viewed as metaphysical).[36] In what has been referred to as the "ontological turn" (which also entails the return of metaphysics), the "intimate relationship between sociopolitical thought and metaphysics," has been affirmed, and the "once celebrated value neutrality of liberalism" has been questioned.[37] Central to this stream of thought are philosophers such as Hegel, Henri Bergson, Gilles Deleuze and Alain Badiou. Rather than seeking to strain out metaphysical assumptions from human thought, these thinkers have sought to recover the respectability of metaphysical speculation and to engage in an account of the Real as such.

My *second* reason for focusing on post-secular theorists who have rejected the postmetaphysical approach concerns a specific critique regarding democracy and pluralism. Several political scientists and legal scholars have argued that the postmetaphysical approach, which makes a particular philosophical outlook foundational for how "religion" should be treated, is excluding large groups of people from active involvement in politics. The target of this critique is the claim that religious citizens are to denude themselves of their particular religious/philosophical particularities if they do not want to be excluded from the public sphere. Habermas' approach, whereby religious citizens are asked to translate their religious reasoning into neutral and secular language, is one example of this position. The British sociologist Austin Harrington has here argued that Habermas "will to include the other," when talking about religion "has a paradoxical tendency to perform the thing it most seeks to avoid, namely to exclude the other or to exclude otherness."[38] Differently put, it is suggested that Habermas' demand that "religious ideas" have to be translated into secular language: that is, "publicly intelligible language" is operating with a very "thin" view of religion that, due to his highly cognitive and rational approach to social life, is missing aspects that lie outside the moral and cognitive (such as "the centrality of spirituality, emotion, and tradition").[39] For example, British sociologist Derek McGhee has argued that Habermas' (and Rawls') account of religion is "built upon problematic assumptions with regard to essentialist, reified and inflexible identities and associated 'mentalities' that these authors assume exist across the so-called immanent and transcendent divide that allegedly structures so-called 'religious' and 'secular' encounters across the public table."[40] The American sociologist of religion, Michelle Dillon, has in a similar manner argued that "Habermas's post-secular – religious turn underappreciates the contested nature of religious ideas, marginalizes the centrality of spirituality, emotion, and tradition to religion, and fails to recognize religion's intertwining with the secular."[41] Others have argued that Habermas' postmetaphysical liberalism tacitly postulates a particular view of religion which tends to assume that religion is a purely private matter, and thereby "overlooks a fundamental dimension of religion: its power of symbolic community institution."[42]

Several other scholars have warned against the dangers of excluding religious sensibilities from politics and argued that "religious arguments are prima facie acceptable or even desirable in political argument."[43] The American political scientist Andrew F. March has here pointed to an "emerging consensus that religious arguments should not be excluded from public life."[44] Against theorists who advocate a rationalized ideal of deliberation aimed at consensus, the American political scientist Bryan Garsten has argued "that the aspects of rhetoric that seem most dangerous – the appeals to emotion, religious values, and the concrete commitments and identities of particular communities – are also those which can draw out citizens' capacity for good judgment."[45] Paradoxically, Garston argues that theorists of deliberative democracy who follow Habermas "in spite of their interest in disagreement, [...] often find themselves opposing rhetorical deliberation and the politics of persuasion."[46] In much the same vein, the American democracy theorist Romand Coles has, against demands to strain out metaphysical and religious points of view from the public sphere, argued that "one can analogously argue that where there are serious disagreements over shared terms across different faith traditions, withholding the metaphysical roots of these differences will also provoke resentment and divisiveness."[47]

Taking both the philosophical and the political critiques of Habermas' postmetaphysical approach seriously, I thus want to focus on postsecular theorists who have chosen to engage questions of ontology and metaphysics. But before we turn to these theorists and their alternative construals, we will start by looking closer at some of the central concepts in these debates.

2
Whose Religion, Which Secular?

In the paradigmatical accounts of religion from the late eighteenth century, such as Kant's *Religion Within the Boundaries or Mere Reason* (1793), and Schleiermacher's *On Religion: Speeches to Its Cultured Despisers* (1799), religion is approached in terms of disembodied thought and feeling. Furthermore, religion was believed to have an essence, and was thus approached as a generic category, as something of its own kind. According to Kant, the essence of religion lies in its moral functions; in "the recognition of our duties as divine commands,"[1] while for Schleiermacher, the essence of religion is defined as "neither thinking nor acting, but intuition and feeling."[2] Kant's disembodied notion of "pure reason," understood as a non-religiously informed reason that is supposed to resolve moral and political matters in a way that is able to convince every rational human being, can in this sense be seen as paradigmatic for the modern notion of the secular as neutral or unbiased. This approach privileges secular reason, understood as a mode of universal discourse able to transcend particular traditions and religious forms of reasoning. According to the American scholar of religion Wayne Proudfoot "[t]he turn to religious experience was motivated in large part by an interest in freeing religious doctrine and practice from dependence on metaphysical beliefs and ecclesiastical institutions and grounding it in human experience."[3] Implicit in this reasoning is the attempt to separate a generic notion of religion from the secular, understood as a neutral, a religious space or standpoint.[4] For example, Habermas has argued that "At best, philosophy circles the opaque core of religious experience when reflecting on the intrinsic meaning of faith. This core must remain so abysmally alien to discursive thought as does the core of aesthetic experience, which can likewise only be circled but not penetrated by philosophical reflection."[5] According to this perspective the secular is viewed as a form of absence: as that which is left when religion has been expelled from the public sphere. This understanding, however, raises questions: Is the secular nothing more than simply absence of religion, or could it in fact, be said to constitute something "in itself?"

Originally, the term "secular" was a theological concept stemming from Western Christianity with no equivalent in other religious traditions.[6] The purpose of the term was to oppose ordinary or profane time to religious or higher time. This binary division, central for structuring the worldview of medieval Christendom, was eventually transformed to denote areas or spheres. For example, to this day a parish priest in the Roman Catholic Church is referred to as secular clergy, as opposed to members of a monastic order, that don't live out in the secular world and are referred to as religious. Used in this sense, secularization denotes the passing something from ecclesial authority to worldly authority: "to make worldly."[7] More recently, however, the distinction between "secular" and "religious" has often been made with the intention to make a clear distinction between a natural and a supernatural sphere, or a "supermundane reality" that "transcends the mundane world revealed by sense perception."[8] A recent attempt to make such a distinction argues that a religion "must include something supernatural of a certain scope."[9] While such an approach might have practical benefits, it is not without problems.

Up until the seventeenth century the term supernatural was used to describe change in the powers of people and things beyond their own capacity, or their "natural" powers.[10] Accordingly, a pig could be supernaturally fat in the sense that the pig had achieved fatness, not by its own powers, but through the intervention of the farmer's feeding. It was not in the pig's own nature to be this fat, but the farmer intervened and supernaturally gave the pig extreme fatness. According to such an understanding of the word, the one thing that cannot be referred to as supernatural is God; at least, not according to an early medieval Christian understanding, which held that nothing could be added to God. Accordingly, as has been objected by Timothy Fitzgerald, the notion of the supernatural is "a dubious crosscultural category," which may not be properly understood separated from a particular cultural context, and is therefore unable to "provide a sufficient basis for a coherent analytical study." More specifically, he argues, it is often unclear "whether the supernatural is thought of as ontologically transcendent or a part of nature, assuming that 'nature' itself is an indigenous concept, which it may not be."[11] Given what he sees as an insufficiently critical perspective of Western ideology and Judaeo-Christian assumptions implicit in religious studies, Fitzgerald warns of the dangers of appropriating certain terms as analytical concepts, which, according to him, rather should be understood in their specific historical and sociological contexts. Instead, while still acknowledging the need for general categories, he argues that the study of religions should be engaged as "a hermeneutical problem of interpreting cultures."[12]

Scholars of religion such as Timothy Fitzgerald and the French anthropologist Daniel Dubuisson, have, along with Russell McCutcheon, argued the constructed and historical nature of the concepts of "religion" and "the secular," and accordingly rejected *sui generis* understandings.[13] Talal Asad has in the same vein argued that "any discipline that seeks to understand 'religion' must also try to understand its other." Asad has approached the concepts "secular" and "secularism" in a way that refrains from reducing them to a by-product of the Western concept of "religion," and instead pays attention to the concept "the secular," as a category that "emerged historically in a particular way and was assigned specific practical tasks."[14] Asad takes the view that "religion" and the "secular" are not essentially fixed categories and that nothing is essentially religious or secular. However, given Asad's claim that "what many would anachronistically call 'religion' was always involved in the world of power" and that "the categories of 'politics' and 'religion' turn out to implicate each other more profoundly than we thought," the concept of the secular cannot do without the idea of religion.[15]

Underlying this critique is the assumption that the project of describing, separating, categorizing and labeling aspects of human existence is by necessity always done from inside a specific tradition, given that no person can stand apart from the universe but always participates from within it. Furthermore, as Michel Foucault has pointed out through his work on the interconnected nature of knowledge and power, practical interests always attend the act of distinguishing a "this" from a "that." In this vein it has been argued that no definition is politically innocent. Instead, it is emphasized that every attempt to separate one sphere of human existence from another begs the question of underlying motives, utility, ontology, or ideological purpose. According to this perspective we have no reason to believe that the act of distinguishing "religion" from "secular," or "religious" from "political," is unaffected by this mechanism. Hence, the notion of neutrality should be viewed with suspicion, and the notion of the secular assumed to be hosting underlying assumptions about reality that display a particular outlook. So, instead of viewing "religion" and "the secular" as once and for all given, it is increasingly recognized that, not only are religion and the secular mutually constitutive concepts, but that it is also possible to speak of secularism's own metaphysics, understood as a set of principles that posit themselves a priori of historical reality.[16] Even secularism operates, according to this perspective, on the basis of certain metaphysical claims about the nature of reality, claims that can be viewed as metaphysical in the sense that they rest on unproven assumptions. The concept "metaphysics" will be explored in greater depth below, but first we will turn more directly to discussions which attempt to transcend the strict dichotomy between "religion" and "secular" – the post-secular.

2.1 Post-secularism

The concept of the "post-secular" has largely emerged in sociological discussion in the wake of the mainly philosophical debate initiated by Jürgen Habermas on rationality and religion in contemporary society. Habermas has, through speeches, debates, and writings, played a central role in the popularity of the concept as well as the broader discussions of the role of religion in liberal democracies.[17] However, given the fluidity and ambiguousness of the term "post-secular," some distinctions are in order. The Spanish sociologist of religion, José Casanova, seeking to grapple with the concept, has pointed out the ambiguities related to any term attached to the prefix "post:" Does "post" intend a subsequent phase within the same phenomenon (like post-modern), or does it mean a radical break with the past that still lacks a proper name?[18] Casanova introduces an analytical distinction between three different meanings of the term "secular." In the *first* sense the secular is intended as part of the religious/secular dyad that structured the medieval world through a separation between the "religious-spiritual-sacred world of salvation," and the "secular-temporal-profane world."[19] According to this understanding, everyone living in a modern society is secular, given that we live in the secular world according to secular time. The *second*, and narrower meaning of the secular denotes a self-enclosed immanent sphere which, rather than contrasting itself against a transcendent sphere, signifies a self-sufficient, exclusive, secularity in which people perceive themselves to be closed off from transcendence and functioning *etsi Deus non daretur* "as if God would not exist." This sense of the secular translates to what Charles Taylor has termed "the immanent frame," denoting the experiences of living in the modern, social and moral order – an experience shared regardless of whether people hold religious or theistic beliefs.[20] The difference here is that belief in God is no longer axiomatically considered a viable option; instead, secularity has become the "default option." Finally, the *third* sense of the secular that Casanova identifies denotes a secularity that employs, what he refers to as, a "stadial consciousness," in which the secular is perceived as the natural historical progression, succeeding an older religious era. This perspective, which has its roots in the Enlightenment, perceives secularization as an emancipatory coming of age, or a maturation, in which the irrationality of belief has been "overcome." Casanova describes this understanding of secularism as "a philosophy of history, and thus an ideology" that seeks to "turn the particular Western Christian historical process of secularization into a universal teleological process of human development from belief to unbelief, from primitive irrational or metaphysical religion to modern rational postmetaphysical secular consciousness."[21] In this sense, to be secular is not an existential choice, but a natural consequence of becoming modern.

Now, to be *post*-secular would mean different things depending on each of the three different meanings of the term secular that Casanova identifies. In its first sense it is not entirely clear what post-secularity would mean, given that the secular in the first sense is part of a spatial and temporal dyad to structure the world of Medieval Christendom. Post-secular would in this sense probably have to entail some sort of re-enchantment that restructured the modern way of perceiving the world. However, being post-secular in the second sense is easier to imagine, given that it merely entails the recognition of a sphere beyond the immanent frame. Such a change of the social imaginary can be the product of a religious revival on an individual or societal level. Finally, to be post-secular in the third sense would, according to Casanova "not mean necessarily becoming religious again, but questioning our stadial consciousness, destabilizing if not our secular immanent frame, at least the possibilities of transcendence within the immanent frame, and being open, receptive, at least curious to all the manifold forms of being religiously human."[22] It is post-secularity in this third sense that is the focus of this book.

However, even understood in this third sense, the post-secular is not to be perceived as a unified field or movement, but rather as a spectrum of concerns and possibilities. Thinkers commonly associated with this spectrum of thought seek to formulate, not only a critique of secularism, but also alternative socio-political visions. A wide variety of understandings concerning central concepts (such as religion and the secular) exist even amongst scholars associated with post-secular perspectives – a fact that has triggered attempts to structure the field.[23] The post-secular spectrum includes liberal political philosophers such as Jürgen Habermas, pragmatist philosophers like Jeffrey Stout, agonistic thinkers like William Connolly, radically orthodox theologians like John Milbank, as well as materialist post-Marxists like Slavoj Žižek.[24] What unifies these diverse thinkers can been formulated in various ways each focusing on different themes of post-secular thought. The two most common themes concern: a) a certain mode of self-awareness concerning the foundation of secular reason, and b) the difficulties of making a strict distinction between the religious and the secular.

a) The post-secular entails a self-reflection regarding the historical roots of the secular, roots which oftentimes and paradoxically, are dependent on religious traditions. Habermas has described the post-secular as responding to a certain lack of "self-awareness" in secular reason, and how the Enlightenment was "unenlightened about itself," but now is becoming aware of its own limits.[25] In this vein, Habermas has stated that "we may call 'postsecular' the situation in which secular reason and a religious consciousness that has become reflexive engage in a relationship."[26] Resonating with Habermas, the Dutch philosopher Hent de Vries claims that "the postsecular invites the secular to historicize and contextualize itself."[27] The American philosopher Eduardo Mendieta has in a similar manner described the post-secular as "the affirmation of a type of subjective reflexivity and intersubjective relationally that neither dispenses with nor affirms a priori either the significance or irrelevance of religion for modern subjects."[28] According to this perspective, also propounded by the Swedish theologian Ola Sigurdson, the concept post-secular should not be interpreted as "non-secularity," but rather as denoting that which "affirms the kind of political discussion coming after secularity."[29]

b) The emergence of problems in attempts to uphold a clear distinction between discourses of religion and those of secular reason. For example, such problems have been experienced when seeking to conceptualize progress (understood as freedom, emancipation, and liberation) in purely secular terms.[30] One example of this is Habermas' recent claim that the "weakness of rational morality" explains why "enlightened reason unavoidably loses its grip on the images, preserved by religion, of the moral whole – of the Kingdom of God on earth – as collectively binding, moral ideals." Habermas' point here is that a strictly secular perspective lacks the sufficient strength to awaken "an awareness of what is missing."[31] In a related manner, the American professor of law and religion, Steven D. Smith, has argued that secular rationalism, through its attempts to filter out appeals to religion or other "comprehensive doctrines," have drained modern discourse and rendered it more shallow. The reason for this, he suggests, is that the "truncated discursive resources available within the downsized domain of 'public reason' are insufficient to yield any definite answer to a difficult issue – abortion, say, or same sex marriage, or the permissibility of torture."[32]

The difficulties in upholding clear differentiations between religion and the secular have here been understood in terms of a blurring of distinctions; widely recognized in discussions concerning liberal secularism and religion, and the post-secular. The British sociologist of religion James Beckford, notes how "the blurring of conceptual boundaries between the private and the public is also at the center of a usage of the 'postsecular'."[33] Others have argued that "post-secular" should be understood in a way that implies "that the borders of previously distinct (secular versus religious) institutions may become, to some extent, blurred."[34] This "blurring" has been described, by the American philosopher of religion Clayton Crockett, as stemming from a critique which attempts to expose secularism as an ideology closely connected to liberalism, based on ideas of "a neutral, value-free space."[35] This critique suggests that, just as religion and secularity are difficult to separate neatly, so is any strict separation between political philosophy and political theology. In line with this critique, Crockett describes a "postsecularist environment," in which "we possess no absolute or certain criterion by which to claim that any phenomenon is theological as opposed to nontheological." This radical claim draws on Crockett's particular understanding of theology as "an open-ended discourse about value and meaning in an ultimate sense."[36] Consequently, for Crockett, it becomes possible to talk about "secular theology" as a non-confessional and non-dogmatic discussion concerning meaning and value. As a result of this, Crockett argues that the "distinction between religious and secular is breaking down, so that it is no longer possible to consistently and rigorously separate and oppose the sacred and the profane."[37] The American political theorist Elizabeth Shakman Hurd has, in a similar manner, argued that the study of the secular and the religious in world politics requires "a reconsideration of the political, philosophical, and religious certainties sustaining the rigid secular/religious binary that has underwritten most social-scientific scholarship to date."[38] Having studied the relations between the United States and Iran, and the rise of the AK (Justice and Development) party in Turkey, Shakman Hurd is arguing that the secular/religious binary needs to be approached as an unstable, historically contingent construct; otherwise, important political developments will be misunderstood. Conventional negotiations of the secular/religious distinction in the discipline of international relations presume a fixed definition of the secular and, correspondingly, the religious. This rules out identifying and framing objects of study that require historicization and politicization of the secular/religious binary to appear in the researcher's field of vision.[39] Instead, Shakman Hurd argues for the need to acknowledge the historical and political contingencies of the secular/religious binary, and for a critical reexamination of the assumptions embedded in hypotheses, empirical tests, and research findings. Such an account actualizes the questions of how "the post-secular" relates to the discussions about value neutrality and normativity. Is post-secular a descriptive term, or a normative program? While in theory it is possible to understand the post-secular in purely empirical terms, as a statement about de-secularization and the new visibility of religion, most scholars associated with the term also take normative positions regarding the construal of religion and secularity. This can be seen in Habermas' claims regarding post-secular society, as well as in the suggestion by post-secular Canadian philosopher James K.A Smith, who has suggested that "perhaps 'post-secular' is less a descriptor and more a normative ideal, a prescription for how society or the sciences ought to be ordered and conducted, countering normative doctrines of secularism."[40]

The post-secular could thus be approached as the end of the secular project understood as the attempt to separate a religious private sphere from a secular public sphere. The secular project entails in this sense, both a distinction between what is deemed to be religious and secular, as well as a boundary between what constitutes a private sphere and a public sphere.[41] Through these demarcations the secular project not only determined what was to be considered religious and what was political, but also designated that the proper arena for politics was the public sphere, and not the private. The post-secular question, which entails a critique of the secular project, could thus be formulated as follows: Despite claims to neutrality, does not the secular project constitute a particular politics of its own? Furthermore, despite its claim to strain out metaphysics, does not the secularist project implicate a metaphysic (in the wide sense of the word) of its own? One might object that it is possible to answer these questions affirmatively, while still holding to a secularist position. However, such a secularism, which rejects claims to neutrality and understands itself as merely one tradition amongst many with metaphysical claims, would be pressed for questions regarding what distinguishes it from "religious" positions, and would perhaps more properly be labeled as post-secular.

In order to better understand what is entailed in the concept of metaphysics, as well as it's centrality for discussions related to the post-secularism of Taylor, Milbank and Connolly, I will in the following seek to give a brief introduction to the concept.

2.2 Metaphysics

In Plato's dialogue *Timaeus* there is a distinction drawn between "that which always is and has no becoming" and "that which is always becoming and never is."[42] This distinction between "being" and "becoming" is central to understanding the history of metaphysics. However, the precise meaning of these terms has been subject to different interpretations, which has resulted in different accounts of the nature of metaphysics. For Aristotle, metaphysics concerned the study of "being qua being:" that is, of things that have the property being, or "of things that can be said to be."[43] However, metaphysics also concerned the attempt to identify the first causes, such as a God, or what Aristotle referred to as the Unmoved Mover or Uncaused Cause. Accordingly, metaphysics in the tradition from Aristotle up until Aquinas generally entails both the study of the first causes including God, and a more general account of everything that has existence.[44] A contentious issue in later accounts of metaphysics concerned how the concept of being should be understood in relation to beings. For example, theists have argued that the notion of an ultimate being or God is qualitatively different from beings such as you and me.[45] Martin Heidegger, however, have argued that the history of Western thought is characterized by a "forgetfulness of Being," or a disregard for the ontological difference between being and beings – which he refers to as ontotheology, due to its tendency to identify the metaphysical account of "beingness" with the theological notion of an ultimate Being.[46]

God is, according to Aquinas' theistic account, understood to be eternal, with no beginning and no end. Furthermore, God is understood as pure actuality – nothing can be added to him and there is no unrealized possibility in him. However, in the High Middle Ages a Franciscan friar and scholastic philosopher, Duns Scotus (1266–1308), introduced a different way of thinking about metaphysics. Scotus argued that being and beings should be understood as existing on one and the same ontological plane; the difference between God and creatures was ultimately one of degree.[47] Put bluntly, for Scotus the difference between

God and humans was quantitative. Metaphysics in the previous tradition as formulated by Plato, Aristotle, and Aquinas, on the other hand, given its two-tiered ontology, can be understood as ordering existence as a hierarchy of levels, requiring ontological differentiation between immanence and transcendence. According to this tradition the difference between God and humans was qualitative. Scotus' ontology, in which being is conflated with Being, or the finite with the infinite, is commonly referred to as the univocity of being, or a univocal ontology.[48] The univocity of being entails the position that there is a fundamental concept or sense of being under which everything that exists falls.[49] Scotus' ontological univocity of being had far-reaching implications for how people came to understand their relationship with God.[50] The old Christianized Platonic worldview understood humans as connected to, or suspended from, God and the whole of creation as participating in the divine life. This worldview was challenged with Scotus' "flat" ontology: both the Creator and the creature were understood to exist in the same way. The consequence of this philosophical move was that "being" became an overarching category that God and creatures shared; or, differently put, that God and humanity existed in the same way. A further consequence was a renewed understanding of God's transcendence and immanence. Before Scotus, God was perceived as transcendent in every category including being, and hence incomprehensible. With Scotus, God was perceived as the highest being amongst other beings. This shift has been described as the "domestication of God's transcendence," a shift that also implicates the end of divine immanence. Where a traditional Christian metaphysics understood God's being as non-spatial, a univocal understanding of God made his presence in creation impossible.[51]

While Aristotle viewed metaphysics as an attempt to identify the first causes in the universe, such as God or the Unmoved Mover, the rationalists of the seventeenth and eighteenth centuries widened the meaning of metaphysics to include, not only God or a Supreme Being, but also broader philosophical issues such as the distinction between mind and body, the immortality of the soul, and freedom of the will. Later on however, Kant along with many empiricist philosophers rejected previous understandings of metaphysics as illegitimate attempts to get beyond the limits of reason. With Kant, metaphysics was reduced to demarcate the more general structures at work in our thought about the world.[52] This Kantian understanding still holds sway amongst many philosophers, who argue that the aim of metaphysics is the characterization of our conceptual scheme or conceptual framework, rather than reality. However, the Kantian understanding of metaphysics, which sets out the limits for human knowledge, has been critiqued with regards to its implicit view of reason as "pure" and unaffected by culture: "for if there are problems with characterizing the world as it is, there ought to be similar problems with characterizing our thought about the world."[53]

One of the earliest critics of Kant's view of reason was the German philosopher Johann Georg Hamann (1730–1788) who was Kant's contemporary. Hamann disputed the possibility of a disembodied pure reason detached from history, tradition, experience, and interpretation. For Hamann "it is pure idealism to separate faith and sensation from thought."[54] Drawing on Hamann, later critique of the Kantian rejection of metaphysics usually targets the idea that the human mind can somehow take a position outside itself and perceive the "bounds" of the phenomenal and the categories supposed to apply to it. In this way, Hamann opened up for approaching reason as a problem of language and thereby setting the stage for postmodernity, and some would also argue, for the post-secular.[55] Against Enlightenment claims of the purity of secular space and religion as a private affair, the revival of metaphysics has in this sense re-actualized the relation between reason and religion, and consequently of religion in relation to science and politics.

Taking this critique seriously, in what has been called "the ontological turn" in religion, philosophy and political theory, questions about ontology, have come to replace epistemology as the main focus of philosophical interest. Against an understanding informed by Cartesian dualism, in which cultures and different religions were viewed as different representations of a single material world "the ontological turn is a turn away from the idea that human difference can be captured by differences in representational states."[56] Positively, in the words of American political theorist Stephen K. White, the ontological turn can be explained as "the result of a growing propensity to interrogate more carefully those 'entities' presupposed by our typical ways of seeing and doing in the modern world."[57] White notes how the social sciences have increasingly come to focus on ontological issues. Central to this "ontological turn" is the claim that every affirmation of a theory also entails a commitment to the existence (or non-existence) of certain entities. This renewed interest in ontology can, according to White, be seen as a reaction to the "disengaged self" of modernity which seeks to "generate distance" from the particularities of its background such as tradition and embodiment. Contrary to this perspective, the ontological turn represents a renewed interest in questions regarding the underlying presuppositions of what we hold to be reality. Rather than assuming a neutral and transcendental account of reason (that is, an account of reason that is unconditioned by external factors) ontological commitments are understood to be bound up with questions of identity, history, and meaning, and consequently how we both individually and collectively make existential sense of the world in which we find ourselves. Accordingly, many theorists now recognize that procedures and methods of knowledge are not neutral; that theories of knowledge rest on deeper presuppositions about anthropology and the way the world is perceived to be constituted (what is sometimes referred to as ontological commitments).[58] Metaphysics is, understood in this way, an inevitable part of being human since any statement about reality in this sense is a metaphysical claim. Or, in the words of the British philosopher and metaphysician E. J. Lowe, metaphysics is "inescapable for any rational being and that they themselves demonstrate this in the objections which they raise against it. For to say that reality is inaccessible to us or that there is no reality independent of our beliefs is just to make a metaphysical claim."[59]

However, a project central to mainstream philosophy of science during the last century has been "to separate scientific method from metaphysics – from prior assumptions about the nature of the world and of ourselves which scientists cannot help bringing to inquiry and which, it is claimed, always distort our understanding."[60] Accordingly, science was supposed to be distinguished from religion, metaphysics, and superstition. Opposing this project, post-colonial and feminist theorists have argued that scientists necessarily bring distorting metaphysical commitments from their roles in social life (including those of class and sex), and that these are reinforced in the social arrangements within science.[61] As an example, American philosopher Sandra Harding argues that Western secularism is deeply Christian and even Protestant in central respects.[62] According to American philosopher Kathryn Pyne Addelson, if we admit Thomas Kuhn's claim that metaphysical commitments are an integral part of scientific activity, then we see that the scientific authority which defines the nature of the world is not limited to laws and theories, but that this authority also shapes our commitments to the world and relations with one another. In this sense, scientists never just tell us about their theories, but also about their metaphysical beliefs. Only by stating "that reality is known through universal laws and predictions," does one, according to Addelson "share an analogous metaphysical assumption," namely that "the scientific enterprise is based on the metaphysical premises that because there is one reality, there must be one, correctly described truth."[63] Entailed in this Kuhnian critique of science allegedly free from metaphysics, is a critique of any strict dichotomy between religion and reason. The Slovenian philosopher Slavoj Žižek makes a similar point with regards to the relation between faith and reason after Kant:

> Kant started as the great destroyer, with his ruthless critique of theology, and ended up with – as he himself put it – constraining the scope of Reason to create a space for faith. What he displays in a model way is how the Enlightenment's ruthless denigration and limitation of its external enemy (faith, which is denied any cognitive status – religion is a feeling with no cognitive truth value) inverts into Reason's self-denigration and self-limitation (Reason can only legitimately deal with the objects of phenomenal experience, true Reality is inaccessible to it).[64]

Central to Kantianism is a "dualistic demand" that claims that: "physical grounding and metaphysical grounding be kept rigorously separate." This implies that "physical ideas should not be explained in terms of nonphysical factors, causes that are not bound by physical laws."[65] Accordingly, Kant refrains from saying anything about the relation of the mind to nature. Within continental philosophy that follows in the footsteps of Kant, the issue of religion and God-talk has been treated in a post- or anti-metaphysical manner, informed by a certain "postmodern" philosophical framework.[66] This anti-metaphysical stance towards religion can be exemplified by the writings of American theologian and scholar of religion John D. Caputo, the Italian philosopher Gianni Vattimo and the American philosopher Richard Rorty, in the sense that metaphysics is used as a pejorative term to denote what is perceived as the futile project of finding an ahistorical, transcultural matrix for one's thinking.[67] However, in the light of recent critiques within philosophy of science and continental philosophy, metaphysics is today being re-actualized in relation to discourse about religions and the secular.[68]

This trend can be exemplified with thinkers such as the French philosophers Bruno Latour, and Quentin Meillassoux, who operate in what has been labeled a speculative realism.[69] Meillassoux argues that the Kantian refusal to think the absolute or the supersensible is in fact religious or metaphysical in itself. The critique of metaphysics, such as "end of metaphysics"-proclamations, is in fact "undermining a particular religion which appealed to 'natural reason' in order to declare the superiority of its particular beliefs over those of other religions."[70] In this sense Meillassoux argues that the "contemporary end of metaphysics is nothing other than fideism," by which he means that talk about the "end of metaphysics," implies a position of having "an authentic access to the absolute."[71] This way of forbidding reason any claim to the absolute, leads, according to Meillassoux, to a return of the religious given that a whole domain of reality is deemed off bounds for reason.

Bruno Latour, who is well known for his work in philosophy of science, has in a related way critiqued the subjective/objective division and argued against the "the solid difference between psychic mechanisms, representations, and causes" as well as attempts to "divide the world into top and bottom, nature and supernature."[72] More recently, particularly in his recent Gifford lectures on "natural religion," Latour has provided tools for thinking about how we conceive "religion" in relation to "nature" in a manner that seeks to move beyond a reductive accounts of materialism and beyond a dualist understanding of the relation between religion and science. More specifically, Latour seeks to deconstruct the amalgam of "religion" and "nature" by showing how our conceptions of nature tend to be informed by a religious or theological understanding.[73]

The ontological turn thus entails a critique of the ability of "pure reason" to account for reality and instead seeks to explore questions concerning the presuppositions entailed in the way we account for the basic structure of the world. Drawing on Kant's distinction between "transcendent metaphysics" and his own "critical metaphysics" where the former "seeks to characterize a reality that transcends sense experience" and the latter seeks to "characterize our conceptual scheme or framework" (rather than the world itself); the ontological turn thus entails a focus on transcendent metaphysics. Or differently put, the set of beliefs that each of us holds about reality and ourselves, and what we take for granted and as given about the world.[74]

2.3 Difference and metaphysics

The Enlightenment ideal of a universal humanity in which all are equal inasmuch as all have a capacity for reason and moral sense has certainly played an important role in the elimination of group difference such as those based on class, race, and gender. However, as proponents of a more recent ideal of liberation have claimed, liberation based on a notion of a universal humanity in which physiological differences such as skin color or gender are assumed to have no significance for a person's sense of identity, implies that certain differences are deemed unimportant. Such a perspective, it is argued, promotes an ideal of assimilation into the majority, rather than a recognition of differing identities, made not despite but because of their differences.[75] Scholarship related to this perspective is commonly referred to as "politics of difference" or "the politics of recognition," and traces its philosophical roots to discussions concerning the relation between identity and difference where, in contrast to classical philosophy, difference is understood to precede identity. The reason for this is that identities are seen as being constituted through processes of differentiation where I am who I am because of my differences.[76] This perspective is closely related to personal and existential perspectives of politics, since, as stated by Jonathan Z. Smith "[d]ifference is rarely something simply to be noted; it is, most often, something in which one has a stake."[77]

In relation to this dilemma, the British political philosopher John Gray has argued that liberal tolerance actually consists of two different traditions, which embody two incompatible philosophies. "Viewed from one side," Gray argues "liberal toleration is the ideal of a rational consensus on the best way of life. From the other, it is the belief that human beings can flourish in many ways of life."[78] In the former view, propounded by John Locke and Immanuel Kant, liberal tolerance is viewed as a universal project, in which differences are seen as possible to reconcile through a specific rational approach. In the latter view, however, propounded by for example Isaiah Berlin, tolerance of competing values is viewed as a mere strategy of coexistence. Drawing on the Greek word *agon*, meaning contest, competition or rivalrous encounter, Gray uses the term "agonistic" to denote a pluralism that stems from value-pluralism.[79] This is one example of how different metaphysical perspectives concerning values and universality can lead to different social visions or different understandings of pluralism.

Another example of how metaphysical or religious beliefs can inform different accounts of pluralism is briefly hinted at by the Dutch philosopher Hent de Vries in the introduction to the collection of essays *Political Theologies: Public Religions in a Post-Secular World*, in which he contrasts Pope Benedict XVI with the former US president George W. Bush. Benedict XVI argues against a notion of pluralism understood as "contradictory and disordered linguistic fragments" as opposed to a notion of "symphony" in which each individual part plays a role in a "unity." "Only that pluralism is great," claims Benedict XVI "which is directed toward unity."[80] A different account of pluralism could, according to de Vries, be found in the administration of George W. Bush. Religious scholar Bruce Lincoln has analyzed the writings of George W. Bush and labeled them as a blend of "an evangelical theology of 'born again' conversion; a theology of American exceptionalism as grounded in the virtue of compassion; a Calvinist theology of vocation; and a Manichaean dualism of good and evil."[81] Lincoln has elsewhere labeled Bush's official rhetoric as marked by "ethical dualism, a theology of election, and a sense of soteriological mission."[82] Hent de Vries, in this context, also quotes former British Prime Minister Tony Blair's remarks concerning his feelings on the decision to invade Iraq "[t]he only way you can take a decision like that is to do the right thing according to your conscience." This quote, for de Vries, serves to confirm "the extent to which a certain liberalized (interiorized, Evangelical, Protestant?) religion has become, if not a ploy or an ideological justification, then at least a welcome vacuum for the (external) powers that be."[83]

The simple observation I wish to make is that metaphysics is not unrelated to differences between social visions and accounts of pluralism. This should not be understood in a deterministic fashion where a particular metaphysical idea by necessity determines a social vision. However, it should be recognized that a pluralism that entails the acceptance of any cultural or religious difference rests on certain metaphysical assumptions, in the same sense that the recent decision by the European court of human rights to uphold the ban on women's right to wear the full-face veil in public, rests on a different set of metaphysical assumptions. The two cases evaluate and negotiate religious difference differently, and in this sense display different accounts of pluralism. The former case might be understood to "recognize," difference, while the latter case was motivated with reference to "the preservation of the conditions of 'living together'."[84] Nevertheless, both stances entail metaphysical assumptions concerning human identity (anthropology) and the common good (ethics).

Traditionally, liberal pluralism has avoided this kind of metaphysical inquiry and often opted for, as in the case of Rawls and Habermas, non-metaphysical or postmetaphysical approaches. The reason for this relates to what Ghanaian-American philosopher Kwame Anthony Appia, has stated as the fact that "disputes grounded in controversies about metaphysics are unlikely to be resolved."[85] However, if peace is the benefit of not describing the precise contours of the good life, there are also problems with this approach. These problems stem, as has been argued by post-liberal philosophers, from delegating religious and metaphysical conflicts to the private sphere. As suggested by the American Religious Studies scholar Charles T. Mathewes, secular liberalism encourages an "ethics of inarticulacy" and a "meta-ethical aphasia," in the sense that it refuses to explicitly ground ethics in metaphysics. This, Mathewes claims, makes it impossible to argue with those who do not share your own fundamental views, eventually leading to situations in which ethics is reducible to will.[86] Differently put, if we can no longer have a rational discussion about values, and where no genuine agreement is possible, force – either through "the tyranny of the majority" or by violence – will present itself as the only remaining alternative.[87]

A theorist who has sought to take seriously both the need to recognize difference as well as metaphysical questions, is the Canadian philosopher Charles Taylor, to whom we will turn next.

3
Phenomenology and Overlapping Consensus

3.1 Charles Taylor

Charles Taylor is a Canadian philosopher best known for his contributions in the areas of political philosophy, philosophy of social science, and history of Western Modernity. Taylor has, due to his willingness to account for dimensions of human experience beyond natural science, along with his emphasis on how ideas shape history, and thus that history and philosophy are deeply intertwined, been linked to the philosophical tradition of Idealism.[1] However, in his attempt to account for the historical developments of concepts and notions such as "the self" or "secularity," Taylor seeks to balance between what he refers to as a "vulgar Marxist" materialism, that focuses solely on structural and material explanations and which tends to "bypass human motivations all together," and on the other hand, a "vulgar Hegelian" view, in which ideas are seen as sufficient to explain the cases behind historical developments.[2] Rejecting these two extremes, Taylor seeks to account for how ideas are "embedded in practices."[3] Taylor here includes practices at all levels of human social life, such as family, village, national politics, rituals of religious communities, and argues that "ideas articulate practices as patterns of dos and don'ts."[4] Taylor has later expressed this position by stating that "our past is sedimented in our present, and we are doomed to misidentify ourselves, as long as we can't do justice to where we come from."[5] Furthermore, central to Taylor's blend of ideas and practices is the view that freedom is achieved – not by rejecting tradition and community – but rather through a commitment to it. Taylor thus argues that an abstract and individualist Kantian notion of morality should be replaced by Hegel's notion of *Sittlichkeit*, which makes particular practices and communities central to ethics. Hegel has in this sense had a strong influence on Taylor's thought.[6]

Taylor here seeks to account for the intersubjective conditions in which beliefs and identity are formed in modern life. Taylor describes modern man as caught in a tension between, on the one hand, an Enlightenment understanding of man as a disengaged, free, and reasoning subject, and on the other hand, the Romantic movement of authenticity on the other. Amongst the central historical shifts that Taylor lists in order to understand how the modern human derives identity, he gives special focus to human welfare and the reduction of suffering, what he calls the "affirmation of ordinary life," and the notion of nature as displaying an inner moral source. At the end of his *Sources of the Self (1989)*, Taylor questions which moral sources are able to support the far-reaching commitments to benevolence and justice present in liberal democracies. Taylor is unsatisfied with Enlightenment naturalism, or "exclusive humanism," which he claims suppresses the spiritual dimension, and thus is unable to serve as a moral foundation. Instead, he claims that "high standards need strong sources."

A Secular Age (2007) constitutes Taylor's grand attempt to account for how the modern West became secular, or why belief in God is radically different today than 500 years ago. Taylor challenges the dominant "master narrative" of secularization understood as the inevitable decline of religion with the advance modernity. In its place, Taylor seeks to put forward an alternative narrative, in which he approaches religion in terms of a transcendence implicit in human aspiration for "fullness." By the term fullness, Taylor here intends the very different ways in which everyone seeks to account for what constitutes a richer, deeper, more worthwhile, more admirable, life. According to Taylor, every person, and every society, has some sort of conception of what this fullness or flourishing is. Taylor argues that a key feature of the secular world is the emergence of a self-sufficient humanism that accepts no other goals beyond human flourishing.

Reason and religion

While Charles Taylor's academic engagements span diverse areas – such as, moral and political theory, epistemology, hermeneutics, and philosophy of mind – his more recent writings have increasingly focused on religion, secularism, and multiculturalism.[7] His standpoints are informed by a distinct philosophical perspective, drawing on thinkers such as, Hegel, Martin Heidegger, Maurice Merleau-Ponty, Hans-George Gadamer, Michael Polanyi, and Ludwig Wittgenstein. Taylor stands in a hermeneutical tradition that sees knowledge as the outcome of embodied existence and experience. What this means more specifically is that the way in which we cognitively encounter the world is seen as always already shaped by the fact that we are bodily creatures, and that we perceive the world through our bodies. Accordingly, Taylor has argued for the need of the social sciences to recognize that knowledge, at its base, is the outcome of embodied existence and experience. In his words "[t]he thinking rational subject can only exist embodied. In this sense we can truly say that the subject is his embodiment, that, e.g., I as a thinking being am my living body."[8]

In line with this particular philosophical outlook, Taylor has leveled criticism against what he sees as a certain narrowness of modern moral theory, as well as certain forms of liberalism, that do not pay attention to the particularities of cultural or religious difference. He has specifically critiqued the underlying notion of what he calls "disengaged reason," by which he means "a reasoning which in no way draws insight from the significances things have for us as embodied, social beings, who mark moral and aesthetic distinctions in things and actions."[9] This critique has immediate implications for Taylor's engagement with liberal secularism and religion, given the contemporary discussion about which cultural expressions, such as religious language and clothing, should be allowed in the "secular sphere."

For other philosophers of Taylor's generation who also stand in the Catholic tradition, such as Alasdair MacIntyre and Taylor's old teacher G.E.M. Anscombe, modernity has largely been perceived as regrettable in its display of disenchantment, secularism, and materialism. For Taylor, however, modernity is far from a bad thing, but is recognized as having brought with it goods such as liberal democracy, which he sees as one of its great achievements.[10] In Taylor's words; "The age of Hiroshima and Auschwitz has also produced Amnesty International and Médecins Sans Frontières."[11] However, Taylor holds that modernity is somehow at odds with itself in the sense that its ideal of freedom is not really met. In this vein, Taylor engages the dilemmas that arise when liberal democracies turn out to be not as democratic as they hold out to be. These dilemmas are, according to Taylor, displayed in the ways such as the exclusion of certain groups, and by a reluctance to recognize and affirm certain cultural and religious particularities, such as the recent legislation in France against wearing the hijab in schools. What Taylor is critical of is a specific understanding of modernity, what he refers to as an "acultural" theory, which views cultural transformations from an allegedly neutral vantage. According to this explanatory model "modernity is conceived as a set of transformations that any and every culture can go through – and that all will probably be forced to undergo."[12] The problem with this account is, according to Taylor, that it is prone to view contingent cultural changes as unavoidable effects of some deterministic notion of "development," and by doing so, overlooks cultural aspects that do not fit the explanatory model. Differently put, there is a stadial, or almost deterministic, account of the way culture will progress. Against the "acultural" view of modernity, Taylor argues for a model that recognizes that Western modernity has been driven by different visions of the good, which have instantiated new cultures, or "multiple modernities." Against the monolithic view of modernity, Taylor argues that "[m]odernity is not that form of life toward which all cultures converge as they discard beliefs that held our forefathers back. Rather, it is a movement from one constellation of background understandings to another, which repositions the self in relation to others and the good."[13] Accordingly, the kind of understanding of modernity that Taylor rejects is underlaid by a supposedly culture-neutral understanding of rationality and progress, and is unable to account for the fact that non-Western cultures have modernized in rather different ways.

Taylor positions himself between what he sees as backward-looking enemies of modernity on the one hand, and enthusiastic modernists (and postmodernists) on the other. In line with critics of modernity, Taylor agrees that not everything is as it should be in contemporary culture; instead, unlike them, he thinks that authenticity, understood as the impulse of being true to oneself, should be taken seriously as a moral ideal. However, against proponents of postmodern subjectivism, Taylor believes that it is possible to argue rationally about different moral ideals.[14] Furthermore, Taylor seeks to articulate his position "from within the achievements of modernity," conceding "the humbling degree to which some of the most impressive extensions of a gospel ethic depended on a breakaway from Christendom."[15] However, Taylor suspects that modernity as a culture "has aimed higher than its moral sources can sustain," and that "the denial of transcendence" can put its valuable gains in terms of rights and the affirmation of life, in danger.[16] Never before, Taylor argues, have people been asked to stretch out so far in solidarity with strangers, or "to maintain standards of equality that cover wider and wider classes of people, bridge more and more kinds of difference."[17] Taylor is thus skeptical with regards to the ability of secular humanism to power the great philanthropic reform entailed in liberal democracy, and he has little hope that "a society of self-fulfillers" or the pursuit of self-interest is the solution.[18] Rather, for Taylor "Christian spirituality," described as a love or compassion that is unconditional and not based on works or merit, points to a way out of this dilemma. However, such a love is for Taylor only possible if transcendence is recognized, or "to the extent that we open ourselves to God, which means, in fact, overstepping the limits set in theory by exclusive humanisms."[19]

The "acultural" model of modernity as it manifests itself in the Enlightenment paradigm, tends, according to Taylor, to draw on a strict distinction between reason and religion. Taylor is highly critical of this distinction and a central part of Taylor's critique of secularism draws on a rejection of the split between "reason and faith."[20] In fact, Taylor suggests that any strict distinction between religious and non-religious discourse seems to be "utterly without foundation."[21] Against a Kantian notion of pure reason, taken as a safe source of knowledge that does not rely on religious or metaphysical sources, Taylor argues that "'reason' is not the name of a reliable source offering univocal and reliable answers; and 'revelation' itself is a category by which we try, rationally, to make sense of the truth we discern."[22] The only domain in which Taylor concedes that reason "comes very close" to providing univocal answers is in formal logic and mathematics, where the reasoning is codified. Here, Taylor admits that belief in "reason alone" is applicable. However, whilst natural science involves applying a correct method and inferring the best explanation, Taylor objects that "good explanation" depends on an adequate conceptualization. Drawing on Thomas Kuhn, Taylor here argues that we need more than observation and explanatory inferences, namely theoretical imagination.[23] It is instead by creative thinking that we transform our understanding in a way that enables us to make sense of anomalies that do not fit the original paradigm. Reason in this sense must include an element of creativity that can't be accounted for in terms of pre-existing models, Taylor argues. Therefore, according to Taylor, once we step beyond the realm of mathematics and natural science, the separation between reason and belief breaks down.

Taylor is thus critical of the view of reason implicit in the writings of John Rawls and Jürgen Habermas to the extent that it reserves a special status for non-religiously informed reason (what Taylor calls the Enlightenment myth of pure reason). This distinction rests, according to Taylor, on the assumption that "reason alone" is able to resolve certain moral and political dilemmas in a way that "can legitimately satisfy any honest, unconfused thinker," along with the notion that a "religiously based conclusion will always be dubious, and in the end only convincing to people who have already accepted the dogmas in question."[24] The basic epistemic distinction between religious and non-religious discourse, supported by Habermas, is rejected by Taylor, due to what he sees as a lack of foundation.[25] In fact, Taylor argues that "the very idea that there is a clear distinction between political thought where theological considerations are at work, and political thought where these are banned is redolent of a certain myth of reason."[26] This distinction rests, according to Taylor, on the view that some immanent or "this-worldly" argument is able to establish a solid moral-political foundation. Against this view Taylor objects that, it is far from clear how the fact that we are rational, desiring, enjoying, or suffering beings is supposed to constitute a more solid moral foundation than the claim that we are created in the image of God. He then goes on to argue that "[t]he two most widespread this-worldly philosophies in our contemporary world, utilitarianism and Kantianism, in their different versions, all have points at which they fail to convince honest and unconfused people."[27]

Accordingly, Taylor rejects the idea that "secular reason" is more rational than reason inspired by, for example, Christianity or Islam. Instead Taylor argues that reason has to be thought of as working in different ways in different departments, as exemplified in the differing ways reason is used in science and moral discourses. Taylor here employs the Wittgensteinian concept of "language games," in which words have the meaning they have only within a certain context, or "game." However, the diverse forms of reason at work in the different language games do not, according to Taylor, imply that the different traditions cannot be moderated by reason. Instead he holds that hermeneutics is a viable tool to bridge such differences.[28]

Taylor's understanding of reason is in this sense connected to that of imaginative and creative reasoning. Taylor here draws an analogy to the motto "faith seeking understanding" (Fides quaerens intellectum) attributed to the medieval scholastic Anselm of Canterbury (1033–1109). While recognizing that it might seem provocative to invoke this motto in discussions relating to science, Taylor nevertheless maintains that there is "a similarity in structure" which can be discerned in all uses of the imagination which "leap ahead and set the path for more certain knowledge." This structure, Taylor, suggests, is vaguely recognizable in the "scientific hunch." [29] Understood in this way, reason includes a moment of articulation in which one gives the reasons one can't say *a priori*, and is according to Taylor, far from incompatible with religious or metaphysical traditions. Differently put, Taylor argues that "faith," understood as an empirically unverifiable claim, is an important condition for the formulation of new paradigms in so far as it leaps ahead of what we know. Commenting on the British biologist Richard Dawkins' remarks about religion as "belief that isn't based on evidence," Taylor has commented that "to hold that there are no assumptions in a scientist's work which aren't already based on evidence is surely a reflection of a blind faith."[30]

Taylor on the secular and secularization

A central aspect of Charles Taylor's work concerns the project of describing the processes and historical shifts related to modernity and how people in the West came to be "modern." Taylor has approached this shift in terms of a turn to subjectivity, and the conditions in which beliefs are formed and deemed (im)possible in modern life. In order to come to terms with this huge question Taylor sketches a secularization narrative that is different from that found in most sociological literature. In his *A Secular Age* (2007), Taylor starts from the observation that belief in God isn't quite the same thing in the year 2000 as it was in 1500. Focusing almost exclusively on the conditions of Christianity in Western Europe, Taylor argues that we have changed, not only from a condition of living "naïvely" in a world dominated by an enchanted worldview to one of disenchantment, but also from a situation in which belief in God was unchallenged, to a situation in which almost everyone views religion as just one option amongst many.[31] It is through the "optionality of faith," that Taylor approaches secularization. He does so by developing a radical critique of the prevailing secularization narratives, due to what he perceives to be the inadequate answers they provide to explain the demise of religion.

In particular, his critique targets two types of explanation for the demise of religion. The first type of secularization narrative that he criticizes is the materialist-rationalist idea, associated with Auguste Comte, which holds that science will eventually do away with religion. According to this projection: "a day will come when humanity will no longer believe, but it will know: a day when it will know the metaphysical and moral world, just as it already knows the physical one."[32] The other narrative of secularization that Taylor is critical of is the theory of differentiation often associated with Max Weber, by which functions that are originally carried out together are perceived as falling into separate spheres with their own norms, rules, and institutions. The medieval household was in this manner a unit of both living and production, whilst today, we tend to have separate, or differentiated, spheres or locations for those activities. The problem with the theory of differentiation when applied to religion is, according to Taylor, the assumption that activity in one sphere is supposed to follow its own rationality and not supposed to permit "religious" norming. However, according to Taylor, the differentiation model doesn't account for the fact that other spheres of life can still be very much shaped by religions. Taylor exemplifies this with how "a modern doctor will not usually send her patient to touch a relic" and is in that sense displaying differentiation between the religious and the medical spheres, but, as Taylor goes on to argue "her vocation to medicine may be deeply grounded in her faith," and does in this sense display no differentiation.[33] This example highlights what he understands as the mistake of identifying secularization with disenchantment. Taylor argues that, if secularization is taken to include some sort of decline of Christian beliefs, this identification does not hold up. Admittedly, Taylor argues, a separation of secular spheres, such as economy and science has occurred, but it doesn't follow that this necessarily leads to privatization and marginalization of religion in the modern world. Instead, he claims, the religious remains very much entangled with other spheres.[34]

The underlying problem that Taylor identifies with the prevailing narratives of secularization is that they contain what he calls "subtraction stories." By this he means that they assume that once we scrape away or subtract religious and metaphysical beliefs, what we are left with are "ordinary" human desires, and that these are the proper basis of modern humanism.[35] Against the implicit anthropology that underlies such subtraction stories, Taylor argues that "Western modernity, including its secularity, is the fruit of new inventions, newly constructed self-understandings and related practices, and can't be explained in terms of perennial features of human life."[36] Critiquing what he perceives as the prevailing but reductive narratives of secularization, Taylor seeks to formulate a more complex story – a different metanarrative. Taylor's rival narrative entails, as previously mentioned, a specific account of secularity understood in terms of the process by which belief in God has gone from being unchallenged to becoming merely "one option among others."[37] Taylor argues that two things needed to happen for this notion of the secular to come about. First, a distinction between the natural and the supernatural had to be developed, and secondly, it had to be perceived as possible to live entirely within the natural, or as Taylor calls it: within the "immanent frame."[38]

The term "immanent frame" is central to Taylor's secularization narrative as he lays out the shift from an enchanted universe to one of disenchantment. By this term he intends a culture in which the immanent world (against a possible "transcendent" one) is perceived as the "natural" order, and in which "instrumental rationality is a key value, and time is pervasively secular."[39] However, the immanent frame is not primarily a set of beliefs that we entertain about our predicament; instead, "it is the sensed context in which we develop our beliefs."[40] In this sense, Taylor's approach to religion and the secular focuses more on the social context and the phenomenological experience of transcendence (or lack thereof), as opposed to creeds and purely theoretical beliefs. It is this phenomenological experience that, according to Taylor, makes our age a secular one. However, according to Taylor, we have become secular not primarily by refuting transcendence, but rather by developing alternative ideological and conceptual systems. Therefore, it is not due to the method of science that religion has declined in terms of belief and practice, but rather due to changes in the narrative that makes sense of the world. As mentioned, Taylor refers to these narratives as "subtraction stories," which typically explain how humans have "liberated themselves from certain earlier, confining horizons, or illusions, or limitations of knowledge."[41] There is, according to Taylor, a certain moral attraction towards immanence at work in many of these narratives, according to which religion is perceived as emanating from a childish lack of courage, and where we "need to stand up like men, and face reality." Taylor here makes a connection between materialist science and a certain humanism where the ideal is "to be a mature, courageous being" in order to face the facts.[42]

Taylor somewhat paradoxically traces one of the root threads of secularization back to Christianity itself. He does so both in terms of the theological distinction between the natural and the supernatural previously mentioned, but also, and more concretely, of the importance that ecclesial authorities of the late medieval and early modern periods put on reform, in order to make the whole of Latin Christendom live up to the same standard of piety. Previously, the church had allowed for a gap in levels of piousness between dedicated minorities of religious elites, such as clergy and monastic orders, and the laity.[43] However, this new "rage for order" in Latin Christendom that aimed to change the whole of society by the implementation of higher moral standards is, according to Taylor, one of the main sources of secularization.

On religion and transcendence

Against William James's classic study *Varieties of Religious Experience*, Taylor argues that there are "important, widespread religious forms that cannot be undistortively understood within his concept of religious experience."[44] Challenging James, who famously defined religion as "the feelings, acts and experiences of individual men in their solitude," religion for Taylor is a more social affair "a collective connection through a common way of being."[45] Accordingly, Taylor does not approach belief and unbelief as rival theories, but rather as "different kinds of lived experience involved in understanding your life in one way or the other, on what it's like to live as a believer or an unbeliever."[46] In this inclusive sense of religion, the different ways that people account for existence or morality, whether by God or by something in nature, is given the same attention. Taylor's approach to religion supplements the usual account of "religion" in terms of belief in the existence of supernatural entities with "the perspective of a transformation of human beings which takes them beyond or outside of whatever is normally understood as human flourishing." [47] Taylor does not theorize generally about "religion," as he perceives any attempt of define religion in general as an "insuperable task," given that "the phenomena we are tempted to call religious are so tremendously varied."[48] Instead, Taylor's approach to religion focuses on the distinction between the transcendent and the immanent, and notions of "fullness" outside, or beyond, human life. Taylor uses the concept of fullness due to what he believes is its general applicability: "[e]very person, and every society, lives with or by some conception(s) of what human flourishing is: what constitutes a fulfilled life? What makes life really worth living? What would we most admire people for?"[49]

Central to Taylor's transcendent/immanent distinction is whether the idea of fullness is found outside or beyond human life (which is the position of religious affirmers of transcendence), or within human life with no reference to transcendent reality (which is the position adopted by secular affirmers of immanence). Taylor argues that in order to understand religion in the West, we have to examine different dimensions of transcendence, and suggests that we need to "see religion's relation to a 'beyond' in three dimensions." [50] These dimensions entail: a "good" higher than human flourishing (beyond merely human perfection), a higher power (such as God), and an extension of life beyond death.[51] Taylor further argues that our experience of living within "the immanent frame" has affected our understanding of fullness, in the sense that modern secularity is coterminous with a humanism that rejects final goals beyond human flourishing. "Of no previous society was this true," Taylor claims.[52] In this sense, the immanent frame directs both our understanding of reality and our sense of the good from within the world.

Metaphysics and the social order

For Taylor, the notion of secularity is related to what he describes as a rupture from a medieval cosmology, entailing a hierarchical and teleological order. Taylor here refers to "a common premodern understanding of the moral/metaphysical order" which involves the idea of an ordered cosmos, very different from the modern understanding of the universe, which is generally seen as unrelated to the modern social order.[53] Taylor describes how, partly as a result of the scientific revolution, the old understanding of an ordered and hierarchical cosmos faded away. However, he argues, the modern view of the cosmos "has its own kind of order, that exhibited in exceptionless natural laws. But it is no longer a hierarchy of being, and it doesn't obviously point to eternity as the locus of its principle of cohesion. The universe flows on in secular time".[54] Taylor here understands secularity in terms of a shift in our understanding of what society is grounded on.[55] Taylor describes the medieval social order as being saturated with metaphysics, in the sense of a social and moral hierarchy stemming from the notion of the Great Chain of Being (*scala naturae*). This concept, derived from Plato, Aristotle, and further developed during the Middle Ages, details a strict, hierarchical structure of all matter and life, which was believed to have been decreed by God. In societies guided by this social imaginary, it was, according to Taylor, clear that a moral order was more than just a set of contingent norms, but that it also contained an "ontic component" which identified features of the world that made the norms realizable. In this sense, what constituted medieval society was the metaphysical order it embodied. People acted within a framework that existed "prior to and independent of their action."[56] However, Taylor not only contrasts secularity with the metaphysics of the Great Chain of Being, or of the divinely established church, but also with an understanding of society as constituted by an eternal law. The notion of a law that transcends particular and contingent regulations (either as divinely ordained or as put in place by ancient forefathers) stands in stark contrast to the modern secular notion of law that can be changed or abolished by a single vote in parliament. The contemporary public sphere is in this sense secular, in that it is constituted by nothing outside the common action we carry out in it. It is this absence of a framework independent of human action that, according to Taylor, makes it radically secular.[57] What Taylor sees as particular to modernity is a secularity where the constituting factor of a community is nothing other than its common action. Taylor's use of secularity is in this sense much broader than "not tied to religion." In fact, he argues that an exclusion of the religious dimension is not a necessary condition of this understanding of the secular since there can be "religious motives for espousing a separation of church and state."[58]

Against the post-metaphysical notion propounded by, for example, Habermas, which claims that we need to discard metaphysical notions of an order anchored in the cosmos in favor of a social order that is constructed and man-made, Taylor argues that metaphysics and ontology are still relevant concepts and that even our modern secular age draws on certain "ontic components."[59] These "ontic components," or implicit metaphysical assumptions (which will be explored further below), can, according to Taylor, be seen in the modern understanding of society, as existing for the mutual benefit of individuals and their rights, prevalent for the last three centuries.[60]

This new secular social order does not invoke transcendent notions of a divine law, but rather draws on what might be called an immanent metaphysics, in which a notion of mutual benefit between individuals becomes central. Taylor's critique of the subtraction at work in the prevailing secularization narrative is that this way of telling the story "'naturalizes' the features of the modern, liberal identity." By doing so, according to Taylor, it runs the risk of missing the "historically constructed understanding of human agency among others norms we live by on our own authority."[61]

Taylor's account of the post-secular

One way to account for the post-secular is in terms of a reversal of the secularization process: that is to say, a retreat of secularity and the return of religions or enchantment. Taylor, however, understands post-secular in a rather different way. His use of the term has rather to do with what sort of narrative we tell in order to make sense of the shifting relation between religion and the secular. According to Taylor, the post-secular is better defined as the situation after which the earlier narrative of secularization has begun to fade and where there is a struggle towards a new narrative.[62] Thus, by "post-secular" Taylor doesn´t mean a situation that is "post" (beyond) secularity, but rather "post" (beyond) the hegemony of the narrative that underlaid the notion of secularity. In Taylor's words "I rather mean a time in which the hegemony of the mainstream master narrative of secularization will be more and more challenged."[63] A central part of Taylor's new and more complex narrative entails a more history-centered account of secularization that avoids the subtraction stories previously mentioned; which, according to Taylor, are "occluding, or belittling, whole dimensions of possible religious life and experience."[64] Taylor sees the exclusion or perceived irrelevance of religion as being part of the unnoticed background of social science, history, philosophy, and psychology. Taylor refers to this as the "unthought" of secularization: that is, "the more subtle way that one's own framework beliefs and values can constrict one's theoretical imagination."[65] This "unthought" of secularization manifests itself by claiming that religion must decline: either because science has proven religion to be false or irrelevant due to technological advance, or because it is hierarchical and infringes on individual autonomy. Taylor's postsecularism wants to tell a rival story that concerns ideology rather than sociology. He thus argues that "[t]he 'postsecular' doesn't refer to a new social condition, but to a changed understanding of our present condition, and even a changed understanding mainly on the part of academics and intellectuals."[66] Taylor's approach to the post-secular can be seen in his attempt to redefine the meaning of secularism from relating primarily to the fixed categories of religion and secularity, towards a more dynamic understanding of how to deal with increasing religious and cultural diversity. Taylor here argues that "[w]e think that secularism (or *laïcité*) has to do with the relation of the state and religion, whereas in fact it has to do with the (correct) response of the democratic state to diversity." Accordingly, it becomes relevant to examine what Taylor means by a "correct" approach to diversity, or differently put, what the political implications of his account of post-secularism looks like.

3.2 Ontology and difference

Central to Taylor's philosophy is, as we have seen, the view that our knowledge depends on our bodily engagement with the world. Our understanding of the world and our sense of identity are in this way dependent on our interaction with the world. Based on this perspective, Taylor has developed a distinct understanding of pluralism which seeks to highlight the link between identity and different ways of being in the world. In his essay *The Politics of Recognition*, Taylor argues that political liberalism has had a tendency to neglect the crucial role society plays in the shaping of identity. Against this, Taylor holds that "our identity is partly shaped by recognition or its absence, often by the misrecognition of others, and so a person or group of people can suffer real damage, real distortion, if the people or society around them mirror back to them a confining or demeaning or contemptible picture of themselves."[67]

A person's understanding of their own identity is in this sense affected by what society perceives their identity is or should be. Given the crucial role societies play in identity formation, Taylor claims that legal and public recognition is a legitimate part of human dignity. However, Taylor points to ambivalence in the meaning of identity: it has come to mean two different things. On the one hand, it is used in a Universalist and egalitarian sense, which draws on "the dignity of all human beings." This understanding emphasizes the equality of all citizens by virtue of their sameness. On the other hand, with the emerging notion of authenticity and individual identity, another account of equality emerges. With this account, recognition is demanded on the basis of the uniqueness and difference of each individual. Taylor goes on to argue that a neutral application of rights fails to account for the importance of society in the shaping of identities. Accordingly, Taylor has sought to critically engage what he sees as the "difference-blind" liberalism which underlies certain forms of secularism. Taylor describes this liberalism as infused with an "epistemological picture," to which certain "priority relations" are central, such as the claims that "[t]he knowledge of reality as neutral fact comes before our attributing to it various 'values' and relevances. And, of course, knowledge of the things of 'this world', of the natural order precedes any theoretical invocation of forces and realities transcendent to it."[68] Taylor rejects this kind of epistemology, along with the related idea that liberalism can offer a neutral ground on which people of all cultures can coexist; and, on which ground it is possible to make distinctions between public and private, and between politics and religion. It is only with distinctions like these, Taylor argues, that one can "relegate the contentious differences to a sphere that does not impinge on the political."[69] Taylor even understands the idea of toleration as supported by the assumption that certain aspects of identity classified as private, are deemed irrelevant to politics and should not be permitted in the public domain.[70] Taylor rejects this model and exemplifies its problem by pointing to how in Islam, the idea of separating politics and religion in a way we have come to expect in Western liberal society, is not an option. In this sense a "difference-blind" understanding of equality can end up "preventing the free exercise of religion of the members of religious minorities."[71]

Instead of the distanced approach of epistemology, Taylor seeks to highlight the phenomenological experience of the world that each of us encounters, and in this sense favors ontology over epistemology. Taylor has elsewhere referred to this as the "principle of embodiment," in which the human subject and her mental life "however 'spiritual' it may appear, are inescapably embodied."[72] Understood in this way, mental life has less to do with introspection of internal data, and more to do with recognizing that mental data are created in the interaction with the external; an interaction to which the body is central.

Phenomenology and ontological pictures

Few thinkers today have done more to highlight the broad ontological questions in relation to politics and ethics than Charles Taylor.[73] An ongoing project, from his *Sources of the Self* to *A Secular Age*, has been to articulate the underlying ontological commitments behind different outlooks on life, or in Taylor's words, the "'background picture' lying behind our moral and spiritual intuitions."[74] However, Taylor rarely talks in explicit metaphysical terms about how he conceives reality to be constituted. Instead he takes a phenomenological approach and focuses on how "realities," "world structures," or "social imaginaries" are formed and experienced. These "ontological background pictures" constitute, what has been referred to as, an "engaged value realism" in which the world we live in is not deemed morally neutral, but laden with normative values.[75]

One of the ways Taylor exemplifies the role that ontology plays in our everyday understanding of the world concerns what he calls an "ontic component," and how it shapes the way we perceive the world to be structured. Taylor describes this ontic component as "identifying features of the world which make the norms realizable," or more specifically like an idea of "what it is in God's will, or the universe, or ourselves, which makes these norms appropriate and possible of realization."[76] Taylor exemplifies this by how in ancient societies a hierarchical differentiation is seen as the proper order of things, such as the great chain of being, or a division of society in terms of a designation of roles, such as those who work, those who fight, and those who pray. Such a social order implies a mutual dependency, but there is a hierarchical order of nobility or a descending scale of dignity. According to the ontic component in this society "the hierarchical differentiation itself is seen as the proper order of things," and any attempt to change the order would be seen as turning "reality against itself."[77]

The modern idealization of order differs radically from this premodern one, partly because of the lack of a Platonic metaphysical hierarchy, but according to Taylor more importantly, because every function in society is deemed contingent; "it will be justified or not instrumentally; it cannot itself define the good."[78] Taylor exemplifies this contingency or lack of ontological grounding with the public sphere, which arose in the eighteenth century and he describes as a "meta-topical" common space.[79] By this he means that the public sphere established itself as a place standing outside every other sphere, and constituted itself by nothing else but that which was carried out inside of it. In this sense Taylor sees the public sphere as radically secular: "an extra-political, secular, meta-topical space, this is what the public sphere was and is."[80] The notion of metaphysics or ontological grounding here presents itself as an important aspect of what Taylor means by secular.

As opposed to a pre-modern social order that was perceived as pre-ordained, the public sphere is contingent; which is what, according to Taylor, makes it secular. He claims, however, that it would be a mistake to assume that the modern social order lacks an "ontic component" altogether. It is however a very different ontic component compared to earlier times. It is now rather "a feature about us humans, rather than one touching God or the cosmos."[81] Taylor exemplifies the modern ontic component with the belief that human life is designed so as to produce mutual benefit. Taylor takes the British philosopher and economist Adam Smith's notion of the "invisible hand," whereby "our search for our own individual prosperity redounds to the general welfare," as an example of this sort of modern ontic component.[82] What is new with this account of the ontic component is that it is intrahuman; it is thought to reside within us rather than as a mind independent reality.

A central part of Taylor's work seeks to describe and investigate "social imaginaries" and examine how different articulations of these ontological background pictures make sense of our moral reactions. Taylor construes religions to be on a par with any other outlook on life, in the sense that he views them as "different kinds of lived experience." He does so in contrast to a perspective that sees belief and unbelief as "rival theories" of existence or morality.[83] A paradigmatic example of Taylor's engagement with "lived experience" is his account of the "immanent frame," which he describes as a sensed and unchallenged (rather than cognitive), framework which structures what we in the modern West perceive as the "natural" order (as opposed to a "supernatural" or a transcendent one).[84]

Taylor's approach to ontology in this way entails both a phenomenological aspect and a realist aspect. In a phenomenological manner, he describes different ontological accounts as social constructs or "social imaginaries" of which the most prevalent one in modern Western societies is constituted by the immanent frame. But the way Taylor evaluates different social imaginaries, and seeks to critique the immanent frame, also implies a realist, non-constructed, ontological ground on which he himself claims to stand. This is exemplified by the way in which Taylor seeks to account for, on the one hand, moral instincts and deeply rooted feelings, and on the other hand, the way our moral convictions also include implicit or explicit ontological claims about nature and what it means to be human. Taylor argues that "[t]he whole way in which we think, reason, argue, and question ourselves about morality supposes that our moral reactions have these two sides: that they are not only 'gut' feelings but also implicit acknowledgements of claims concerning their objects."[85] In this sense Taylor seeks to hold together the subjective and affective aspects with the objective and theoretical accounts of human attempts to make sense of the world. Instead of focusing on theory and epistemology, Taylor puts "background beliefs" and conditions of belief at the center, beliefs which are often largely unformulated.

Central to Taylor's task in *A Secular Age* is to approach religion as defined by a double criterion: on the one hand, the belief in a transcendent reality; and, on the other, the related aspiration of a transformation which goes beyond ordinary human flourishing.[86] By the term "flourishing," Taylor seeks to capture accounts of what makes life really worth living. More specifically he is interested in the question of whether what we consider the highest, or the best, lives "involve our seeking, or acknowledging, or serving a good which is beyond, in the sense of independent of human flourishing."[87] Taylor is interested in the role that a transcendent reality, understood as the source of fullness, plays in our conception of flourishing. Taylor argues that modern secularity emerges at the same time as the rise of a society "in which for the first time in history a purely self-sufficient humanism came to be a widely available option." [88] This "exclusive humanism" stands out in the sense that it doesn't accept any final goals beyond human flourishing, or any allegiance to anything else beyond this flourishing. Taylor here contrasts believers, whose accounts of fullness require a reference to God or something beyond human life/or nature, against unbelievers, who understand fullness in immanent terms.[89] Taylor argues that everyone has some conception of fullness, but that we interpret our accounts of fullness differently. However, at the end of *A Secular Age*, Taylor goes on to argue that exclusive humanists who only recognize modes of fullness within the immanent frame are in fact responding to a transcendent reality, but are "misrecognizing it." Taylor clarifies this by stating that "If I am right that our sense of fullness is a reflection of transcendent reality (which for me is the God of Abraham), and that all people have a sense of fullness, then there is no absolute point zero."[90] In this passage Taylor's double approach, as both a social philosopher and a Christian apologist, comes to the fore. Furthermore, this passage also serves to exemplify his double approach to metaphysics, which he accounts for both as a description of modernity from a phenomenological point of view, as well as what might be called a cultural critique of a disenchanted modernity based on a Christian ontology.

Taylor suggests that the modern disenchanted world is unable to provide a sufficient moral source to sustain its high universal standards of justice and benevolence, due to its disengaged understanding of human agency. By moral sources Taylor means the constitutive goods, which "makes certain of our actions or aspirations good; it is what constitutes the goodness of these actions or motives," and have an empowering or motivating role.[91] Against the tendency in liberal political theory to favor epistemology over ontology, Taylor argues that "high standards need strong sources."[92] Our normative commitments do, according to Taylor, in this sense need to be anchored in a deeper underlying ontology. Taylor is furthermore negative regarding the possibilities of materialist reductionism to account for what he sees as central features of human fullness – such as, creativity, moral capacity, and the ability to respond to beauty – and asks: "Can you really give ontological space for these features short of admitting [...] some reference to the transcendent, or to a larger cosmic force, or whatever?"[93]

Taylor is here concerned with the correlation between our ontology and our ethics, or differently put "whether our moral or ethical life" can "be captured by the accounts which fit with our favoured ontology."[94] Without coming down with a definite stance on this matter, though he admits that he has his own "theistic hunches," Taylor seems skeptical of the idea that a naturalist ontology can make sense of what he calls "the phenomenology of universalism." By this he means: the bonding notion of an overarching, higher solidarity between humankind which bridges narrow conceptions and divisions of ethnicity, religion, and culture.[95] Taylor is thus effectively arguing "that a purely materialist ontology, as well as a utilitarian account of ethics, cannot make sense of our moral experience."[96]

A broader horizon of diversity

Taylor has noted that there is a certain ethnocentricity bound up with the claim that states have to be "secular."[97] In his essay *Why We Need A Radical Redefinition of Secularism*, Taylor goes on to construct an alternative – and, he argues, a more inclusive – understanding of secularism.[98] Taylor argues that democratic societies must promote respect for various religious creeds, and refrain from focusing on religion as a problem. In his alternative account, Taylor draws on three principles, which he classifies in terms of the French Revolutionary trinity: liberty, equality, and fraternity.[99] By liberty he means the free exercise of religion – no one should be forced in the domain of basic belief; by equality, that people of different faiths or basic beliefs should be treated the same; and, by fraternity, that all religions must be heard and included in the ongoing process shaping society and its political identity. The reason Taylor gives for taking liberty, equality, and fraternity as a starting point for his revised secularism, is that "people can relate to those coming out of very different religious traditions," and furthermore that it is possible to secure them in ways that "make sense in very different religious environments."[100]

The great challenge of the coming century – both for politics and for social science, dealing with an increasingly diverse world – is, according to Taylor, to understand "the other."[101] Taylor's response to the challenges of plurality in a political community which, on the one hand, seeks to be inclusive of diverse ways of being, but which, on the other hand, draws on sameness to strengthen its identity as a national community, entails what he calls "deep diversity." This idea seeks to promote multiple forms of belonging and to recognize many forms of difference within the same state, as well as to abandon the uniform notion of citizenship.[102] Taylor here draws on the theories of the German philosopher Hans-Georg Gadamer; in particular, his concept of "fusion of horizons." The meaning of this concept entails the idea that one should seek to acknowledge one's own prejudices and bring them into a meeting with a new text or culture in order to have one's presuppositions (or horizons) challenged. As a consequence of making room for a new subject, which did not fit within one's old framework, ones horizons become extended. Following Gadamer, Taylor argues that when we allow ourselves to be challenged, two connected changes follow: "we will see our peculiarity for the first time, as a formulated fact about us, and not simply a taken-for-granted feature of the human condition as such; and at the same time, we will perceive the corresponding feature of their life-form undistorted."[103] Taylor utilizes Gadamer's account of the challenge of the other, as well as the fusion of horizons, and applies them to how we understand alien societies and epochs. With Gadamer, Taylor underlines the need to avoid thinking of one's own perspective as neutral and universal. This perspective has immediate implications for discussions about post-secularism in the sense that it recognizes the problems with broad categories, such as "religion" and "secular." According to Taylor, such categories run the danger of becoming mere labels that do little more than reflect our own prejudices in ways which make us prone to read "religion" only in terms of what it means in our world, and hence slide towards an ethnocentric reading. But, Taylor argues, if our understanding of the other is to be construed as a fusion of horizons, and not as possessing a science of the object, "then the slogan might be: no understanding the other without a changed understanding of self."[104]

Implicit in both Gadamer and Taylor's thinking is that ontology is central for hermeneutics: an attempt to understand something new is already present, or based on a prior "ontological" understanding. A different way to put this is that our understanding is dependent on our perspective, on where we stand. Thus, the central hermeneutical task becomes to "make explicit" the structure of such situatedness. This perspective stands, as we have seen, in opposition to that propounded by Enlightenment thinkers such as Kant, which tended to accept the epistemological model of "objective knowledge" that excluded from the realm of "truth" all human experience not produced through adherence to the scientific method.[105]

3.3 Taylor's post-secularism in practice

The challenge that Taylor identifies for our plural societies, where large numbers of citizens also belong to cultures that question liberal philosophical boundaries, concerns the balancing act between, on the one hand, recognizing their sense of marginalization and, on the other hand, standing firm on our basic political principles.[106] Accordingly, Taylor's version of secularism entails the challenge of implementing a system of governance that seeks to enable democratic states to promote "equal respect to individuals with different worldviews and sets of values."[107] In order to grant this to all citizens, Taylor argues that the state must be able to legitimize its decisions to everyone in a way that draws on a "minimal political morality" that is at least in theory acceptable to all citizens.[108] But equality of citizens is not a sufficient condition for secularity, according to Taylor. An equally important aim of secularism is to protect citizens' freedom of conscience and to thereby recognize the sovereignty of the individual person in his or her choices of conscience, including religion.

Overlapping consensus

One of the challenges that Taylor identifies with regards to the renegotiation of religion and the secular in relation to the state, concerns the balance between, on the one hand, being neutral concerning different conceptions of the good (including religious ones) and, on the other hand, not seeking to promote an anti-religious form of secularism.

Instead the state must, according to Taylor, seek to become "politically secular but without promoting social secularization."[109] Taylor here encounters the dilemma of securing certain values that, without being perceived as belonging to one particular tradition, will grant all citizens the maximum amount of freedom. In response to this dilemma of neutrality, Taylor holds that there are certain constitutive values to which "a liberal and democratic state cannot remain indifferent" since they provide the system with their foundations. Taylor admits that "although these values are not neutral, they are legitimate," given that they "allow citizens espousing very different conceptions of the good to live together in peace."[110] Taylor motivates this pragmatic approach further by emphasizing how these values "…allow individuals to be sovereign in their choices of conscience and to define their own life plan while respecting others' right to do the same. That is why people with very diverse religious, metaphysical, and secular convictions can share and affirm these constitutive values."[111] Taylor here invokes the liberal political philosopher John Rawls' concept of an "overlapping consensus."[112] This term refers to how proponents of different philosophical or religious conceptions of the good can find common ground and agree on certain basic public values. A typical example of this can be seen in the different motivations behind certain fundamental human rights: a Christian will motivate these rights by drawing on how humans were created in the image of God, while a Kantian will typically argue for the need to protect the equal dignity of all rational beings, a utilitarian will make the case that human rights will lead to a maximum of happiness, etc. While they may not agree with each other on how to motivate or legitimatize the principle or value, the point is that they agree on the principle itself.[113] In this way agreement can ideally be reached in a way that also sidesteps division along religious and secular divides.

> Peaceful coexistence will be based not on the secular equivalent of a religious doctrine but, rather, on a range of values and principles that can be the object of an overlapping consensus. The aim of relying on common public values is to ensure the moral equality of citizens so that, potentially, they can all embrace the state's broad orientations on the basis of their own conception of the good.[114]

However, Taylor is critical of Rawls' original interpretation of the overlapping consensus, and argues that Rawls holds to the notion of an ethic allegedly independent of any tradition. Against Rawls, Taylor seeks to modify the overlapping consensus by suggesting that such a concept means we should "converge on some political principles, but not on our background reasons for endorsing these."[115] Taylor is not willing to limit peoples' claims to what Rawls calls "comprehensive doctrines" – that is, their views about God and life, right and wrong, good and bad – but argues instead "let people subscribe for whatever reasons they find compelling, only let them subscribe."[116] Given that more and more societies are becoming multicultural, in the sense of including more than one cultural community, Taylor argues that "the rigidities of procedural liberalism may rapidly become impractical in tomorrow's world."[117] The kind of alternative secularism that Taylor propounds, which is a modified version of Rawls' overlapping consensus, is not to be understood as an optional extra for modern democracies, but as the *only* viable alternative for peaceful coexistence in a diverse society. Thus, Taylor argues "whether we like it or not, the overlapping consensus has got to be made to work."[118]

The Bouchard-Taylor Commission on Reasonable Accommodation

In 2008, Charles Taylor served as co-chair (together with Gérard Bouchard), of the *Consultation Commission on Accommodation Practices Related to Cultural Differences* in Quebec, Canada. The Commission was set up by the Quebec government in response to public discontent with multiculturalist accommodation of religious and cultural practices. The commission's report contains empirical material stemming from consultations with the citizens of Quebec, public agencies, and government officials, as well as a normative framework for how religious and ethnic minorities are to be treated in modern liberal democratic states. The report draws on themes previously developed in Taylor's essay *The Politics of Recognition,* and in particular the idea that recognition by the state is demanded on the basis of uniqueness and difference, rather than sameness. This comes to expression in the principle of "reasonable accommodation," which Taylor and Bouchard explain in terms of how "equality sometimes demands differential treatment."[119] Such an account of equality stands in difference to the principle of uniform treatment, which stipulates that everyone is to be treated in exactly the same way, regardless of their individuality. The report describes Quebec's political system as liberal given that "it protects rights and freedoms from possible abuse by the majority." However, and more specifically, the kind of liberalism propounded draws on what Taylor has called a substantivist model, which seeks to recognize the important role that society plays in shaping identity, as opposed to a procedurial model that applies a neutral understanding of rights. This can be seen in the way in which conflicting rights should be dealt with: "When two rights come into conflict, the courts do not seek to determine which of the two is superior to the other, i.e. to organize rights along hierarchical lines, but endeavour to hand down a decision in which the level of infringement of the two rights is 'minimal'."[120] This approach emphasizes an understanding in which basic rights are of equal importance, and where a hierarchy of rights is refused. Of particular interest for our purposes is the distinction the report makes between public and private, as well as the notion of state neutrality. Seeking to address the argument that "religion belongs to the private sphere," the report distinguishes two meanings of "public:" whether relating to the state, as in "public institutions," or as accessibility to everyone in the sense of "a park open to the public." Depending on which meaning of "public" is intended, the place of religion varies dramatically. The report argues that the first meaning is in line with the secular principle that the state should be neutral with respect to religion and, accordingly, supports the position that religion must be "private." However, the report does not hold it to be a legitimate secular claim to demand that religion should be absent from the public space in the broad sense. Instead the report points out that "religions already occupy this space" and that "religious groups and the faithful have the freedom to publicly display their beliefs."[121] By this claim the report seeks to establish a view where the public visibility of religions are seen as a natural part of an open society.

As we have seen, Taylor argues that the state must be neutral with respect to religions and ideologies. However, being a secular and democratic state, it has to rest on at least some substantive values. This paradox is negotiated with reference to an overlapping consensus approach in which "the secular State defends certain principles but it does so without taking sides in respect of the deep-seated reasons that citizens may cite to justify their adherence."[122]

The kind of secularism propounded in the report, which the authors refer to as "Open secularism," differs notably from the French model of *laïcité*. The French model has been criticized for holding the position that cultural and religious identities obstruct social integration, and suggesting that secular schools should aim to emancipate students from religion in a way that encourages a citizenship void of any particularism. Against this model, Taylor and Bouchard argue in favor of a model based on the belief that a diversified society is achieved through intercultural exchanges between citizens. Religion is in this sense not perceived as a problem, but as a possible means for integration. Accordingly, they argue that "Cultural, and, in particular, religious differences need not be confined to the private domain. The following logic underpins this choice: it is healthier to display our differences and get to know those of the Other than to deny or marginalize them."[123] This position is manifested in the report's recommendations concerning the wearing of religious signs by government employees. Given the particular brand of neutrality that Taylor and Bouchard propound, they don't believe that the wearing of religious signs would bias the impartiality of public servants. Instead, they believe that such a prohibition would prevent believers of certain religions from pursuing careers in the public service, therefore violating the freedom of conscience and religion, held to be of central importance in Taylor and Bouchard's "Open secularism." They further reason that such a prohibition would make it difficult to create a public service reflective of the religious diversity of Quebec's population, which in its turn would risk violating the equality of citizens (a principle also of central importance to their "Open secularism"). Therefore, with regards to the wearing of religious signs, Taylor and Bouchard conclude that "We do not believe that a general prohibition concerning the wearing by all government employees of religious signs is warranted, except in a certain number of functions that imply a duty of selfrestraint, e.g. the President of the National Assembly, judges and police officers."[124] This approach draws on a particular understanding of "religion," which resists viewing it as a whim or "mere choice." Instead "religion" is seen as "a deep-seated conviction" and a question of conscience oftentimes "experienced as non-optional."[125] This understanding is referred to as the "subjective conception" of religion, and is pragmatically motivated by "the virtually insolvable problem of trying to define what is or what is not a religion." Amongst the benefits of this understanding, the report argues, is the avoidance of a situation in which the state can be accused of promoting one particular understanding of religion, as well as having to act as a religious court.[126]

Furthermore, a striking theme in the report is that it seeks to avoid the formal legal realm in favor of what it refers to as "citizen action:" that is, intercommunity initiatives that encourage active deliberation. Against the idea that high-level constitutional amendments and institutional arrangements are enough to deal with cultural diversity, the report stresses the importance of individual groups or cultures having to work out conflicts between themselves. This approach puts less emphasis on the state and more on interaction and deliberation between different groups.

A post-secularism that welcomes difference

Taylor has argued for the need to recognize moral sources that lie outside the subject; or, differently put, sources that transcend the immanent frame. For Taylor personally, these sources are to be found within the tradition of Judeo-Christian theism.[127] However, Taylor readily rejects the idea that there could ever be a perfect match or a total fusion between his Catholic faith and any particular society.[128] Despite his critique of procedural liberalism, he is appreciative of the modern rights culture that has produced "the attempt to call political power to book against a yardstick of fundamental human requirements, universally applied."[129] In fact, Taylor argues that secularism in some form is "necessary for the democratic life of religiously diverse societies."[130] However, given that modern democracies require the notion of a "people" that is unified around a common identity, Taylor is highly attentive to the exclusion of any group from this common identity. Whereas in the past, parts of the population were excluded or unheard on the basis of class, poverty, or gender, Taylor highlights exclusion on the basis of religious identity as a democratic problem. Accordingly, the kind of secularism that Taylor propounds should not be understood as a bulwark against religion but rather as a way to secure "the basic goals of liberty and equality between basic beliefs." [131] It is in relation to this perspective that Taylor states that secularism does not primarily concern the relation between the state and religion, but rather the way that the democratic state responds to cultural and religious diversity.[132] Where liberalism has often been viewed as a possible meeting ground for all cultures, Taylor argues that liberalism is in fact a particular political expression compatible with certain cultures and incompatible with others. Taylor here suggests that, "...as many Muslims are well aware, Western liberalism is not so much an expression of the secular, postreligious outlook that happens to be popular among liberal intellectuals as a more organic outgrowth of Christianity – at least as seen from the alternative vantage point of Islam."[133] However, Taylor is not arguing in favor of some "postmodern" perspectivism in which everyone is entrapped within his or her own perspective, and where debate is futile. Instead, as we have seen, Taylor believes in rational discourse and the possibility of an overlapping consensus, although "this task is very difficult, and what is more important, it is never complete." [134] Taylor is here in a sense stuck between the seemingly incompatible positions of, on the one hand, propounding state neutrality with regards to any religion or ideology, and on the other hand, having to recognize that the state, out of necessity, has to recognize at least some values as fundamental, which in Taylor's post-secularism is equality and justice. Taylor acknowledges the problems related to the task of the state not to frame its decisions in a way that gives special recognition to any particular interest or group (religious or secular). However, he argues "this is not easy to do; the lines are hard to draw, and they must always be drawn anew. But such is the nature of the enterprise that is the modern secular state. And what better alternative is there for diverse democracies?"[135] Nevertheless, Taylor's distinct perspective, with regards to the debate on secularism and religiously diverse democracies, is to be found in his critique of the notion of the secular as an epistemologically neutral position. Against the notion of "religion" as a faulty mode of reason, Taylor has highlighted the ontological assumptions underlying every perspective, even secular ones.

Another theorist seeking to highlight what he sees as the ideological grounding of the secular is the British theological John Milbank, to whom we will turn next.

4
Analogy and Corporatist Pluralism

4.1 John Milbank

John Milbank is a Christian theologian and the Professor of Religion, Politics and Ethics at the University of Nottingham where he also directs the Centre of Theology and Philosophy. Milbank gained wide recognition after the publication of *Theology and Social Theory* (1990), in which he laid out the theoretical foundations for the theological sensibility which later became known as Radical Orthodoxy. In his most recently published monograph, *Beyond Secular Order* (2013), which is intended to be the first of a two-volume sequel to *Theology and Social Theory*, Milbank continues his project of tracing the roots of "the secular" by focusing on the genealogy of modern thought, and in particular on political ontology. Milbank argues that what is apparently secular in modern ontologies in reality derives from particular accounts of theology. As an alternative to modern secular ontology, which Milbank paradoxically argues has theological roots, he presents an alternative theological ontology, or a counter-metaphysics and politics.

The opening sentence of Milbank's major work *Theology and Social Theory* reads "Once there was no secular."[1] This introduction is reflective not only of the book, but also of the broader work of Milbank and the theological school of Radical Orthodoxy (which I will account for in more detail below). With this opening Milbank seeks to establish what he refers to as the constructed and mythical nature of the secular. The secular, he argues, had to be imagined.[2] Milbank's central theme is that we shouldn't understand the secular as natural, neutral, or as simply given. Instead, he claims that all political and social theory rests on myth, or an underlying narrative. Milbank uses the concept of myth, or *mythos*, to denote a kind of basic story, system, or paradigm, and suggests that even the secular is an expression of a *mythos* in the same way that religions are, and that secular modernity is "no more rationally 'justifiable' than the Christian positions themselves."[3] By way of example, according to Milbank, the notion of a natural state and a social contract in the thought of Hobbes and Rousseau, are both founded on myths. In fact, Milbank argues that the modern distinction between religious and secular is itself mythical, or even theological. In this way Christian theology and secular social theory constitute two different narratives of origin, or two competing myths. Milbank refuses any philosophy or position that claims the existence of a neutral "reality" that limits the reach of the Christian narrative in history. Instead, he argues that "There is no independently available 'real world' against which we must test our Christian convictions, because those convictions are the most final, and at the same time the most basic, seeing of what the world is."[4] In this way, Milbank attempts to level the playing field so that the secular and the religious are on the same epistemological ground given that they both rest on non-provable assumptions. This epistemological stance is further reflected in Milbank's view of how theology should relate to the secular liberal state. According to Milbank, if neither the secular nor the religious rest on verifiable assumptions that can be falsified, but rather on stories, it follows that traditional, rational argumentation in the classical sense, is not a way forward. Milbank in this respect takes a different stance on the possibilities of dialogue than, for example, the philosopher Alasdair MacIntyre (whom he otherwise is indebted to) in seeking to enable ways of argumentation between different traditions. Against MacIntyre's willingness to "argue against [the] stoic-liberal-nihilist tendency, which is 'secular reason'," Milbank claims that "secular reason" is "only a mythos, and therefore cannot be refuted, but only out-narrated, if we can persuade people – for reasons of 'literary taste' – that Christianity offers a much better story."[5] The radical consequence of this is that Milbank seems to reject any sphere of overlapping rationality or of a neutral shared social space. Instead he sees theology as the primary discourse, and the church as the social space in which societal pluralism should be negotiated. Instead of letting what he refers to as secular reason position theology, he seeks to have theology position every other discipline. Milbank warns that "if Christianity seeks to 'find a place for' secular reason, it may be perversely compromising with what, on its own terms, is either deviancy or falsehood."[6] Accordingly, Milbank seeks to reclaim theology's position as the hegemonic perspective, or as the Queen of the sciences. This understanding is reflected in his account of other religions. Milbank is critical of the traditional Western notion of religion, given that he understands the very concept of religion as merely reflecting the construction of religion within Western modernity. By contrast, he argues "what we are often talking about when we speak of the religious, are the basic organizing categories for an entire culture: the images, word-forms, and practices which specify 'what there is' for a particular society."[7] It is, in Milbank's view, a liberal understanding of "religion in general" that is to blame for the fact that religion is not perceived in political terms, but that religion in liberal democracy has been relegated to "the private sphere of private inspiration for the individual activist."[8]

Milbank on the secular and secularization

Perhaps the most central theme in John Milbank's work is his interpretation of the secular as heresy. When Milbank claims that the secular is heretical he means it in the sense that it is either an "exaggeration or thinning-down of the truth."[9] The truth, for Milbank, is the teaching of Catholic Christianity; conversely, he perceives the secular as a distortion or "a parody" of Christian doctrine.[10] What constitutes the heretical nature of "the secular" is, for Milbank, the notion of an autonomous sphere separated from God. In Milbank's view, the imagining of this sphere derives from the emergence of particular theological dogmas concerning power and autonomy on which liberalism and the secular rests (this is where Duns Scotus' theories about univocity of being play a central role in Milbank's work, a theme which will be explored later). Accordingly, in playful contrast to the German philosopher Hans Blumenberg's defense of the legitimacy of the modern age, Milbank's perspective could perhaps be called *The Illegitimacy of the Modern Age*.[11] Both Blumenberg and Milbank would agree that the secular was invented, in the sense that the secular, understood as an autonomous sphere, is a construct. But, where Blumenberg defended the notion that modernity had invented something new, Milbank argues that the secular is a distortion of theological creeds, and not a theologically neutral sphere. Milbank rejects the possibility of any neutral account of reality and refuses to depict the secular as "the realm of pure reason, pure nature, natural law or natural rights and so forth."[12] Once theology surrenders its claim to constitute the master narrative, another discourse based on different assumptions will, according to Milbank, inevitably take its place. In Milbank's words "If theology no longer seeks to position, qualify or criticize other discourses, then it is inevitable that these discourses will position theology."[13] This "secular imagination," or way of construing the world without God, is according to Milbank, a product of historical and contingent processes, and it is particularly in the discourses of liberalism "scientific politics" and political economy, that the secular is first constructed.[14]

> The abstraction of "politics," the turning of it into a new sort of deductive science based on accident not substance and on "artificial" and arbitrary causal connections, was the achievement of a voluntarist political theology. Here the "secular" as an area of human autonomy is actually promoted by a theological anthropology for which human willfulness, in certain circumstances, guarantees divine origin.[15]

What lies at the heart of Milbank's critique of the secular is, differently put, its "unhooking" or detachment from the supernatural. The result of such a secular worldview, in which a secular sphere is strictly delimited from a supernatural sphere, has for Milbank far-reaching philosophical and political consequences. Milbank claims that "without a realist belief in a transcendent God and heaven, the ontological ground for hope for a transformed human future is removed."[16] Accordingly, Milbank argues that the various spheres of human life would lack depth and meaning and inevitably end up in nihilism if it weren't for their relation to the transcendent.[17] Against a worldview in which the secular is viewed as autonomous, Milbank's metaphysics emphasize an "integralist" or an "analogical" account of transcendence in which any attempt to analytically separate "natural" and "supernatural" is rejected.[18] Milbank's refusal of any clear distinction between a transcendent and an immanent dimension, or in his own theological terminology, between grace and nature, is reflected in his refusal to separate or delimit any social space as secular.

However, Milbank's suggested alternative to the liberal account of the secular public sphere is not one of "faith" or revelation, as a distinct layer, added to reason.[19] Milbank rejects such a solution given that he discards any clear distinction between the natural and the supernatural, or between faith and reason. Instead, Milbank claims that these boundaries are always messy, and here follows Aquinas claim that "there can be no reason/revelation duality."[20] In fact, Milbank states that the very notion of a reason–revelation duality is part of the heretical secular mode of knowledge. It is not to say that revelation has priority over reason, but that reason and revelation are impossible to separate. Thus, Milbank rejects any reference to the purely religious or purely transcendent, along with its mirror images, the purely secular or the purely immanent.

John Milbank was one of the first to argue against the view that one becomes "rational" and "secular" simply by subtracting religion and superstition; what Charles Taylor later referred to as the "subtraction theory" of secularization.[21] Hence, Milbank (and Taylor) refute the idea that secularization is a process of removal of religion understood as a "layer," under which a more basic and natural core of secularity is to be found. Instead, as we have seen, Milbank argues that the secular had to be imagined and constructed.[22]

In Milbank's story of how the secular came into existence, the process of secularization is closely tied to the intellectual history of different interpretations of metaphysics. Milbank stands out, amongst the three theorists surveyed here, in the sense that he employs a thoroughly idealized account of secularization, tied to developments in theology. Milbank here lists four dimensions that he sees as contributing to the notion of the secular as a separate sphere.[23] First, he lists the emergence of a non-theological mode of knowledge. Milbank sees this as being made possible through the philosophy of Duns Scotus, who elaborated the notion of "Being" as such, abstracted from any link to God. Secondly, and closely related to the first, is what Milbank sees as the destruction of the notion of "analogy of being" and "participation," after which "finite and infinite beings 'are' in the same univocal sense." As we shall later see when we turn more specifically to Milbank's account of metaphysics, the notion of the analogy of being (*analogia entis*) is central to Milbank's theological metaphysics. Briefly stated, the analogy of being entails an understanding in which the being (*entis*) of the created world offers an analogy by which we can (in a very limited way), comprehend God. Thirdly, Milbank points out a significant break in how religion ceased to define public virtue, and instead became associated with private piety. This is for Milbank related to the change from where the state was seen as divinely ordained, to a situation in which it has become unhooked from, or lost its relation to a cosmic hierarchy. Milbank notes how the notion of "religion" in this new situation came to serve the state in the sense that it privatized political notions that otherwise could challenge the state's sovereignty. Whereas before, religion had claims that concerned public justice, it later became reduced to inner sentiment, and thus de-politicized. Fourth, the emergence of "ritual" activity as separated from other activities. Given the prevailing transcendent cosmology of the Middle Ages there was, according to Milbank, no strict distinction between ritual and non-ritual actions. But, with the changed understanding of religion to primarily denoting a set of theoretical beliefs, actions that related to those beliefs came to be perceived as strange. It was here, according to Milbank, with the loss of the enchanted worldview, that the realm of "ritual" and "symbolic action" was born as separate practices.

The disjunction between faith and knowledge lies, according to Milbank, at the heart of modernity.[24] Milbank sees this dualism in the theology of Luther and his account of "knowledge by faith alone," but he traces its roots further back to the Scholasticism of the Middle Ages, and particularly to the nominalism of Duns Scotus. As we have seen, the consequence of this philosophical position was that "being" became an overarching category in which God and humans existed in the same way. In this way, according to Milbank, Scotus and later medieval theologians "managed to construct the theological preconditions for the modern autonomy of philosophy and secular practice."[25, 26]

Milbank further traces the origin of the political, understood as an autonomous field of pure power, to the writings of Hobbes and Spinoza, and particularly to Hugo Grotius' account of natural law in the form of something that could be known *"etsi Deus non daretur:"* that is, even if there were no God.[27] With this move, Milbank argues, morality became increasingly a matter of inner will and conscience, and no longer about virtues shaped in community. It was this modern understanding of natural law, which in Milbank's understanding enabled a sealed-off totality of nature where justice no longer was perceived to relate to theological notions of the good, but to "mere" theoretical reflection.

In his review of Charles Taylor's *A Secular Age,* Milbank dwells on the relationship between disenchantment and secularization: that is, the connection between the loss of an enchanted worldview and the decline in religious beliefs and practices. Milbank here takes Calvinism, Bible belt fundamentalism, and Wahhabism, as examples of how "the disappearance of enchantment does not equate with decline of religion," or differently put, how disenchantment doesn't necessarily lead to secularization in the sense that all religious movements would disappear.[28] He nevertheless maintains (along with Taylor) that disenchantment encourages secularization. Milbank restates one of Taylor's basic arguments of how behavioral reform in Latin Christendom, which aimed to make people more pious, tended to dampen the popularity of festive and carnivalesque elements in popular piety (closely linked to enchantment), and eventually led to secularization. Milbank goes on to condense Taylor's thesis as "reform engendered secularization in the Latin West," and finds beneath it an underlying thesis about religion which he finds convincing.[29] The conception of religion – or rather, the popular understanding of the religious person – that Milbank supports, is the paradoxical combination of, on the one hand, the Dionysic aspects of someone that goes beyond the conventions in terms of beliefs and experiences, paired, on the other hand, with someone who is leading a moral and ordered life. Milbank claims that "the religious" will be reduced to the "merely ethical" if it ignores the mystical, the ecstatic, or the transcendent. By "merely ethical" Milbank intends the secular, immanent practice of grounding the ethical in pre-ethical notions such as happiness, freedom, and sympathy. However, Milbank is deeply skeptical of this strategy given what he perceives as the futility of grounding a notion of mutual benefit, or common good, on what he perceives as the "amorally pre-ethical."[30] In brief, Milbank's argument is that "by ignoring the more-than ethical one eventually gets the less than ethical," or differently put, that ethics can't be detached from religion (understood as transcendence) if nihilism is to be avoided.[31]

Milbank finds several affinities with Taylor's account of the driving forces behind secularization and what he denotes as the Radical Orthodox position. Milbank's way of telling the history of secularization puts emphasis on what he (with Taylor's terminology) calls "the intellectual deviance theory," which gives prominence to "bad theology" propounded by Scotus and univocal ontology. In particular, by "bad theology" Milbank is targeting the philosophical position of voluntarism, which emphasizes that nothing can limit the will and power of God, a position which he argues leads to the separation of "faith and reason." Milbank argues "We [RO] are saying that overpiety (Franciscan voluntarism) paradoxically undermines theology; he is saying that hyperreform of the laity paradoxically undermines belief."[32] Taylor, in *A Secular Age*, tells a somewhat different story and puts emphasis on what he refers to as the "Reform Meta-narrative," understood in a simplified way as the story of how the desire for reform in the late medieval period led to secularization in the Latin West.[33] However, Milbank admits that Taylor's account of the "Reform Meta-narrative" is more fundamental than the "the intellectual deviance theory," given that that story combines both theory and practice.[34] Nevertheless, he claims that in order to get an even more adequate account of secularization, one would have to bring together the "Reform Meta-narrative" and the "the intellectual deviance theory" in order to account for how scholastic theology relates to "disciplinary, pastoral, and legal practice."[35]

Milbank's account of the post-secular

Despite the fact that Milbank is widely viewed as representing one stream of post-secular thought, he rarely uses the term "post-secular" himself.[36]

What defines and separates Milbank's brand of post-secularity from someone such as, for example, Jürgen Habermas' draws in particular on his understanding of the "secular." For Milbank, the term "post-secular" describes a state in which "the secular" has been deconstructed, and where the assumption that religious traditions need to be mediated through a neutral secular discourse in order to make sense, are rejected in favor of a view that underlines the impossibility of neutrality. But, not only is the idea of the secular as a neutral sphere rejected, furthermore, the very distinction between religion and the secular is put into question.

The Australian philosopher Wayne Hudson, commenting on the German philosopher Friedrich Schelling, has described what he denotes as the standard view of the philosophy of religion as: first, that religion is an intelligible historical generic category; second, that philosophy can comprehend and restate what religion is *really* about; and third, that what is significant about religion is its "depth."[37] Milbank rejects all three of these statements by arguing that: (A) Attempts to construe "religion" as a genus is a futile project that most of the time ends up describing nothing but basic organizing categories for an entire culture, and furthermore, oftentimes embodies covert Christianization.[38] (B) The idea of a neutral and secular philosophy that, from a perspective untainted by "faith" can tell us what "religion" really is about, is, according to Milbank, the product of a mythical worldview. As already mentioned, Milbank calls this the myth of the secular, and understands it to be "but another 'religion'."[39] Instead, Milbank seeks "to challenge both the idea that there is a significant sociological 'reading' of religion and Christianity, which theology must 'take account of', and the idea that theology must borrow its diagnoses of social ills and recommendations of social solutions entirely from Marxist (or usually sub-Marxist) analysis, with some sociological admixture."[40] (C) Milbank rejects the idea of religion as a distinct sphere of human life given that it encourages a view in which ethics, aestethics, and politics are viewed as somehow separated from religion.[41] Instead he propounds a view in which religion is not seen as an analytical category, or as the natural manifestation of species' diversity, "but embodies in its practices and beliefs a continuous reading of the world."[42]

So, in conclusion, from Milbank's perspective Habermas' usage of the term post-secular is not post-secular enough, given that it doesn't question the modernist presumptions that underlies its understanding of concepts like "religion" and "the secular."

But, what does Milbank seek to accomplish with his particular brand of "post-secular" thought? By rejecting Kant's account of a neutral and pure reason, and by pointing to the interconnection between politics and religion, Milbank's post-secularism is perhaps best read as a critique of the Enlightenment presuppositions underlying liberalism. In fact, Milbank's emphasis on the non-avoidability of the theological and metaphysical makes his post-secularism not just post-liberal, but blatantly critical of liberalism. Contrary to a liberal understanding of the secular as a means of liberation from religious oppression and violence, Milbank understands the secular to be totalitarian and even "terroristic" since "it acknowledges no supra-human power beyond itself by which it might be measured and limited."[43] Milbank's post-secular political hope for a new state of affairs is linked to the possibility of a new universal discourse. Since he deems that the old attempt of reaching universality on the basis of "enlightenment rationality" in the form of liberalism has failed, Milbank instead looks to "a newly serious post-secular, rather than neo-modern, investigation into the universal."[44]

4.2 Milbank's metaphysics

In the following I will account for the relation between John Milbank's metaphysics and his particular brand of post-secularism. Specifically, I will focus on how his analogical view of metaphysics has implications for his view of pluralism and religious difference.

Secular ontology against theological metaphysics

How did the secular come to be perceived as "natural?" This is a central question for Milbank, who argues that the secular was constructed, not by philosophers hostile to religion, but by theologians who constructed a "de-sacralized backdrop" to reality.[45] Milbank claims that the rationale behind this move within medieval theology was to secure the freedom of God against conceptions of nature that could be understood as setting limits to God's omnipotent freedom. The issue at hand concerned whether God's power could be limited by some other normative power or moral requirement existing prior to God's willing them. This dilemma was expressed in the scholastic distinction between God's declared will *(potentia ordinata)*, which could be precisely known and serve as a basis for law, and the infinite power of God *(potentia absoluta)*, which is unknowable for humans. This distinction – which separated what God could do hypothetically in the abstract given his absolute power, and the consideration of what he had chosen and willed to do in actuality – gave rise to speculation about the relationship between God's capacity and volition. The question of whether God commands that which is morally good because it is morally good, or if it is morally good because God commands it, is the essential example of this dilemma. The reason that this seemingly obscure theological question is central to the emergence of the secular, Milbank argues, is that it makes possible a non-theological sphere from which it is possible to judge God's action. Milbank here construes the emergence of a secular sphere in two steps: first, due to an "overwhelming nominalist stress on the gulf" between God's declared will and God's absolute power; and, secondly, a theological stream of thought that emphasized God's will over his reason, known as voluntarism.[46] Milbank in this way puts nominalism and voluntarism at the root of the secular, and thereby makes theological positions concerning the nature of God's will (and not secular philosophy or historical materialism) central to the emergence of the secular. From this perspective, God is neither bound by the laws of nature, nor by his previous determinations. Instead, God is free to do whatever he wills, not bound or limited by reason or an immutable order of nature. As a consequence, the only source of knowledge of God available is through revelation. The theological claim that God's infinite power *(potentia absoluta)* is unknowable for humans, as opposed to Aquinas' view that we can have a limited knowledge of God's will through nature, leads according to Milbank, to a radical separation between God and the world, and consequently to a separation of philosophy from theology.[47] Since God's will is no longer understood to be revealed in nature, the world becomes understandable in itself without reference to God. It is this ontology that, according to Milbank, lies at the heart of the modern creation of a secular sphere.

Of particular importance for Milbank's ontology is the difference in "being" or existence between God and humans. However, in order to make sense of Milbank's theologically infused ontology, it is necessary to have an understanding of the historical debates regarding the meaning of the term "being" to which Milbank refers. During the Middle Ages a theological shift took place that made being in general (God included) the prime object of metaphysics. This shift was essentially brought about by Duns Scotus' theories on "univocity of being," which held that "The difference between God and creatures, at least with regard to God's possession of the pure perfections, is ultimately one of degree."[48] This theological shift has been linked to what later came to be called "ontotheology" (a term which has oftentimes been used as a pejorative label to reject metaphysics in general), and points to problems related to describing God in generic philosophical categories such as omnipotent, omniscient, and benevolent. According to Heidegger, and Kant before him, such an approach transgresses the radical divide between knowledge and faith, and between philosophy and theology, and masquerades as a being based on a secure knowledge about the ultimate. The problem with metaphysics understood as ontotheology is thus, according to Heidegger, that it represents "a thinking that is not wholly thoughtful of its self-imposed limits."[49]

Opposing the depiction of his thinking as ontotheological, Milbank claims to profess a different sort of metaphysics. He understands God (or Being), as the transcendent source of all that exists (or has being), and thereby rejects an account of metaphysics that seeks to include God in a metaphysical scheme which puts God and humans on the same ontological plane, as opposed to an account of metaphysics which emphasize the qualitative difference between God and humans.[50] In this sense Milbank claims to escape the problem of ontotheology, since he perceives his metaphysics to be subject to a transcendent God and not based on a rationalistic approach of pure reason. Given Milbank's critique of Scotus' univocal ontology where God (or Being) is put on the same ontological plane as beings. Milbank argues that his (Aquinas) understanding of metaphysics escapes the charges of ontotheology as it doesn't conflate Being with beings and thus resist to "idolatrously describe God as 'an individual'."[51] Bluntly put, Milbank is sharply critical of any metaphysical account that he understands as failing to recognize the ontological difference between God and humans. This theme will be explored in more detail in chapter 6, under the heading *Different accounts of being: univocity vs. analogy*.

According to Milbank, modernity reinterprets metaphysics (drawing on Scotus) as a transcendental ontology in that it seeks to establish finite bounds for the knowable.[52] The term transcendental ontology here refers to an account of being that disregards any particularities of different beings, and instead focuses on what is common to all forms of beings (including God). The problem with this, he claims, is that it leads to a foundationalism in which the conditions for the possibility of knowing (the transcendental) are grounded in an assumed "secure" and immanent position from which the limits of knowledge can be determined (and thus rules out any reference to the transcendent).[53] This secure position is commonly referred to as the Kantian transcendental subject since it takes it starting point and derives it horizons from the scope of the human subject (and thus claims that there can be no knowledge of the divine). However, Milbank rejects this position, given his claim that "no such fundamental account, in the sense of something neutral, rational and universal, is really available."[54] Differently put, Milbank rejects a transcendental account of ontology due to what he argues is an illegitimate assumption about being in general as "simply the 'matter of fact'," where it is assumed that "a priori structured thought-processes of the mind can be somehow 'matched' with empirical information."[55]

Milbank instead seeks to ground his metaphysics in theology: "it is theology itself that will have to provide its own account of the final causes at work in human history, on the basis of its own particular, and historically specific faith."[56] What Milbank seeks to develop in his work is, in his own words "first and foremost an ecclesiology," rather than an abstract metaphysical theory.[57] What this means, along with its sociopolitical implications will be addressed in more detail in Section 3.3, where I account for *Milbank's post-secularism in practice*.

Difference, nihilism and violence

A key part of Milbank's central work, *Theology and Social Theory*, is focused on how his theological account of virtue and goodness relates to difference. Milbank understands the concept of difference in a broad sense to denote the classic philosophical dilemma regarding the relation between difference and sameness (or identity), and applies it with regards to conflicting ethical and social views. According to him, our conception of difference has consequences for how we socially relate to that which is unlike us. One of Milbank's central claims is that his account of Christian theology constitutes a unique way of resolving conflicts stemming from difference. During modernity, Milbank suggests, it was possible to reduce religion to something more basic: such as social control, discipline for production, or psychological needs. However, the new "postmodern mode of suspicion claims no ground upon which to decode the hidden truth underlying religion's spurious truth-claims. It cannot demythologize, nor question the content of belief over against a standard of truth. It can, however, relativize and question claims to universality."[58] So, whereas it was previously acceptable to compare differences based on "universal" categories, Milbank depicts the contemporary "postmodern" condition as one where every truth claim is deconstructed into mere "difference." Thus "postmodernity" offers no platform from which one can adjudicate differing claims; all that can be said is that the claims are different. The obvious implication of "many incommensurable truths" leads, and here Milbank follows Nietzsche, to a situation in which "every truth is arbitrary, every truth is the will-to-power."[59]

Milbank understands the postmodern condition to be secular and nihilistic in the sense that it is unhooked from any metaphysical account of virtue or goodness. Consequently, what is considered good or evil in the secular realm is, according to Milbank, entirely contingent. Or differently put, it is arbitrary and could have been construed differently. The notion of arbitrariness leads, according to Milbank, to the subjection of morality to the will to power; all that remains is "the irreducible difference of opinion and aspiration, or the arbitrariness of impulse and invention."[60] This means that discussions of good and evil will be subjected to power struggles in the wake of the death of God as a transcendent guarantor of values. Since there is no longer any hope of finding a solution that is deemed ultimate and objectively good, the conflict will eventually come down to violence.

If one wishes to escape the problems of nihilism related to the secular, the only possibility is, according to Milbank, a social order grounded on virtue. However, the complications related to talk about "virtue in general" are numerous. One of Milbank's concerns is absence of specificity: *which* tradition of virtue is to be propounded? Milbank thus rejects the approach to propound virtue in general as some sort of secure foundation against nihilism. In fact, Milbank rejects the idea that there are any arguments against nihilism of a general kind.[61] Milbank further argues that Kant's attempt to ground virtue in the human will soon collapse when it is realized that will and reason are not ahistorical facts about an essential human subject. Milbank here follows Foucault in his claim that reason, freedom and the human subject are far from neutral, but always biased and tangled up in power struggles. It is here that Milbank sees the real problem arising, since, if there is nothing but abstract power, and if the Kantian (or Habermasian) call for emancipation is equally involved in power struggles, what alternatives are there? Milbank's here suggests that "[t]o say 'emancipate' is only to say maximize negative freedom of choice, and to say 'freedom' is to say arbitrary power."[62] Milbank is thus equally critical of a foundationalism that seeks to counter nihilism by propounding virtue in general, and of a foundationalism based on the objectivity of reason.

Milbank describes the contemporary condition as the "postmodern" affirmation of "infinite difference" that sees reality as inherently conflictual.[63] Milbank refers to this condition as an "ontology of violence," which he explains as a view of the world which "assumes the priority of force and tells how this force is best managed and confined by counter-force."[64] This ontological priority of violence assumes a naturally given element of chaotic conflict at the root of human existence. Milbank sees this ontology as central in the modern, secular legitimation of the role of the state. Violence and specifically religious conflicts must, according to this view, be tamed and ordered by the stability of the state. A further and equally important point for Milbank concerns the political and societal implications of this understanding of the state. Milbank argues that modernity, in its emphasis on a powerful secular state as the facilitator of peace, tends to cut out societal "middle associations" and establish a direct relationship between the "sovereign" state and the "private" individual.[65] On the other hand, Milbank argues, in a social order based on virtue, the role of the state is changed from mere policing of order and implementing the will of the majority. Instead, in Milbank's own theologically infused social vision, the role of the state includes the moral education of its citizens about what is considered "objectively desirable goals for human beings."[66] However, as Milbank puts it "[t]he possibility of such a politics depends upon the acceptance of the view that there is a 'right', and in this sense a 'natural' way for human beings to be, although this cannot be discovered from an empirical survey of our pre-cultural constitution."[67] Milbank further argues that the only virtue tradition able to sustain such a project is the Christian tradition.[68]

As a contrast to the ontology of violence, which Milbank links to Nietzsche's moral ideal, he positions the Christian ontology of peace. Milbank points to the North African, fourth century Church father Augustine, and in particular to his theological and social vision *City of God*. In this treatise Augustine depicts the city of God as a non-antagonistic, peaceful mode of life, in contrast to the earthly city, characterized by self-love, pride and arbitrary, and therefore violent, power over others.[69] A central point for Milbank with regards to Augustine's ontology of peace – that is, the ontological priority of peace over conflict – is that it is anchored in a narrative, or a *mythos*, not in abstract universal reason. So, against the ontology of violence, Milbank suggests that we propound the equally unfounded and mythical story of the ontological primacy of peace.

Difference and analogy

As we have seen Milbank's theological vision contrasts an ontology of violence, anchored in chaos, or nihilism, with an ontology that assumes the "sociality of harmonious difference" – an ontology of peace.[70] But, what is meant by "harmonious difference?" The question of how we can live together in mutual agreement despite our differences, depends, according to Milbank, on whether it is possible to find "an 'analogy' or a 'common measure' between differences."[71] However, it is important for Milbank to do so in a manner that does not reduce differences to mere instances of a common essence. Put another way, Milbank seeks to find a "commonness" that does not "flatten out" difference, but which respect differences in a way that finds likeness, not despite, but through differences. This paradoxical claim draws on Milbank's understanding of the metaphysical notion of "analogy."

Milbank is, as we have seen, deeply critical of the Enlightenment attempt to reconcile difference through reason. Instead Milbank argues for an understanding of virtue that is "not deconstructible to difference, but that also embraces an analogically understood difference."[72] The notion of analogy draws on a metaphysical understanding in which everything is understood as to "participate in being." Milbank's idea of participation draws specifically on Plato's theory of the "five meta forms" in *The Sophist*: "being," "rest," "movement," "same," and "difference." According to Plato, everything participates in being to the extent that it has existence. Milbank here emphasizes how, not only everything participate in the "same," but in addition, everything also "participate in difference (thateron) because even the same is different from difference, and being is different from motion, as motion is not the whole of being."[73] The fact that difference, and not only being, is understood to participate in everything is key to understanding Milbank's analogical account of participation. This understanding stands in opposition to postmodern philosophers like Jacques Derrida and Gilles Deleuze who emphasize difference against sameness. Instead, Milbank claims that difference is a necessary participant in the divine whole; unity or beauty would not exist without difference.

Milbank claims that the analogical participation is one of the most distinctive features of Christianity.[74] Milbank here invokes the theological doctrine of the Trinity and the relations between Father, Son and Spirit in order to make this harmonious, or "charitable difference," possible.[75] In an analogous way with the Trinity, Milbank understands all of reality to be relationally joined together. Within the unifying frame of the Trinity as the transcendent source of all being, everything that exists is in Milbank's understanding mutually constituted by its opposite. This understanding of the triune God, as in itself displaying difference, leads Milbank to claim that God *is* difference, in the sense that analogy implies "identity and difference at once."[76]

It should again be pointed out that Milbank doesn't seek to ground his beliefs on a universal base of reason, but instead turns to the Church Fathers, and seeks to elaborate a Christian "reason;" a "reason that that bears the marks of the incarnation and Pentecost."[77] Milbank thus paradoxically propounds Christian theology insofar as it is a narrative, and rejects nihilism insofar as it is "positivist" or "metaphysical." That is, he acknowledges his own position as being predicated on a story, and rejects the claims of any rival perspective to be grounded on a foundational account of reason or reality.

Milbank further claims that, because his account of Christianity is a story or a *mythos*, it can't be refuted "but only out-narrated," and that Christianity, for reasons of "literary taste," offers "a much better story."[78]

However, as has been pointed out by the British philosopher, Gavin Hyman "even when nihilism is itself 'unmasked' as being itself just an unfounded mythos, Milbank continues to oppose it on the grounds that Christianity tells a much better story."[79] The critical question posed to Milbank thus becomes: On what grounds are one supposed to choose one story over another if no overarching meta-narrative exists to provide criteria and enable such a choice? Differently put: Is there no foundation from which it is possible to claim that one narrative is better than another? Confronted with this critique Milbank admits that his narrative of ontological peace is "not really an ungrounded decision;" instead, he appeals to "a certain inchoate current human preference for peace over violence" along with "a certain bias towards reason rather than unreason," both of which he understand to some extent as "innate" and as a cultural product of Christian civilization.[80] However, Milbank maintains that his ontology of peace is "a debatable account of actual real history – in relation to which one could urge facts, reasons, probabilities and persuasions both for and against."[81] Given that Milbank's theological account is subject to rational inquiries, we will move on by investigating the political implication of his *mythos*.

4.3 Milbank's post-secularism in practice

What does a society shaped by Milbank's account of analogy look like? What are the political implications of Milbank's ontology of peace, and how do these relate to religious difference?

Milbank labels himself a Christian socialist, deeply critical of neoliberal politics and its dismantling of the welfare state. However, he does not align himself with leftist thinkers like Jürgen Habermas who seek to retrieve Enlightenment ideals against "postmodern" relativism.[82] Instead, Milbank seeks to formulate a new way of pursuing the tradition of socialism, one that is freed from modernist understandings of progress, and materialism, and less reliant on the state. He combines this with "a conservative anti-capitalist thematics" which entails "the traditions of classical and biblical political thought." Central to this ideal is an openness to religion and the claim that "a just politics must refer beyond itself to transcendent norms."[83]

As we have seen, Milbank is highly critical of developments within liberal democracy, which he perceives as being plagued by an "indifference to truth," a "manipulation of opinion," and an inevitable drift towards "populism."[84] At the root of his critique is the contention that liberalism is based on an ontology of violence, which entails the assumption that we are to nurture our own self-interest, and also to seek protection from the egotism of others. Milbank here targets Adams Smith's model of the market and society since it subordinates sympathy to self-interest, and assumes that every man "by nature" is "principally recommended to his own care."[85] In the end, Milbank argues, this leads to a liberalism that is unable to defend the very freedoms it once set out to defend, and which eventually is overcome by a neo-liberalism which only endorses "the free market along with the nation-state as a competitive unit."[86] Against the liberal emphasis on abstract contract and a "naturalization of original sin as original egotism," Milbank argues for the importance of mediating institutions between the state and the individual, such as the family, the church, and local business, which will be able to constrain the greed of the individual and the market.

Complex space

Milbank depicts the modern liberal social order as "simple space" in which citizens are viewed as isolated individuals that all have their counterpart in the sovereign state.[87] Against this view, Milbank holds that his version of "trinitarian transcendence," which emphasizes analogy and participation, calls for a "corporate," or "complex" understanding of society and authority.

Power in this corporatist view is spread out on several societal bodies, as opposed to being centralized in the all-powerful state. Milbank here draws on the notion of "subsidiarity," characteristic of Catholic social thought, in which society is perceived in organic terms: social bodies higher up the societal hierarchy should support, rather than constrain and control, lower levels of social bodies.[88] The "complex space" in this sense entails an understanding of society where the relations between citizens and different social bodies – such as guilds, unions, clubs, churches and business – are made central, and in which different people and groups are thought to have different talents and insights, which "they share for the good of the whole body."[89]

Milbank describes the enlightenment "simple space" as secular and the "complex space" as sacred. In the "simple space," which presupposes a distinction between sacred and secular, God, or Nature, commands the sovereign who then rules according to a logic in which the parts are subsumed to the whole. Counter to this perspective Milbank propounds a form of pluralist distribution of sovereignty that emphasizes the importance of civil society and of intermediate associations. According to this model "every act of association, every act of economic exchange, involves a mutual judgment about what is right, true and beautiful, about the order we are to have in common."[90] Furthermore, in the "complex space," by contrast, the secular/sacred distinction is undone and the sacred is no longer understood as a distinct source of power which can be manipulated by law. Rather the social order is perceived to be infused with the "sacred."

One controversial aspect of Milbank's Christian democracy concerns his hierarchical view of society, or more specifically "the reservation of a non-democratic educative sphere concerned with finding the truth, not ascertaining majority opinion."[91] Milbank advocates a "mixed government grounded in eternal law." What this means is that he propounds a form of government that integrates elements of democracy, aristocracy, and monarchy, where some issues are decided by the majority of the people, some other issues by few, and other issues by a single person. Milbank justifies this constitutional arrangement with the need for a mechanism that can limit the scope of what the majority can decide on. As we saw in the section on Milbank's account of the secular, he also calls for "monarchic commitment." By this he means a notion of justice guaranteed by "a transcendent 'One' [...] that is unmoved by either the prejudices of the Few or those of the Many."[92] This is Milbank's attempt at a constitutional safeguard against the whims of the majority on the one hand, and against the tyranny of the sovereign ruler, on the other. In fact, Milbank argues that "democracy, as 'the rule of the many', can only function without manipulation of opinion if it is balanced by what we might call an 'aristocratic' element of the pursuit of truth and virtue for their own sake."[93]

Differently put, Milbank argues that democracy needs a hierarchical or "monarchic" element that is able to disregard popular opinion.

Milbank's political vision has, perhaps not surprisingly, been accused of displaying theocratic tendencies.[94] In fact, when confronted with this critique, Milbank himself admits that his vision is a form of "democratized theocracy."[95] However, Milbank qualifies this by making certain delimitations. For example, he argues that the power that is controlling legislation and punishment mustn't be "directly in the name of God, and there mustn't be certainly a quasi-sacral caste that is performing these actions." However, when it comes to political bodies dealing with education and economy, he is more open to "the permeation of church into all these functions."[96] Furthermore, Milbank points out the paradox that the notion of theocracy is inconceivable without a certain level of secularization since "a theory which limits rule only to a sacral class with a monopoly on divine mediation, requires there to be a distinct secular sphere over which to exercise this authority."[97] Against an understanding of the secular and the sacred as distinct spheres, Milbank argues that the divine is mediated through participation. Theocracy, Milbank argues, becomes problematic when the secular is seen as a separate sphere. As opposing examples Milbank mentions the societies of ancient Athens and Israel in which he argues that transcendence was not delimited to a specific sphere, but understood as being mediated through all of society. At the other hand, he argues "[o]nce the political is seen as a permanent natural sphere, pursuing positive finite ends, then, inevitably, firm lines of division arise between what is 'secular' and what is 'spiritual'."[98]

Milbank furthermore provocatively rejects the distinction between Christianity and Christendom. Traditionally the former denotes the religion that gathers "believers," and the latter term is used to designate the cultural and political impact of the former. However, Milbank argues "Christians rightly believe in the paradox that true power is attained through receptive weakness, in self-offering unto death, infinite forgiveness, and ecstatic reciprocity and reconciliation," then they "must believe that such stances should prevail."[99] Milbank takes this to mean that Christians must implement these stances in all of culture and politics, since failing to do so would undermine the belief in the incarnation as reality. Accordingly, the distinction between Christianity and Christendom is abolished.

Given Milbank's view of his own project as an ecclesiology, as an account of the church as a society, it becomes in his words "possible to consider ecclesiology as also a 'sociology'."[100] Against the accusation that talk of "a Christian sociology" would be equally silly as talking about "Christian mathematics," Milbank argues that there "can be no sociology in the sense of a universal 'rational' account of the 'social' character of all societies," and that Christian sociology just explains "the vantage point of, a distinct society, the Church."[101] The task of Milbank's project is in this sense rather to combine the Christian "mythos" with a Christian praxis in a manner that refuses to treat reason and morality as ahistorical universals. Instead Milbank seeks to establish Christianity as a narrative, which, as we have seen, has political consequences. But what implications does Milbank's Christian, theocratic democracy have for other religions? How does his account of pluralism relate to religious difference?

Organic pluralism and religious difference

Milbank has called for the invention of a new sort of politics, which he refers to as "traditionalist socialism" or "Red Toryism."[102] This politics entails the corporatist vision of society just mentioned, and "links egalitarianism to the pursuit of objective values and virtues."[103] This approach has interesting implications for questions related to religious difference, as Milbank argues it has the capacity for a "more heterogeneous pluralism and tolerance of differing groups."[104] This is a reaction to the liberal democratic notion of tolerance which Milbank seeks to counter, due to what he understands as its individualism and abstract social contract (as seen in Hobbes and Locke). Moreover, Milbank argues that liberalism, given its reluctance to commit to "thick" or substantive accounts of the good life (as opposed to negative accounts of freedom) self-deconstructs, as its sole focus on the individual is unable to sustain an account of community. As a consequence, Milbank argues that liberal principles, in the end, will prioritize the rights of the individual over those of the group, and will thus be unable to defend corporate religious freedom.[105] Instead, Milbank boldly claims that the origins of pluralism lie in Western "corporatism." This "organicist pluralism," which Milbank depicts as Catholic and Thomist, is, he argues, able to embrace elements that are foreign to it as long as it shares an overarching vision of the good society. In Milbank's words: "political society as a whole need not entirely agree with the premises of the Baptist Church, nor the Muslim *umma*, to be able nonetheless to accept that they are performing roles that contribute to the cohesion of the entire political body."[106] It is thus possible "to cope with a certain degree of 'dissenting pluralism' within an 'organically pluralist' framework."[107] The primary reason that Milbank argues that "organicist pluralism" is superior to liberal tolerance has to do with what he sees as liberalism's inability to account for the whole, or to give a positive account of society in terms of purpose or *telos*.

Milbank provocatively argues that a "secular, neutral, liberal perspective" is unable to "advance the search of 'human dignity as such'." The reason for this, he argues, is that it lacks a substantive notion of what this dignity or human value consists of. What is needed is according to Milbank, is "a specific religious mindset – one that provides a definite metaphysical framework within which it makes sense to talk of such a thing at all."[108]

In his essay *Shari'a and the True Basis of Group Rights*, Milbank outlines his understanding of the problems related to issues of religious group rights. He starts by identifying two common positions regarding religious group rights, which each represent different understandings of religion, as well as what constitutes a group. Central to Milbank's distinction between these two positions is the issue of whether the difference, or otherness, that is central to the group's identity is perceived to be "appearing" or "non-appearing" (or differently put, visible or non-visible).[109] The first position, which Milbank associates with the thought of the French philosopher Emmanuel Levinas, seeks the respect of the general public on the basis of the appearing "otherness" of religion, in virtue of its "mystical" character. Milbank finds this strategy unviable given what he sees as "the increasing secular rejection of any truths outside those guaranteed by science" and "little admiration for any values other than those of extending freedom of choice."[110] If, according to the second position, one considers the otherness of the religious group as "non-appearing," this leads to questions regarding the identity of the group. The problem thus concerns what it is exactly that is to be respected, since according to Milbank "one can universally respect the freedom of the other insofar as this is publicly verifiable. But respect for something that does not appear is a blank cheque."[111] According to these two positions, one is, according to Milbank, stuck with the choice of either "exotifying" religion, as in the first position, or, legitimizing the group *qua* group and thereby ignoring the possible destructive, or anti-civil purpose of a group, as in the second position. Milbank ascribes this seemingly unresolvable dilemma to problems that he takes to be inherent to liberalism and its atomistic emphasis on individual rights. Given that liberalism is based on the notion of a freely choosing, and self-determining, individual, Milbank asks "If one treats the group as such an individual, then how can the group take precedence over the members of the group who have contracted into it – and therefore must be free to break their 'original' contracts at any time in the face of new collective developments?"[112]

In response to this account of liberalism Milbank controversially claims that only a hegemonic Christianity can provide the basis for religious group rights, or perhaps even more provocatively, that only a "Christian outlook, and nor a secular one, can accord to Islam respect as Islam."[113] Milbank acknowledges that he as a Christian holds much in common with Muslim beliefs, but that this does not lead him to suppose that that there are secular reasons to acknowledge Muslim sacrality. Instead he argues that a Christian polity can support sacrality insofar as it is similar to Christianity's own sense of sacrality. Given that Milbank rejects the idea that a culture or polity can be religious in general (as opposed to only in a specific way), he consequently argues that "a neutral religious pluralism of the multiculturalist variety can only be an expression of secularity."[114] Instead, Milbank argues that religious liberty can only be safeguarded by "a religious perspective – one which affirms that a 'faith' beyond reason is needed in order to establish the socio-political order." "Faith," in this context, denotes a "necessary but unprovable 'trust'" that Milbank holds to be necessary "for any human project to get going."[115]

The kind of "post-secular, rather than neo-modern" universalism that Milbank propounds represents a pre-modern blend of ontology and religion in the form of Platonism and Christianity.[116] This perspective stands in stark opposition to the Enlightenment account of rational universality that seeks to make strict distinctions between religion, politics and the secular. Milbank agrees that there is a need for a universal discourse if we are to sustain political hope in the midst of what he sees as our fragmented time. This universal discourse is however, according to him, not to be found in "procedural secularity" as represented by Habermas, and which presents itself as supposedly neutral with regards to nonbelief and religion. The problem with such an account of neutrality is from Milbank's perspective that it is itself entirely secular (and not neutral), and "therefore unable to accord the religious perspective equal protection."[117] As we have seen, Milbank instead grounds his project on a theological account of metaphysics that holds that "politics must refer beyond itself to transcendent norms."[118] Milbank's understanding of transcendence is mediated through a platonic notion of analogy and participation in the divine being. In turn, this enables him to go beyond what he sees as "mere" mutual liberal tolerance to an understanding in which difference is harmoniously incorporated. He can then in an exclusivist manner go on to argue that only Christianity is able to provide a framework "that is able to comprehend 'the other'."[119]

Sharing in Milbank's critique of the secular as a neutral sphere, while subscribing to a very different account of metaphysics, is the American democracy theorist William E. Connolly, to whom we will turn next.

5
Becoming and Rhizomatic Pluralism

5.1 William Connolly

William Connolly is an American political theorist primarily known for his work on democracy, pluralism and secularism. His political philosophy is geared towards an understanding of pluralism that extends beyond the traditional liberal pluralism, and he draws his inspiration from a range of thinkers associated with both the pragmatist tradition, such as William James, and the continental tradition such as Friedrich Nietzsche, Michel Foucault and Gilles Deleuze. Connolly's work has therefore been described as an attempt to combine pragmatist political thinking with contemporary continental European philosophy.[1] Throughout his career, Connolly has engaged the conditions of democratic life in the twenty-first century. As a consequence, his political theory has touched on such topics as pluralism, materialism, religion, secularism, capitalism and neurobiology. At least two phases can be detected in his scholarship. In his earlier monographs Connolly explores different dimensions of identity and difference, pluralism and secularism. He has here reacted against what he perceives to be accounts of biased pluralism "in which some concerns, aspirations, and interests are privileged while others are placed at a serious disadvantage."[2] In his later works, Connolly has focused more on issues such as neuroscience, self-organizing processes, and critique of neo-liberalism. He has here engaged more deeply with issues related to immanent metaphysics and developed his own position of "immanent materialism." However, despite his interest in immanence he has continuously engaged with questions related to religions and the existential aspects of different worldviews and philosophies.

Connolly has, in relation to his critique of the "biased pluralism" of secularism (to which I will return below), written about the relation between religion and politics. He has done so with the purpose of working against what he sees as a certain secular dogmatism, and with the aim of upholding a dialogue with "believers" and "non-believers." This is seen most clearly in his *Why I am Not a Secularist* (1999), where Connolly engages more specifically with religion in liberal democracies and argues that secularist critique of religion too often embodies a narrow and intolerant understanding of public reason. As an alternative, Connolly seeks to formulate a new model of public life that, in a more inclusive way, seeks to reflect what he sees as the needs of pluralist societies. However, Connolly has also voiced critique of religions that have failed to embody inclusiveness. In *Capitalism and Christianity, American Style* (2008), Connolly engages the theme of religion and politics from an American perspective, and seeks a way for the democratic left to fight what he describes as the "evangelical-capitalist resonance machine's grip" on American religious and economic culture in order to put egalitarianism and ecological integrity on the political agenda. Connolly here argues that the liberal distinction between secular public and religious private life must be reworked.

Central to Connolly's understanding of pluralism is the relation between difference and identity. Our differences as human beings, social groups and cultures, are, according to Connolly, what constitute our identities. Understood in this way "to confess a particular identity is also to belong to difference."[3] This theme is most clearly developed in *Identity/Difference* (1991), where Connolly explores the relationship between personal identity and democratic politics, particularly in the domains of religion, ethics, sexuality, and ethnicity. Connolly's emphasis on how identity requires difference leads him to emphasize difference and otherness as central political questions. As a consequence Connolly has been quite critical of attempts to naturalize commonalities and identities at the expense of difference; to enforce identity over difference. This can be seen in various attempts to make commonalities "appear as unambiguous goods lodged in nature or consent or reason or the universal character of the normal individual or ideal dialogue or a higher direction in being."[4] Connolly is here equally critical of certain forms of liberalism that attempt to naturalize a certain type of rationality, as well as certain religious traditions that preach fixed and naturalized gender roles. Against such a position, Connolly seeks to establish a more inclusive and generous pluralism by examining how conceptions of identity are taken for granted in pluralist celebrations of "diversity." Instead of liberal tolerance Connolly is introducing the notion of "agonistic respect," by which he intends an attitude that acknowledges the need to limit ones own self-assertion "so that other faiths can count for something too."[5] Agonism emphasizes the importance of conflict and otherness to politics. Identity is here understood as depending on otherness in the sense that one's identity only makes sense in relation to that which it opposes. The wider import of this conception amongst proponents of agonistic theory, such as Connolly and the Belgian political theorist Chantal Mouffe, is that democratic theory and politics should not assume a fixed or autonomous identity from which politics should emerge. Rather, it is argued that "a vibrant clash of democratic political positions" is a mark of a well-functioning democracy.[6] According to Connolly's agonistic theory, this has important implications for the relation between pluralism and democracy. First, against the traditions of Rawlsian theories of justice and Habermasian theories of deliberative democracy, agonistic theory doesn't start out by seeking a rational consensus, but acknowledges instead the complexities of the construction of identities. Secondly, it opens up space for the recognition of difference in the public sphere, instead of relegating it to the private sphere. And third, it opens up the notion of identities able to transcend that of the national state. The notion of agonism is more fully developed in *Pluralism* (2005) where Connolly further expounds on a multidimensional pluralism: what he calls a "deep pluralism," where participants from multiple minorities bring multiple dimensions of their social and personal lives with them into the public realm, including existential creeds.[7] Connolly further argues that deep, multidimensional pluralism is the best way to promote justice and inclusion without violence. Connolly contrasts his account of "deep pluralism" with what he perceives to be a shallow, secular pluralism, and seeks to make room for different groups to bring their religious beliefs into the public realm. He also engages pluralism in relation to evil, ethics, relativism, globalization, and sovereignty. This multitude of difference is, in Connolly's view, not managed by liberal tolerance since, as he puts it "people seldom enjoy being tolerated that much, since it carries the onus of being at the mercy of a putative majority that often construes its own position to be beyond question."[8]

With the publication of *Neuropolitics* (2002), Connolly starts his engagement with neuroscience in order to explore the way brain activity is influenced by cultural conditions. Connolly draws on recent brain/body research to explore the blurring of the nature/culture distinction and to develop the political aspects of this condition, which he refers to as "micropolitics." With this concept Connolly seeks to highlight the bodily aspects of culture and they way in which the senses can be educated in specific ways through practices and institutions, all with the agenda of advancing a political pluralism. In *A World of Becoming* (2011), Connolly outlines a political philosophy suited to account for a world whose powers of creative evolution he perceives to go beyond what reductive materialism can account for. Connolly approaches complex, interacting systems, including those of climate change, biological evolution, economic practices, and geological formations, and uses the ontological concept of becoming to account for them in a way that, he argues, better captures their complexity than traditional reductionistic science. It is through this ontological account of becoming that Connolly seeks to develop an alternative account of transcendence that, while still rejecting the idea of God or a spiritual realm, affirms an immanent account of transcendence. Connolly in this way seeks to find a third way between a Christian account of transcendence and mechanical materialism, which he critiques for being unable to capture the richness of reality. Connolly continues this line of thought in *The Fragility of Things* (2013) where he focuses on self-organizing systems such as ecological, biological, and climate systems, and financial markets, which he argues display creative capacities that resist a strict division between nonliving nature and human agency. Connolly here argues that the fragility of these systems, in terms of the way they impinge on politico-economic life (and vice versa), calls for a politics of radical pluralism. In this sense, Connolly uses a blend of modern science and postmodern theory to construe an ontology that, he claims, calls for an alternative politics.

Connolly refers to his own philosophical perspective as "immanent naturalism." By this term Connolly intends an understanding of the world in which human activity takes place without the involvement of any supernatural force. However, at the same time, Connolly rejects any account of the universe that makes it reducible to strictly mechanistic accounts, given what he sees as the inability of efficient causality to explain the complexity at hand in the interaction between phenomena such as neural, viral, climatic, chemical and civilizational force-fields.[9] Connolly's examples of the interaction of complex systems ranges from "when a period of capitalist growth accelerates a process of climate change that has a momentum of its own and that then recoils back upon the self-sustaining capacity of capitalism" to "when a virulent virus jumps from birds or pigs to human beings and then mutates again as it rides around the world through air travel."[10] In this sense, Connolly emphasizes how cultural and natural processes mix with different modes of being. Connolly's claim is not that efficient causality never operates, but rather that it is unable to deal with the various forms of agency and self-organization in processes such as these. Instead he seeks to convey an understanding of the world as being richer, more complex, and more fragile than we have come to perceive it during modernity.[11] Accordingly, Connolly claims a middle position between radical transcendence and the sufficiency of the immanent law-like model of nature endorsed by classical natural science. Connolly's position is thus related to what has been called an "immanent transcendence," understood as the reconfiguration of transcendence in immanent or materialist terms.[12]

The paradoxical term "immanent transcendence" is intended to react against an understanding of transcendence as that which is beyond immanence. The use of "immanent transcendence" aims to surmount the dualism of transcendence and immanence by subscribing to a non-reductive view of materialism. According to such a stance, matter will no longer be accounted for in terms of Newtonian mass, but is described as "spontaneous" and "energetic." Connolly's immanent transcendence thus seeks to materialize transcendence so that it occurs completely on the immanent plane. In fact, while Connolly clearly subscribes to a philosophy of immanence "the very point of his immanent naturalism is to blur the stark division between immanence and transcendence."[13] This "blurring" is in Connolly's writings often exemplified by the emergence of complexity theory in natural science, which he understands as drawing natural science closer to cultural theory given that it surmounts reductionism. Complex systems deal with change by generating new possibilities or forks in the road, and "the direction selected affects everything else that later emerges, without determining everything else in a simple, linear way."[14] Connolly understands these changes as a form of emergent causality that are "neither reducible to chance, nor to explanation according to a classic concept of causality, nor to probability within a known distribution of possibilities."[15] What make this form of causality emergent are, according to Connolly, three things: it is not knowable in precise detail prior to the effects "the new effects become *infused* into the very being or organization of the second level in such a way that the cause cannot be said to be fully different from the effect engendered and, third, a series of loops and feedback loops operate between the first and second levels to generate a stabilized result."[16] Emergent causality is in this sense producing effects which are not open to full explanation or exact prediction in advance. Connolly employs this account of causality to take seriously what he feels traditional cultural theory, philosophy, and political theory, have ignored, namely:

> ...the biocultural organization of perception, the layered complexity of thought, multiple modes and degrees of agency in the world, innumerable intersections between nonhuman force-fields of several types and cultural life, the role of multi-media micropolitics in organizing nonconscious registers of intersubjective life, the critical role that cultivation of the visceral register of being plays in ethical life, the connections between natural and cultural time, and other issues besides.[17]

These complex systems and processes, along with their conjunctions, which transcend our ability to articulate them in advance, carry, according to Connolly, implications for how we construe the relation between nature and culture.

One of the defining characteristics of Connolly's contribution to political theory is his insistence on the inseparability of politics and metaphysics. According to Connolly, politics and metaphysics are inescapably bound insofar as "political interpretation projects presumptions about the primordial character of things."[18] In *The Augustinian Imperative (1993)*, Connolly engages the church father Augustine in light of Nietzsche and Foucault. Connolly here touches on themes such as the relationship between fundamentalism and heresy, arguing that the temptation to convert difference into heresy often flows from the effort to conceal uncertainties in one's faith or identity, but also pointing out the difficulties of criticizing fundamentalism from a positive position without that position itself being implicated in fundamentalism. Connolly here resists the idea of grounding morality in a fixed and fundamental account of reality, and instead propounds an ethic that, inspired by Nietzsche, finds inspiration in the experience of the "abundance of life." Furthermore, Connolly argues that every religion, existential outlook, worldview, or method of research, expresses an "ontopolitical interpretation," or a set of metaphysical presuppositions. In this way, to say that either something is fundamental, or that nothing is fundamental, are statements equally bound up with metaphysical assumptions. Thus there is no neutral position available, but every perspective is, according to Connolly, committed to certain unprovable assumptions about the nature of reality. Consequentially, Connolly uses "metaphysics" almost interchangeably with "existential faith."[19] Connolly here resists the Kantian tendency to translate "meta" in metaphysics as "beyond." Instead, he construes metaphysics as dealing with the fundamental character of things, and concludes that "every positive cultural interpretation is inhabited by a metaphysical dimension."[20] Connolly is therefore critical of any order that attempts to portray itself as natural or given, and has accordingly critiqued modern, secular perspectives, which are often thought to escape the realm of metaphysics or "ontopolitics."[21] Connolly rejects the philosophical position that conflicts and disagreements in politics and ethics do not require us to enter into discussions about metaphysics. John Rawls' claim that his theory of justice is political, rather than metaphysical, is a clear example of the position that Connolly rejects – the assumption that the central disagreements of today "do not reach this deep."[22] Despite the strong influence of Rawls' anti-metaphysical liberalism in contemporary political philosophy, Connolly, who draws no sharp distinction between the terms "metaphysics," "ontology," "faith" or "religion," thus argues that politics is inseparable from metaphysics.[23] Furthermore, Connolly doesn't recognize any sharp distinction "between philosophy and faith;" a distinction which, he admits, has formed the hallmark of secular thinking.[24] Instead, Connolly claims that every religious belief or creed has a philosophical component, and that every philosophy is invested with faith. Accordingly, he argues that " ... once you come to terms with the element of faith in utilitarianism, Kantianism and Hegelianism, and then re-encounter the philosophical components of Christianity [...] the academic marginalization of both Catholicism and Nietzscheanism loses much of its intellectual grounding. The modern, secular line of distinction between philosophy and faith begins to blur."[25]

Connolly defines "faith" as "a lived interpretation which so far has not been subjected to definitive demonstration, one that involves both refined reflection and a gut commitment below the threshold of complex intellectualization."[26] Consequently, Connolly's use of the word "faith" shouldn't be understood in traditionally religious terms as having to do with the supernatural. Instead, faith is here understood as an unavoidable condition of what it means to be a human. Subsequently, Connolly makes no strong distinction between "secular" and "religious" faiths. Instead he is interested in how different existential outlooks or "faiths" (religious or secular) are infused with both a "creedal dimension" and "lived sensibilities."[27] In particular he is interested in the relation between these two dimensions, and how creeds get incorporated into conduct (and vice versa). Connolly here argues that even "the way secularists dress, express themselves, fold hesitation into their speech, and practice methods of inquiry both expresses and helps to express their creeds."[28] Thus, Connolly argues in favor of "reworking the global distinctions in secular culture between 'religion' on the one side and 'science' and secular doctrines on the other."[29]

Connolly describes his own faith as a cultivation of a certain attentiveness to the manner in which nature brings about constant change – to "the fecundity of the moment from which new twists and turns can flow."[30] Connolly doesn't mind referring to this stance as a religion, and alternatively refers to his position as a non-theistic creed, or spirituality; by which he means "the most basic disposition toward the fundamental terms of existence."[31]

Connolly on the secular and secularism

Liberalism and secularism are, according to Connolly, related, and differ mostly in what they choose to emphasize. Where liberalism focuses on issues like rights and justice, secularism emphasizes public discourse and the role of religion in public life. Connolly himself "aspires to a critical liberalism that both expands and thickens the range of secularism;" so, while appreciative of certain elements in the liberal tradition such as rights and democratic institutions, Connolly is critical of liberal secularism in its dominant Western form.[32] Or, as he succinctly puts it "[i]f the nobility of secularism resides in its quest to enable multiple faiths to coexist on the same public space, its shallowness resides in the hubris of its distinction between private faith and public reason."[33] In particular, Connolly is critical of the negative Kantian and Rawlsian attitude towards metaphysics, and the attempt to separate private and public life, and dismisses this strain of secularism as being "too constipated to sustain the diversity they seek to admire."[34]

Connolly's understanding of the terms "secular" and "secularism" is perhaps best perceived as a development of his view of "interconnectedness" and "embeddedness" as central features of the human condition. According to Connolly, there is, as we have seen, no strict separation between nature and culture, given that every conception of culture, identity, ethics, or thinking, contains an image of nature. But, according to Connolly, the reverse is also true, so that "even the most adamant realist in, say, physics presupposes a cultural conception of how scientific cognition proceeds."[35] Connolly exemplifies the latter point by how the correspondence model of truth presupposes a relation between, on the one hand, our human capacities for cognition, and on the other hand, the world independent of those capacities. Drawing on Nietzsche, Connolly views such an outlook as containing "the remains of a forgotten theology:" that is, that it operates with the assumptions that the world has "a deep, unchanging structure" and that "such a structure is available to the cognition." According to Connolly (and Nietzsche), such beliefs would be deemed "highly improbable" in a culture that had not been conditioned by "faith in a world created by a universal, omniscient God."[36] In this sense Connolly wishes to point out that science, insofar as it presumes a law-like model of science, is insufficiently secularized. Instead, he propounds a view of the world that lies between a deterministic world and an arbitrary world of pure chance. As Connolly sees it, the inability to find an elevated, unconditioned, transcendental platform to be used as a secure ground for objective knowledge, is part of the human condition. In his words "[e]very cultural interpretation expresses an idea of nature; but because the partisans of each interpretation are themselves sunk in nature and culture, they lack a position above this field from which to reach definitive judgments about it."[37]

At the core of Connolly's critique is what he sees as liberal secularism's failure to realize that no position is entirely above faith and can therefore lay claim on the right to regulate other faiths. Connolly understands secularism, in its dominant expression, as combining "a distinctive organization of public space with a generic understanding of how discourse and ethical judgment proceed on that space."[38] Accordingly, Connolly's engagement with the secular concerns the connections between belief, embodiment, and practice, and in particular, the problems related to an agreed authoritative mode of public discourse. For this reason, Connolly argues that the "thin, intellectualist conceptions of public life advanced by secularists [is] insufficient," for reasons having to do with "the density of culture and the inspirational elements in ethics."[39] The secularist story prevails, according to Connolly, because it presents itself as "a self-sufficient public realm fostering freedom and governance without recourse to a specific religious faith."[40] Many secularists tend, in Connolly's words, to "reduce the self-understanding of their own faith to a set of abstract beliefs while concluding that a Muslim minority lacks the secular division between private belief and public behavior marking a tolerant society."[41] In this sense Connolly argues that secularism has become precisely what it initially sought to overthrow: a dogma stemming from overconfidence, or blind faith in reason, which excludes those who fail to abide by it. This is one of the reasons why Connolly claims that "secularism is coming apart at the seams."[42] Connolly further argues that, while secularism pretends to come to public life under a neutral flag, it actually comes with a set of deep convictions and philosophies that block out other deep convictions. In this sense he argues that "[s]everal variants of secularism kill two birds with one stone: as they try to seal public life from religious doctrines they also cast out a set of nontheistic orientations to reverence, ethics, and public life that deserve to be heard."[43] Instead of assuming a false neutrality, he argues, secularism ought to have an "agonistic respect for minorities who draw ethical inspiration from alternative sources, including nontheistic and asecular sources."[44] Connolly's goal therefore is to de-center the center: to sweep away the idea of a homogenous core in order to incorporate a plurality of ideologies.

According to Connolly, faith is a necessary part of what it means to be human, since "no secularist or rationalist since Spinoza has demonstrated the sufficiency of reason to itself."[45]

Connolly goes on to claim that any method (empirical, hermeneutical, etc.) assumes certain creeds, and thus sees faith and method as interconnected. Consequently, for Connolly, secularism is a "faith/method" aimed to deal with a plurality of faiths, which itself entails a "faith." But, if method in general, and secularism in particular, according to Connolly, are affected by existential faith, how does one judge between rival methods or faiths?[46]

Connolly perceives politics as braided into various other practices – cultural, economic, religious – and, accordingly, claims that there is no such thing as pure politics. In fact, he states: "there is nothing further from my thinking than to search for 'the autonomy of the political'."[47] Consequently, given what Connolly perceives as the impossibility of pure politics, the secular, understood as a sphere free from religion, also becomes an impossibility. Accordingly, he argues "a cautious reconfiguration of secular conceptions of theory, thinking, discourse, subjectivity, and intersubjectivity is needed to come to terms more actively with these registers of being."[48]

In his *Why I am not a Secularist*, Connolly sets out to refashion secularism beyond what he perceives to be the narrow conceptions of "religion" and "the secular." Connolly argues for a "more vibrant public pluralism" that will engage both religions and "irreligions."[49] Connolly's challenge consists in reimagining secularism as "a model of thinking, discourse, and public life," while at the same time rejecting the "opposite" view that "Christianity" or "the Judea-Christian tradition" should set the authoritative matrix of public life. Instead, he argues, we need to "renegotiate relations between interdependent partisans in a world in which no constituency's claim to embody the authoritative source of public reason is sanctified."[50]

Connolly's account of the post-secular

Given Connolly's claim that "secularism needs refashioning, not elimination," the term "post-secular" is, in Connolly's writings, related to various attempts to overcome what he perceives to be the shortcomings of traditional secularism in general, and pluralism in particular.[51] In this sense, Connolly's "post-secular" is perhaps best understood as an ethics of deep pluralism; or, in his words, a "postsecular ethos of public engagement between diverse spiritualities."[52] Accordingly, Connolly's post-secularism is one of radical inclusiveness that puts every worldview on the same epistemological level when it comes to its relation to faith. Connolly's "nontheistic, post-secular ethic" rejects the notion of solid grounds for morality.[53] Instead it affirms "the constitutive indispensability and fragility of ethics" and emphasizes the importance of an attitude of gratitude stemming from what he perceives as the abundance of life. Connolly here argues in favor of cultivating a "critical generosity" to those differences and distinctions that are central to one's own identity.[54] Central to Connolly's post-secular pluralism is what he calls "an ethos of engagement." This ethos is thought to open up conversations between different "faiths" (theist and atheist), and enable them to question their own creeds in a self-reflective manner. Connolly argues that we don't need external commands or guidelines to act ethically, and claims that "the dissolution of foundations does not automatically dissolve ethics."[55] Instead, Connolly contends that generous engagement with differences can be cultivated, both inside as well as outside religious traditions. In fact, he states that "the formation of multiple lines of connection across these spaces of difference is crucial to a generous ethos of engagement in a postsecular society."[56]

In order to uphold the connection between practice and belief, Connolly's deep, post-secular pluralism seeks to welcome each faith practice – along with all of that faith's particularities – into the public realm. In a manner that differs from Habermas' requirement to translate religious arguments into secular terms, Connolly seeks to overturn "the impossible counsel to bracket your faith when you participate in politics."[57] In an attempt to make his own post-secular perspective clear, he contrasts it to both orthodox Christianity (what he calls an Augustinian moment), and a typical secular position. Where Connolly imagines a traditional Christian to say: "we are fragile; god is perfect; the earth is solid and bountiful; we have been given dominion over it," he imagines the traditional secularist reply to be: "we are powerful; the old god is good only for marriages and funerals; nature is pliable and bountiful; we will attain mastery over it."[58] Connolly describes his own position, which he in this context labels "The posttheist, postsecular rejoinder," in relation to the previous positions, as "the earth is fragile; highly organized human economies are interwoven with its fragility; the sovereign god was on balance a destructive construction; the hegemony of the modern project of mastery results in the globalization of contingency;

nontheistic reverence for life and the earth remains to be cultivated."[59] Connolly is thus equally critical of the "projects of mastery" as they appear in the form of orthodox Christianity's assumption of a transcendent God, and assumption of scientific control. Rather, he seeks to embrace what he sees as the radically contingent nature of reality which evades both divine or human mastery.

Connolly's ethics is linked to his creed of a "postsecular, nontheistic reverence."[60] Central aspects of this creed include what Connolly calls a critical responsiveness. By this he means the attitude of self-revision and a willingness to modify one's own position, or in his words "a disposition to listen with new ears to a movement that may jostle elements in your identity."[61] This ethic is not derived or grounded in anything higher or transcendental. Instead, Connolly claims, it emerges out of a sense of gratitude for the abundance of the world of becoming (a term which will be explained further below). It is Connolly's conviction that "this impious, nontheistic reverence for life, can render a postsecular ethic both more alert to the fragility of ethics and more open to the play of difference in cultural life."[62] In brief, Connolly's post-secularism seeks to take seriously cultural pluralism in a globalized world. While rejecting the dogmatism seen in some religious traditions, Connolly is equally critical of the dogmatism of the predominant secularism, and rejects a postmetaphysical perspective which puts itself in a privileged position, away from "religious" views. Instead, Connolly seeks to rewrite secularism in pursuit of "an ethos of engagement in public life among a plurality of controversial metaphysical perspectives."[63]

5.2 William Connolly's ontology

As we have seen, Connolly has sharply criticized the secularist demand to strain out metaphysics from politics. He further holds that the claim to be "postmetaphysical" is highly problematic as it represses its own ontological assumptions and therefore displays a sort of hypocrisy. Another problem that Connolly sees with the attempt to abolish metaphysics has to do with the ambiguity of the term metaphysics itself. On the one hand "metaphysics" can signal that which is most fundamental, and on the other hand "that which goes beyond the physical, the sensible, or the realm of appearance."[64] In either case, Connolly argues, it is impossible to leave metaphysics entirely behind, if you understand the term to denote the fundamental character of things "every positive cultural interpretation is inhabited by a metaphysical dimension."[65] On the other hand, if you take metaphysics to denote that which is beyond the empirical, Connolly argues, as we shall see, that reality is not limited to that which reductive materialism can account for. Connolly has further criticized the presumption that modern, secular perspectives can escape the realm of ontology by giving "primacy of epistemology." By this he means a kind of thinking that assumes it has "access to criteria of knowledge that leave the realm of ontology behind or that your epistemology provides neutral test procedures through which to pose and resolve every ontological question."[66]

Against this perspective Connolly argues that the "primacy of epistemology" itself entails an ontology. The empiricist version of this attempt to screen out ontology is, according to Connolly, the tendency to reduce human beings to "subjects or agents of knowledge." In a similar way, Connolly argues that "invocations of overlapping consensus, ontological minimalism, nonfoundationalism, and the primacy of epistemology" are strategies used by certain social scientists to screen out the ontological dimension of any interpretation of reality. [67] By contrast, as will be more fully explored below, Connolly argues that any interpretation, or method to account for reality, by necessity has an ontological dimension.

Connolly sees Kant as a forerunner to the Habermasian version of postmetaphysical post-secularism that tends to make a sharp distinction between religion and the secular in the public sphere.[68] In order to understand Connolly's critique of this kind of secularism it is important to recognize his rejection of Kant's construal of Christianity as a "rational religion," which he sees as morphing into secularism.[69] Connolly is particularly critical of Kant's attempt to anchor rational religion in an allegedly independent law of morality, rather than the other way around (that is to say, to anchor morality in an ecclesiastical faith). By doing so, Connolly claims that Kant "retains the command model of morality from Augustinian Christianity, but he shifts the proximate point of command from the Christian God to the moral subject itself."[70] Connolly further critiques Kant's rational religion for being structurally similar to the "dogmatic" ecclesiology he seeks to replace. At the core of this critique lies, what Connolly perceives as, Kant's construal of as a too narrowly defined conception of rationality, and how this narrow account of rationality is used as the highest authority to settle disputes between religious sects. As a result of Kant's conception of rationality, Connolly argues, the sensible aspects of life and the body is depreciated, and the supersensible, along with a law-like understanding of morality, is elevated. Connolly goes on to link Kant's philosophy to post-Kantian secularist slogan-like talk about "political not metaphysical," "postmetaphysical," and "beyond metaphysics."[71]

However, the separation between religion and secular is not the only distinction that Connolly seeks to overcome. Against Kant's notion of religion primarily understood as "the good will," Connolly draws on the philosophy of Nietzsche, Foucault, and Deleuze, who suppose that "the will itself is conceived as a complex cultural/corporeal formation."[72] Inspired by these thinkers Connolly argues that:

> We participate in a body/brain/culture network that confounds or challenges the reductionism of sociobiology, the eliminative materialism of physicalists; the stark dualism of Cartesians; the explanatory hubris of classical empiricism; the flatness of rational choice theory; and, perhaps, the quest for deep, authoritative interpretation in some versions of phenomenology.[73]

Given the overturning of traditional dichotomies and the blurring of established borders that have regulated the liberal secularist understanding of the public sphere, Connolly argues for the need "to draw a larger plurality of metaphysical/religious orientations into public life."[74]

Nothing is fundamental

Where ontology in the traditional sense has been understood as something static, Connolly has explored the notion of "being" as something dynamic and ever-changing. Connolly here draws on Nietzsche, as well as the English philosopher Alfred North Whitehead, who has critiqued Western thought for its tendency to describe reality in static terms. Instead, Connolly makes categories denoting process, such as becoming and change, primary. Against the traditional understanding that ontology concerns the study of "the fundamental logic of reality apart from appearances," Connolly suggests that this is an all too limited understanding, and argues that "the most fundamental thing about being is that it contains no such overriding logic or design."[75] However, according to Connolly, this is still an ontological or metaphysical claim: "to say either that something is fundamental or that nothing is fundamental, then, is to engage in ontopolitical interpretation."[76] I will later account more precisely for Connolly's concept "ontopolitical," but his point is that we cannot escape ontology. The claim that "nothing is fundamental" is important if we are to understand Connolly's ontology. Connolly here uses the word "nothing" in two senses. In the first sense the emphasis lies on "fundamental," meaning there is no fundamental metaphysical law, purpose, deity, or contract to govern things. In the second meaning the focus is on "nothing," where "nothingness" is meant as a characterization of reality, in the sense that the most fundamental thing about being is that there is no overriding logic.[77] In the first sense "nothing is fundamental" means that nothing can encapsulate being; in the second, paradoxically, nothing is meant as a something, or a positive description concerning the "nothingness" of reality. Connolly here utilizes the Derridean notion of "différance" to denote the idea that words and signs can never completely communicate what they mean, but can only define themselves by referring to other words from which they differ. It is these "gaps," or "lack of meaning" that according to Connolly make "nothing" fundamental to his ontology.

From this latter understanding of the fundamentality of nothing, Connolly draws the implication that no identity is complete, but is always in some sense marked by what it is not, and that difference in this sense is constitutive for identity.[78] It is this understanding which underlies Connolly's alternative understanding of pluralism, for which I will account later on.

Being as becoming

As mentioned earlier, Connolly is skeptical with regards to the ability of reductive materialism to give a full account of the world. A reductive account of materialism is a mode of explanation where everything is assumed to be reducible to sub-atomic particles. This sort of materialist explanation (the traditional scientific method) is today being challenged by non-reductive approaches. An umbrella term for many of these perspectives is "new materialism." Central to this stream of thought are the Italian philosopher and feminist theoretician Rosi Braidotti, the Mexican-American philosopher Manuel DeLanda, and political theorists like Jane Bennett and William E. Connolly.[79] On the one hand, these thinkers critique the dualistic framework through which spirit and matter, mind and body, are conceived dichotomously. At the same time, there is an emphasis on certain problems related to reductive accounts of matter: such as, the inability to account for central mind-related features of our world, like consciousness, intentionality, meaning, value, etc. Common themes further concern post-humanist perspectives that view matter as "lively" or as displaying agency, along with an interest in the political and ethical implications that come with viewing matter in terms of processes from which humans can't be separated.[80]

This broad stream of "new materialism" seeks, on predominantly non-theistic grounds, to affirm matter, not as an inert substance subject to predictable causal forces, but as "always something more than 'mere' matter: an excess, force, vitality, relationality, or difference that renders matter active, self-creative, productive, unpredictable."[81] In this sense it challenges both dualism and reductive materialist accounts of monism. It is further argued that "complexity and nonreductive significance is always already operative within matter, which is not really matter at all but matter energy."[82] Matter is thus described as "lively," or as displaying agency: a position which brings along a number of ethical and political questions. These issues concern the deconstruction of the nature/culture distinction, which stems from viewing matter in terms of complex and open processes (climactic, viral, neurological) in which humans are fully emerged; and further, the status of life and of the human.[83] Traditionally, natural science has studied reality as being reducible to mechanistic efficient causality (that which causes change and motion to start or stop). However, Connolly argues that this model of causality, which is often exemplified by one billiard ball striking another, fails to account for the full complexity of the world. Given that Connolly is also critical of final causality (the end, that for the sake of which a thing is done) in so far as it implies a *telos*, or an overarching purpose directed by God or Nature, Connolly seeks to "move beyond both mechanistic and finalist readings of the world" into an understanding of the world as "becoming."[84] The notion of becoming in relation to "new materialism" entails an understanding of material realities that are infused with "vitality" and a teleological meaning traditionally linked to spiritual or religious language.

The transcendent, that which exceeds our experience of the mundane, is, according to Connolly, to be found in the process of continuing fecundity of creation. Transcendence is in this sense understood as "that which is *coming* into being rather than a Being beyond being," or differently put, transcendence is not understood as a deity beyond, but rather as an immanent vitality.[85] Connolly's philosophy of becoming in this sense seeks to break down the separation between nature and culture, science and spirituality, in a way that at times borders on pantheism. More specifically, the case has been made that Connolly's philosophy bares traces of Spinozan pantheism, in the sense that he "imagines that forms of regularity and order tend to emerge spontaneously from the immanent movement of social and cultural forces."[86] The reason for Connolly's interest in complex processes such as "the complexity of lava flows that issue in unpredictable patterns of granite," or "the simple, unconscious intentionality of a bacterium as it adjusts its movements up a glucose gradient," is that he identifies self-organizing processes within them; processes that entail a level of creativity traditionally reserved for human action.[87] Connolly recognizes two prevailing models of nature: the "theo-teleological" tradition that he associates with Aristotle and Aquinas; and the law-like mechanical model of science propounded by Galileo, Newton and later by Kant, that sets itself against the first tradition. Connolly identifies the first model with an anthropology of embodiment that emphasize the role of the body in shaping the mind, and which operate with "thick universals or an intrinsic purpose," and the second model with a disembodied conception of cultural life that operate with a non-biological, ahistorical, unemotional, and asocial view of the mind.[88] Against these models Connolly seeks to establish an account of the world that rejects any strict border between nature and culture, and perceives nature to be "more diverse and interesting than any god," and perceives the body to be "more layered, rich, and creative than the soul."[89] Connolly's world of becoming, therefore, does not fit neatly into either the old enchanted world or the disenchanted world.

Rejecting the notion of a teleological order that gives an inherent and determinate order to the universe, Connolly suggests that time itself is "becoming," and that "the future of the universe – and the multiple, interacting, and partially open temporal systems through which it is composed – is really open to an uncertain degree."[90] Connolly rejects law-like, mechanical naturalism due to what he perceives as its degrading account of human beings, given that it only allows for a flat or reductive account of existence. He has questioned intellectualist and cognitive models of science, politics, and ethics, due to their lack of attentiveness to accounts of subjectivity, since he perceives these models often to be "too sucked into a reductive model of science and unappreciative of the need to enter into communication with phenomenological experience."[91] Against the reductive accounts of nature, Connolly utilizes insights from complexity theory which, he understands, "moves natural science closer to the concerns of cultural theory as it surmounts reductionism."[92] Instead, Connolly seeks to cultivate belief and affirmation of a world of becoming, a world composed of heterogeneous force-fields. However, Connolly's world of becoming does not recognize divine meanings of providence or horizontal transcendence. Instead, he emphasizes the "immanent transcendence" at work in the interaction between different complex systems that render surprising effects, along with the possibility of human participation in processes that surpass human understanding.[93]

Connolly's philosophy of becoming calls attention to "messy states" between subjects and objects and processes that are "neither reducible to chance, nor to explanation according to a classic concept of causality."[94] Connolly here uses the term *autopoiesis* to describe sources of fecundity from which new things and processes emerge through self-organization, in ways which he claims exceed human powers of prediction. Connolly understands such events to occur between different force-fields, such as "neural, viral, bacterial, geological, climatic, species, electrical, chemical and civilizational."[95]

Through his philosophy of becoming Connolly seeks to relocate "the element of mystery" from traditional, or vertical, accounts of transcendence into natural and cultural processes.[96] In this sense Connolly can be understood as translating the notion of transcendence into immanent conceptions of time, causality, and freedom. By "immanence" Connolly means an outlook in which "the universe is not dependent on a higher power" and where "becoming" is "reducible neither to mechanistic materialism, dualism, theo-teleology, nor the absent God of minimal theology."[97] Connolly further denies both the possibility and the necessity, of any element of transcendence in the sense of "a God who creates, informs, governs, or inspires activity in the mundane world while also exceeding the awareness of its participants."[98] The kind of transcendence that he does admit to, and combines with his otherwise radical immanence, he refers to as "mundane transcendence." Connolly describes his mundane transcendence as "any activity outside a nonhuman force-field or human awareness that may then cross into it, making a difference to what the latter becomes or interacting with it in fecund or destructive ways, often without being susceptible to full representation before the crossing or explanation by means of efficient causation after it."[99] Connolly refers to his position as immanent naturalism, a position he describes as keeping "an open temporal horizon exceeding human mastery and irreducible to both closed naturalism and radical transcendence."[100] Connolly argues that this position is "open," both to time as becoming and with respect to God; even though "it does not project an image of divinity."[101]

In the next section I will connect Connolly's ontology of becoming to his particular brand of post-secularism by drawing out its political aspects, and I will give particular focus to his alternative account of pluralism.

5.3 William Connolly's post-secularism in practice

Central to William Connolly's philosophy is the notion of everything's connectedness. Any strict border between science, religion, and politics is in his view untenable, and as we have seen he uses recent findings in natural science, regarding complex and interacting systems, to support his thesis that we need to rework the binary model we previously have used to describe the world. Rejecting a model where we have posited "secular, linear and deterministic" accounts on the one hand, against "divinely touched voluntaristic, providential and or punitive" accounts on the other, Connolly suggests that we have to start looking at the world in a way that recognizes "our modest participation in modes of creativity that extend beyond the human estate."[102] Connolly here rejects Kantian attempts to uphold the distinction between philosophy and theology and claims that the terms "'ontology', 'creed', 'theology', and 'metaphysic' slide toward each other."[103] Connolly contends that the strict separation between these terms, along with the bracketing of the existential dimension, has obscured the profound importance of ritual, and micropolitics, understood as the bodily aspects of culture. Connolly here argues that the fact that we all since childhood have been shaped by a combination of physical, mental, theoretical and existential events, forces and anxieties, some of them occurring below our reflective attention, testifies to the inseparability of habits, dispositions, metaphysics and "faith." It is under such conditions, he claims "a laugh to purport to be post-metaphysical."[104] The central point that Connolly here seeks to make, and which he draws from Foucault and Deleuze, is that "ritual and micropolitics do not simply represent beliefs or desires already there; they also *educate* the senses in specific ways; they *accentuate* some modes of conduct as they dampen others; and they help to *compose* embodied public virtues."[105] Connolly here seeks to point out what he sees as interconnectedness between natural science and existential issues. These intersections are not confined to the inner feelings of individuals, but are, according to Connolly, institutionalized through practice and political conflicts, which infuse churches, patterns of consumption, and scientific studies alike. In this sense, there is a close connection between nature, science, the existential, and the political; or in Connolly's words "the quality of existential orientations to the human predicament plays a significant role in ethical, political and economic life."[106] Connolly makes the same point in a different way by claiming that "existential issues do not remain confined to the late night anxieties of isolated individuals. They become burned into institutional practices and political conflicts."[107]

What Connolly is getting at here is what he refers to as the ontological dimension of political thought, by which he claims that "every interpretation presupposes or invokes some [...] stance with respect to the fundamental character of being."[108] One particular way in which Connolly exemplifies this is by referencing the close connection between evangelical Christianity "cowboy capitalism," the electronic news media, and the Republican Party, in what he calls the "evangelical-capitalist resonance machine."[109] Connolly here points out the intimate relation between political economy and religious practice in ways which are never self-contained. Rather, diverse elements infiltrate into the others in a manner that "fold, bend, blend, emulsify, and dissolve into each other" and which resists classical models of explanation. Connolly further suggests that what draws "[Dick] Cheney, Fox News, the Republican Party, and Enron [Oil] together" is in fact that they "share a spiritual disposition to existence;" or, put in ontological language, that they "express a fundamental disposition toward being in the world."[110] Here we can see how Connolly's ontology becomes inseparable from both politics and spiritual dimensions, both of which according to him, can be labeled as religious. This perspective radically reconfigures previous attempts to keep these aspects of human culture separated. As a consequence, Connolly construes ethics and pluralism in ways quite different from the political liberalism of which he is critical.

Connolly's critique of liberal pluralism

Connolly has critiqued liberal political theory for its tendency to reduce the political to the juridical: "to condense most issues of politics into the juridical categories of rights, justice, obligation, and responsibility and to treat the remaining issues instrumentally."[111] What this approach fails to account for is, in Connolly's view, the complex, constructed, and contingent nature of human interaction that goes beyond rational principles. Rather than accounting for the complexities underlying its ontological presumptions, liberalism has resorted to what Connolly refers to as "a single model of the generic individual," and to "deflate the politics of identity and difference."[112] This should be understood as a critique of an all too limited conception of what constitutes a human being. In line with this, he levels critique of the "normal individual," which in liberal theory tends to be a secular one, and which "establishes its parameters of normality not so much by specific argumentation as by omissions in its generic characterization of the individual."[113] Against the notion of a generic individual based on a "secular" anthropology, operating under the assumption that "religion" is irrelevant for what it means to be a human, Connolly argues that "religion" is a dimension of being that needs "to be engaged more openly."[114] For Connolly, however, this entails the view that religious difference isn't special in relation to other differences, but is one aspect of being that applies to deep cultural differences in general.

Deep, rhizomatic pluralism

William Connolly has been recognized for the attempt to formulate a new and "postmodern" theory of pluralism, against the "old" pluralism, which he links to a certain generation of post-war political scientists.[115] As we have seen, Connolly is critical of the political liberalism propounded by thinkers like John Rawls, in which one authoritative center (the secular state) is set to preside over numerous minorities, and where "public reason" sets the limits of the public sphere. Rawls' model assumes that it is possible to reach appropriate principles of justice by agreeing to be reasonable in deliberation with other people, as well as seeking agreement without bringing one's foundational commitments into the discussion.[116] Where the Rawlsian solution entails an overlapping consensus in which one brings "selective dimensions" of one's religion, philosophy or existential stance into the public sphere, Connolly rejects such limitations. His reason for doing so has to do with his suspicion that secularism, when propounded as an alternative to monotheism in public life "often retains a unitarian conception of morality remarkably close in structure to that supported by the Christian faith that originally spawned the space of the *seculere*."[117] Connolly furthermore raises the question whether in fact the presumptions of a Rawlsian overlapping consensus "contain dangerous demands and expectations."[118] The danger that Connolly identifies entails what he refers to as "strategies of concealment," which he sees as prevalent not only in the notion of overlapping consensus, but also in "ontological minimalism, nonfoundationalism, and the primacy of epistemology."[119] At the heart of this concealment lies the screening out of ontological questions and assumptions about the world. It is this concealment that, according to Connolly, constitutes the truncated pluralism of liberalism.

Against this liberal understanding of pluralism, in which religious beliefs as well as ontological commitments tend to be relegated to one's private life, Connolly argues for a pluralization "along multiple dimensions," and for "the procedures of governance" to be adapted accordingly.[120] In line with this perspective "public culture inside and outside the state" needs to reflect that it is "constituted by multiple minorities, divided along more numerous lines of religion, linguistic habit, economic interest, irreligion, ethnicity, sensuality, gender performances, and moral sources of inspiration."[121] Perhaps the biggest difference compared to traditional pluralism is that Connolly's account doesn't entail a strong, authoritative center, but is instead made up of "intersecting and interdependent *minorities* of numerous types and sorts who occupy the same territorial space" who are supposed to negotiate the terms of their relations between themselves.[122] Talal Asad has fittingly described Connolly's political strategy to affirm diversity in terms of a "decentered pluralism."[123] The decentered aspect of Connolly's pluralism draws on a model developed by the French theorists Gilles Deleuze and Félix Guattari, in which the notion of rhizome is invoked.[124] A rhizome is a subterranean plant stem that grows horizontally by shooting off sprouts and roots. The rhizome lacks a trunk, or a central, unifying stem, from which branches grow. Deleuze and Guattari's rhizomatic model of pluralism rejects hierarchical models in which difference is identified and positioned in relation to a center, or in transferred meaning, a tree trunk. Accordingly, Connolly's multidimensional and rhizomatic pluralism rejects the attempt to reduce difference to a unitary base, and encourages participants from multiple minorities to bring multiple dimensions of their social and personal lives with them into the public realm, including existential creeds and religions. So, rather than leave one's "metaphysical baggage at home," or "adopt an overarching faith acknowledged by all parties who strive to promote the common good," Connolly argues for the incorporation of a "deep plurality of religious/metaphysical perspectives" into public discourses.[125]

Given what Connolly sees as liberal pluralism's tendency to quench diversity, his own deep pluralism is in this sense critical of any overlapping consensus, as well as overarching religions, or notions of the good. Instead, Connolly's model assumes that "each faith practices its specific rituals, and each faith minority brings pieces and dimensions of its faith into the public realm with it."[126] However, three ingredients are, according to Connolly, necessary for this multidimensional diversity to be established. Firstly, an affirmation of a pluralism that entails dimensions of diversity beyond just religion and ethnicity, to other areas like gender practices and household organization. Ideally, Connolly envisions that this will result in a situation where everyone is perceived to be part of a minority in at least some dimension of diversity. Secondly, Connolly calls for the recognition of incompleteness, dissonance, or mystery within every philosophical stance or religion, which displays itself as internal inconsistencies or problem areas. It is these "creedal insufficiencies" that Connolly sees as inspiring generosity towards other creeds by making it impossible to disregard the flaws of your own position when criticizing other religions or philosophical perspectives. Thirdly, Connolly seeks to encourage the cultivation of a mix between "faith-imbued" practices and civic virtues in a way that does not require you to "leave your religion at home." However, Connolly's "deep pluralism" should not be understood as a form of universalism which sets the same standard everywhere, nor as a form of relativism.[127] Rather, Connolly seeks to navigate between universalism and relativism. Connolly here argues that his conception of a deep and multidimensional pluralism is able to defeat "cultural relativism, shallow conceptions of secular diversity, and unitarian ideals of politics alike."[128] Against charges of relativism, he makes a strict distinction between "pluralism" and "cultural relativism" and argues that "cultural relativism is the view that you should support the culture that is dominant in a particular place." Central to Connolly's understanding of relativism is the condition of being totally subjected to a monolithic conception of culture that dominates a certain "place." This might cause some confusion, given that such a position might elsewhere be labeled absolutist. However, against the "cultural relativist" position Connolly argues for the need to "militantly defend" his creed of deep pluralism.[129] Thus, Connolly argues that his account of pluralism should be understood as entailing a specific ethic that stands in sharp contrast to relativism. He thus acknowledges the necessity of setting limits, as well as the impossibility to accommodate every difference at the same time, and argues that "it is necessary to organize militantly when pluralism is under grave duress from unitarian movements"[130] However, at the same time Connolly paradoxically seeks to avoid universalism in the sense of a standard that should be imposed everywhere. Connolly here claims to apply, what he refers to as a "double-entry orientation:" that is, a simultaneous act of affirming the importance of universals along with an awareness of the extent to which they are revisable and contestable. Connolly thus calls anyone to "honor the terms of your faith, while acknowledging its contestability in the eyes of others."[131]

As we have seen, Connolly sees different conceptions of what is sacred as stemming from different confessions, theistic or non-theistic, as an inevitable part of being human. He furthermore sees it as natural that these will be displayed publicly in our increasingly diverse societies, and that legitimate contestation and disagreement will be the result of this situation. But when these conflicts arise, Connolly emphasizes three strategies as important for maintaining a deep pluralism: first, to maintain a respect for the sovereignty of the democratic institution in place; second, to seek to pluralize "existential faiths" (nontheistic faiths included) within the democratic institutions; and third, to assume an attitude where what is considered as attacks on "existential faith," or ideas of what is sacred, are relaxed.[132] Connolly's account of pluralism, and in particular the latter of the three strategies above, draws on a particular ethic, or a certain ethos, which I will turn to next.

Connolly's pluralizing ethic

The most fundamental problem of ethics does not, according to Connolly, concern the lack of moral adherence amongst people who share the same religion, transcendental arguments, or ideas of a social contract. Instead, Connolly sees the most basic problem as stemming from the fact that we honor different moral sources, and are unlikely to be moved by arguments or sentiments from other traditions. Connolly does not suggest that these differences might be overcome if everyone simply acted rationally. Instead, against an approach where the state seeks to consolidate one unified theological or secular source as a foundation for public morality, Connolly seeks to go in a different direction. His approach entails the cultivation of those elements in your existential outlook that admit a generous relation-building with other religions and traditions, and also, to open yourself up to criticism from other traditions when they question the foundations of your own. This strategy differs from that of secular liberalism in that it refuses to bracket your "fundamental religious/existential faith" to the private sphere, as well as to "confess faith in the sufficiency of reason, procedure, or deliberation in the public realm."[133]

Connolly's understanding of post-secularism in this sense functions as a way to "open up ethical space between monotheism, mono-Kantianism, and monosecularism," and thus challenge "monocultural" conceptions through ethical and cultural pluralization.[134] Connolly further recognizes that the notion of a common good is essential to sustain any particular set of identities and to promote values and virtues necessary to uphold a society. However, as mentioned before, Connolly is also critical of notions of the common good. The reason for his skepticism is his claim that the project of defining such virtues has the ambiguous effect of naturalizing them; "to make them appear as unambiguous goods lodged in nature or consent or reason or the universal character of the normal individual or ideal dialogue or a higher direction in being."[135] Against such foundationalist strategies, Connolly contends that the ethical life is not "derived" but "fragile." What Connolly wants to point out is that the "earthy, familial, educational, and social practices" that sustain and foster our different notions of the ethical are contingent, and display a tension between habits tied to the past and corrections and adjustments that need to be made in light of new events. Connolly here admits that his account of ethics – which is tied to an ontology of becoming – contains an "element of tragic possibility"[136] The notion of "tragic possibility" for Connolly denotes encounters with evil and violence. However, Connolly does not provide a framework which will enable a clear account of what constitutes evil (since this, according to him, would lead to a sort of universalism), but rather maintains that one should seek to cultivate an existential stance in which new events which might contain "tragedy" and evil are viewed as part of the contingencies of life. Connolly admits that it seems unavoidable to claim that some of one's own dispositions are more ethical than others. But, one should do so, he claims "less because one takes one's particular identity to be intrinsically true than because one's reflective experience of contingency and relationality in identity elicits a reverence for life responsive to the politics of difference."[137]

Connolly does not ground his ethics in the notion of a primordial law, nor in a universal obligation or duty in a Kantian sense. Instead, he seeks to "cultivate" a particular stance of gratitude towards life.

> We cultivate care for the abundance of life and the earth in a world ungoverned by a Transcendent Power. We then seek to weave this spirituality into our pursuit of self interest, identity, judgment, and responsibility.[138]

Connolly's ethic is in this sense grounded in an ethos of what he refers to as a "nontheistic gratitude for the rich diversity of being."[139] Connolly here draws on Nietzsche's account of a sense of gratitude for the abundance and rich diversity of life. This nontheistic gratitude for existence, Connolly argues "redraws the line between secularism and religion by refusing either to eliminate reverence or to bind the element of reverence to theism."[140] However, Connolly admits the inevitability of conflict stemming from different conceptions of the sacred. As a means of dealing with these conflicts, Connolly calls for a more open and welcoming debate climate with regards to religions and issues of ultimate concern.

Connolly is seeking to replace the "Christian sacred/secular division," since he argues that this conception, in pair with the notion of "secular reason" has been "the most powerful barriers to pluralization" due to their tendency to "seek a secure 'ground' for morality, either in the commands/purposes of a god or in commands/purposes of a natural or rational subject."[141] Against the "sacred/secular duopoly," Connolly seeks to pluralize the notion of the sacred in order to make it open to other outlooks of life that operate with different ontological and ethical perspectives. However, while he takes seriously this diversity of conceptions about what is sacred, or worthy of respect, he does not want to sacralize (in the Christian sense) difference, since he fears this would lead to the entrenchment of positions.

Connolly understands his vision of deep pluralism as drawing on an "agonistic respect," which he sees as being quite different from liberal tolerance. Where liberal tolerance is endowed to minorities by a majority that is holding the authoritative public center, by contrast, with regards to agonistic respect "the public center becomes more thinly sliced and diffuse."[142] Instead of relying on a secular authoritative center that seeks to root conflict out of politics, agonistic democracy can be put into practice by allowing a diversity of perspectives to "work themselves out" in the public sphere. From Connolly's agonistic perspective, conflicts, or different perspectives, are not problems to be solved but rather a natural state of order that provides resources to question one's own presuppositions. In fact, he argues that it is the mutual and respectful engagement between adherents of different moral sources and metaphysical orientations, what Connolly refers to as an "ethos of engagement," that will serve as his ethical foundation.[143] A foundation that will find its motivation in a sense of gratitude for the "abundance of being" that according to Connolly is to foster a sense of respect for difference.[144] The real challenge, however, Connolly identifies in the task "to embed such an ethos of engagement in churches, families, schools, consumption practices, media dramas, education, and state priorities."[145] Connolly argues that it is increasingly important to publicly articulate the "philosophy/faith that infuses your participation in public life and ethically honorable to come to terms with the degree to which it remains contestable on comparative terms."[146]

What makes Connolly's philosophy relevant to study from a religious studies perspective, I would argue, is: not only his critique of secularism and aspiration to formulate a post-secular alternative to the modern construal of the relationship between "religion" and politics, but also Connolly's account of an immanent naturalism as an existential outlook (what he would call "faith"), along with his intention to "blur the lines between philosophy and theology, and between science and faith, while giving argument a role of importance in all four."[147] In this manner he intends to develop an "existential faith" which positions itself "between monotheistic faith and rationalistic orientations that purport to eschew faith altogether."[148] As we have seen, this position entails the confession of a "mundane transcendence." Furthermore, Connolly understands "faith" differently from how it has been traditionally understood within Christianity: that is, as belief and trust in God. Instead, according to his immanentist perspective "faith" recognizes the radical uncertainty of each perspective, in a way that makes room for doubt within any philosophical claim or existential position, atheism included. Connolly emphasizes that "existential faiths" are not merely epistemological beliefs, but are also organizations of bodily experience and habit, in the sense that "to be human is to be inhabited by existential faith."[149] It is this understanding of faith that makes it an unavoidable part of being human, since everyone, according to Connolly, holds views and claims about the world which go beyond that which is possible to prove scientifically.

At the center of Connolly's particular brand of post-secularism, which entails a reconfiguration of the relation between religion, politics, and the secular, stands his "ontology of becoming." As we have seen, this ontology has normative implications for his understanding of pluralism. Against a conventional understanding of pluralism which, according to Connolly, has a state-centered ideal, and which has tended to ossify its moral standards of judgment according to old monotheistic or monosecularist moralities, he argues for a more generous, pluralizing ethos. Connolly anchors this pluralization in his understanding of the universe as creative and diverse, and as continuously bringing forward new constellations and new identities, forged out of old differences. Accordingly, Connolly understands pluralism in terms of a goal or process rather than a fixed state. Just as the universe is continuously becoming, so Connolly argues, our account of pluralism should entail a constant process of reconfiguration. Another way Connolly explains the link between his account of ontology and his social vision is by drawing on the American philosopher William James' claim that "pluralism is the philosophy of a messy universe."[150] This means that the universe is composed of multiple elements that elude our understanding or attempts to systematize them, and we should therefore resist the temptation to impose an "all-form," – an absolute – system which doesn't leave room for continuous becoming. Instead, Connolly argues, the urgent need today is to forge an ethos of public engagement between alternative faiths.

Having accounted for Taylor's, Milbank's and Connolly's account of metaphysics and pluralism, I will now discuss their post-secularisms in relation to each other.

6
Post-Secular Visions

In the introductory chapter I accounted for what Jürgen Habermas has depicted as the paradoxical return of both naturalistic worldviews and religious orthodoxies. The dilemma at hand concerned the mediation of "uncritical faith in science" and religious traditions critical of "the liberal assumptions of the Enlightenment."[1] Habermas has, in an essay titled *The Boundary Between Faith and Knowledge* (2008), described the inability of pure reason to generate values which can sustain a liberal democracy, by claiming that "pure practical reason can no longer be so confident in its ability to counteract a modernization spinning out of control armed solely with the insights of a theory of justice."[2] Habermas' "solution" to this dilemma involves the idea of context-transcendent validity claims, accessible through a discursive and postmetaphysical procedure.[3] It is on this discursive account of reason that Habermas bases his strict distinction between faith and reason – a distinction central to his account of the post-secular. Thus, Habermas does not actively engage with metaphysical questions since he chooses to draw a strict distinction between religion and the secular, faith and reason, and between the transcendent and the immanent.

Against Habermas, each of the theorists at the center of this study has engaged with these questions, arguing that metaphysics is an inescapable aspect of any philosophical or religious account. Instead of taking a postmetaphysical stance and emphasizing "the difference that exists between faith and knowledge," Taylor, Milbank, and Connolly have each actively engaged ontological questions and emphasized what they perceive to be a blurred line between religion and the secular, belief and knowledge.[4] As we have seen, the post-secular approaches taken by Taylor, Milbank, and Connolly, are skeptical regarding the prospect of finding value neutral analytical concepts. Rather than seeking objectivity from a supposedly neutral point of view, they emphasize the tradition-based nature of all reasoning, and seek to think "with religion" rather than at a distance from it. In this sense, Taylor, Milbank, and Connolly are, in Jonathan Z. Smith's terminology, less interested in "processes of proof," and more, in "rhetorics of persuasion."[5] However, a central theme in Taylor, Milbank, and Connolly's thought is that they all question the very possibility of making a clear distinction between "proof" and "rhetoric," and instead emphasize that reason and fact-making are dependent on language and tradition. In this sense they are all following Johann Georg Hamann who, in his response to Kant's *Critique of Pure Reason*, argued against what he saw as flawed attempts to treat reason as a purified object detached from culture and religion.[6]

Instead of de-linking the connection between religion and the secular, Taylor, Milbank, and Connolly, have approached the emergence of the secular as related social and historical processes. Perhaps this comes across most starkly in their genealogies of secular consciousness, in which all three theorists highlight the theological disputes during the scholastic period. Such an approach stands in tension with attempts to explain secularization as resulting from non-religious forces such as modern science, or more material conditions of human existence that seek to instrumentalize a religious cosmology.[7] Instead, what stands at the center of their respective approaches is the refusal of any strict distinction between ideas and the material conditions of reality, between nature and culture, in a way that seeks to highlight how beliefs and practices are inseparable from any account of the world.

However, important differences remain between Taylor, Milbank and Connolly. I have sought to approach these differences from two perspectives: through their accounts of metaphysics, and through the socio-political implications of those metaphysical beliefs. The first perspective concerns the way my three theorists construe reality with regards to transcendence and immanence and being and becoming, while the second perspective concerns their ontological creeds in relation to differing views; or, how they negotiate religious difference or seek to construe an alternative to liberal pluralism. This latter aspect has important implications for the connection I am interested in regarding the connection between their ontologies and the ethical-political values that guide their social visions.

In the following, I will contrast Taylor, Milbank, and Connolly with regards to these two perspectives. Starting with their metaphysics, I will first account for differences in their ontological accounts concerning being and becoming, and more specifically to univocal and analogical accounts of being. The reason for my focus on this seemingly obscure difference in scholastic metaphysics has to do with the fact that all three theorists make reference to a specific shift in medieval philosophy in order to explain the emergence of secularization. I will then proceed by developing a typological scheme based on how they construe the relationship between transcendence and immanence.

6.1 Different accounts of being: univocity vs. analogy

One theme that unites Taylor, Milbank, and Connolly is the importance they attribute to the debates within medieval scholastic thought as a historical factor for the emergence for secularism. More specifically, they all agree that, to various extents, the theological dispute regarding nominalism and realism played an important role in the process of secularization; or, differently put, that secularization has theological roots.[8] For this reason, it is relevant to look closer at what this dispute concerned, how it is relevant for contemporary discussions about pluralism and the post-secular, and in particular, how this conflict is interpreted by Taylor, Milbank, and Connolly.

Discussions concerning nominalism have played a significant role in metaphysical debates since at least the Scholastic era. Broadly stated, these discussions concern the existence of universals. Universals are general properties or concepts such as "redness" or "human" (of which red things such as apples and cherries, or the human beings man and woman, are particular instantiations). The philosophical problem that emerges from the concept of universals is the question of whether there is anything in reality to match this commonality, or if commonality is just a mental concept. Realism is in this context understood as the position that a genuine commonality exists in nature. Against such a view, nominalism is generally understood to denote the position that universals are mental concepts that do not refer to real things, and that only individual entities or particulars exist.[9]

A central point of medieval nominalism concerned the independence of God in relation to nature. In the realist theology of Thomas of Aquinas, nature and the supernatural were seen as parts of a composite whole, not as separate "things:" God's supernatural grace was in this sense seen as perfecting or fulfilling nature, not as disrupting or destroying it.[10]

Aquinas consequently argued that grace and revelation did not negate reason, and that it was possible to attain knowledge of God through the knowledge of nature.[11] However, such an understanding was, from a nominalist perspective, understood as limiting God's sovereignty in the sense that the laws of nature could be perceived as circumventing God's will, or setting limits to God's freedom.[12] In order to protect God's sovereignty from the notion of an independent and intrinsic purpose in nature, nominalism consequently asserted a rupture between God and nature. Thus, nominalism has ontological implications insofar as it concerns both the function of language and what it is taken to refer to. As stated in Chapter 2, ontology is traditionally explained to be the study of "being qua being." What is meant by this seemingly opaque term is "being" divorced from all qualifications (such as color, smell, etc.), and quantifications (such as weight and length, etc.).

Milbank, Connolly, and Taylor all attribute importance to the emergence of nominalist philosophy in their different accounts of secularization, but they do so in different ways and focus on different aspects of this philosophical shift. What – according to William Connolly, who here follows Hans Blumenberg's account in *The Legitimacy of the Modern Age* – is driving secularization is that the omnipotence of God is emphasized "so stringently that it extracts faith in divine providence from nature and history."[13] Conversely, the notion of contingency in nature was emphasized in order "to obey more completely a God of absolute sovereignty."[14] Connolly in this way argues that nominalism made it possible to imagine nature as self-sustaining, against enchanted conceptions of the world. Nominalism in this sense "ironically opened the door to secularist conceptions of mastery over a disenchanted nature."[15] Connolly further identifies classical political themes concerning the legitimation and sources of power in the nominalist debate, in his words "between the effective and authoritative dimensions of sovereignty."[16] This debate concerns questions regarding the source of legitimate authority. In more concrete terms this discussion for Connolly concerns how secularized societies that have discarded the notion of "Divine Right," traditionally invested in the king, now seek to make sense of the "the micropolitics of sovereignty," that is how "in democratic, constitutional states sovereignty circulates uncertainly between the multitude, traditions infused into it, and constitutionally sanctioned authorities."[17] Where the medieval nominalist thinkers emphasized contingency in nature in order to "obey more completely a God of absolute sovereignty," Connolly, who also seeks to emphasize the contingency in nature, does so for a radically different reason.[18] Connolly seeks to underscore how, rather than perceiving the sovereign as the *one person* in power, sovereignty is "composed of a plurality of forces circulating through and under the positional sovereignty of the official arbitrating body."[19] This is a somewhat bewildering claim for anyone used to the idea that a unified consciousness is a condition for sovereignty. Connolly, however, draws on Nietzsche, and argues that the disenchantment of the modern world, which has undermined the possibility of an agreement of a metaphysically founded conception of the good, should not be perceived as an abyss, but as "an abundance that enables the production of greater diversity and generosity in life."[20]

It is not immediately clear why an understanding of the universe as radically contingent would support the ethic of "goodness as generosity," rather than resentment.[21] But Connolly here argues that such an ethic "proceeds from the abundance of being," even though "sources of goodness and obligation are fragile and fugitive."[22] Instead of "insisting upon the incontrovertibility of a particular metaphysical faith or to pretend to bypass this dimension of politics altogether," Connolly argues that a condition for our peaceful coexistence is that we embrace "the deep contingency of things."[23]

Taylor's account of secularization tells the story in much the same way, but also emphasizes how "nominalism contributed to the development of a clear distinction between nature and super-nature, immanent order and transcendent reality."[24] Another aspect that Taylor brings up is nominalism's consequences for the instrumental stance of human agency, which along with "science, mechanism, the instrumental stance – contribute to disenchantment."[25] What Taylor is getting at in terms of consequences of the nominalist shift for "human agency" is "a purely instrumental, 'rational' stance towards the world or human life."[26] This is directly related to Taylor's depiction of the modern self as a "buffered self" and the loss of "the expression-embodiment of higher reality in the things which surround us."[27] However, in everything central Taylor sees his understanding of the consequences of nominalism as "complementary" to that of John Milbank.[28]

Milbank makes nominalism central to the overall story he wants to tell about what has gone wrong with modernity, or what he refers to as "the theological construction of secular politics."[29] Perhaps not surprisingly, Milbank's highly negative account of nominalism as the starting point for the secular as an autonomous sphere has been critiqued for being employed as a "fall narrative" – "a fall from a past society structured on the basis of an external transcendent realm (the legacy of Western Platonic philosophy)" – as a way to account for what is wrong with modern society in general.[30] More specifically, Milbank locates the fall into immanence to the late medieval thought of John Duns Scotus and William Ockham, and in particular the account of univocity of being. Milbank, and to some extent also Taylor's, account of the implications of these historical shifts stands in contrast to Connolly's account. Their differences concern, not so much the historical developments (all three consider the emergence of nominalism a key event in the history of metaphysics), but rather how they evaluate the implications of the shift. In particular, their differences concern the different ways in which they utilize religious language. In the following I will address these differences more specifically.

Milbank and Connolly draw on separate philosophical traditions in their understanding of being. Milbank draws on Aristotle and Aquinas and talks in analogous terms of our being as grounded in a transcendent God, in the sense that God is "the beginning and end of all things."[31] Connolly, on the other hand, draws on Deleuze, who, inspired by Scotus, talks about being in a univocal sense, as determined by becoming.[32] Although Connolly himself does not talk about "the univocity of being" in explicit terms, he clearly follows Deleuze in making the idea of "difference in itself" central to his philosophy.[33] Furthermore, what Deleuze identifies as the three moments of univocity in the history of philosophy (that is, Scotus, Spinoza, and Nietzsche), are all central sources of inspiration for Connolly in his development of an "immanent naturalism."[34] Scotus' univocal understanding of being, which paved the way for a collapse between God's being and the being of man, constitutes a revolutionary moment in medieval scholastic thought, and his concept "univocity of being" can be traced both to Deleuze's "difference in itself" and to Connolly's "immanent naturalism." The concept "univocity of being" made possible a "neutral" reference point which enabled immanent criteria for the comparison between God and man. The metaphysical implications of Scotus' view are so important that some scholars have suggested one should refer to it as a "second beginning of metaphysics;"[35] at the time, Scotus' theories about the univocity of being were accused of "destroying the whole of philosophy."[36] Against a metaphysical understanding that posits a great divide between the transcendent and immanent, or between God and the world, Scotus' univocal understanding entails an ontological "flattening out," in which any absolute ontological difference between humanity and the divine is rejected. Deleuze has, in this sense, described the univocity of being as signifying an "equality of being" in which being is of "one and the same time."[37] This leads, according to Deleuze, to a situation in which it becomes possible to account for differences, not only by describing them in relation to God, but to account for "difference in itself."[38] This is the shift which Deleuze refers to as the "Copernican revolution" of viewing difference as being a concept independent of identity or sameness. This revolutionary change of perspective claims that identity, or sameness, is no longer perceived to be primary, but rather secondary in relation to difference. So, rather than having to relate differences to a God whose being was understood as constant and never changing, Deleuze argues that Scotus' univocal account of being should be understood as a process of continuously "becoming" and ever-changing. In his words "returning is being, but only the being of becoming."[39] This understanding resonates strongly with Connolly's term "politics of becoming," "by which a new entity is propelled into being out of injury, energy, and difference."[40] Rather than positing a "natural or intrinsic identity," or assuming that humans are "predesigned to coalesce smoothly with any single, coherent set of identities," Connolly argues that "power is always inscribed in the relation an exclusive identity bears to the differences it constitutes."[41]

As Deleuze, as well as Taylor, Milbank, and Connolly, points out, this shift has had important implications, not only for Christian theology, but for metaphysics in general and for broader religio-political thought.[42] This can be seen in Spinoza's account of God/nature as an ultimate, infinite substance (*Deus sive Natura*); or, as Connolly argues, in Nietzsche's announcement of "The death of God," understood in the sense that "breaking the link between world and creation, unchains humanity from truth."[43] In this sense, any transcendent reference point is discarded in favor of what Deleuze calls a "plane of immanence" so that "the philosopher and the pig, the criminal and the saint" all sing the same song in which "each chooses his pitch or his tone, perhaps even his lyrics, but the tune remains the same, and underneath all the lyrics the same tra-la-la, in all possible tones and all pitches."[44]

The point I wish to make here is that the difference between "being," understood analogously or univocally, is reflected in the differences between Milbank's and Connolly's post-secularisms. More specifically, I want to suggest that we can understand the differences in how Taylor, Milbank, and Connolly construe pluralism as related to their different conceptions of being. This is perhaps most clearly seen in their respective accounts of how difference is to be understood and negotiated. Milbank sees the possibility to construe "differences as analogically related," according to his account of being.[45] However, such an account necessitates a transcendent *telos*, a *telos* that Milbank finds in his theological metaphysics. For Milbank, the analogical way of construing difference is destroyed with Scotus' emphasis on univocity. This understanding is, according to Milbank, later picked up by Deleuze, in the sense that "'difference' has now become the sole 'transcendental';" that is "difference" is now the only thing that unites humanity.[46] Against

Deleuze (and Connolly), Milbank argues that "infinite difference" will only amount to violence, since "the univocal process is absolutely indifferent to each particular difference," whereas "the analogical process is a constant discrimination of preferences and erection of hierarchies."[47] Milbank here posits the notion of hierarchical ordering of differences as a condition for peaceful coexistence.

Connolly, is "with Deleuze," "drawn like a magnet to the idea of radical immanence" as well as to the notion of "difference in itself."[48] This leads to a quite different understanding of pluralism, compared to Milbank's analogical account. As the Australian Deleuze scholar Paul Patton points out in his book about the political implications of Deleuze's philosophy "a philosophy that seeks to make difference an object of affirmation, and to produce a concept of difference in itself, must therefore overturn the traditional hierarchy between identity and difference."[49] Such a philosophy leads to a distinctive kind of pluralism, which in Connolly's case can be seen in his notion of "rhizomatic pluralism." For Connolly, identity is always shaped through differentiation and distinction. But, in contrast to Milbank, he does not posit anything to reconcile these differences. Instead, Connolly seeks to balance the demands of old and established identities against the emergence of new identities. For Connolly, difference is the natural state of things, whereas for Milbank difference is, unless subjected to his theological metaphysics of a divine whole, linked to violence. Connolly's "solution" lies in learning to live generously with difference by viewing one's own position and identity as contingent. For Milbank, difference is overcome by the possibility of hierarchy in which difference is harmoniously overcome through reconciliation.

But where do these exercises in the metaphysics of difference leave Charles Taylor? Taylor, who has continuously argued for the centrality of recognizing difference in order to have a well-functioning democracy, has also explored the philosophical aspects of "recognizing the equal value of different ways of being."[50] However, in this context Taylor posits the question concerning on what basis it is possible to claim equal value of all people. Taylor here suggests that humanity is united by something more than mere "difference." Consequently, according to Taylor, difference is not, as Deleuze would have it, the sole transcendental. Rather, Taylor argues "[m]ere difference can't itself be the ground of equal value. If men and women are equal, it is not because they are different, but because overriding the difference are some properties, common or complementary, which are of value."[51] This position is a rejection of Connolly's hopeful affirmation of "difference in itself," without the means of evaluating or structuring it. In this sense, Taylor is similar to Milbank regarding the emphasis on something to unite all differences. Yet, Taylor's transcendental anthropology, according to which he argues that human agents are necessarily "strong evaluators" – or, differently put, that qualitative distinctions concerning the worth of options is a condition specific to human agency – puts him in a slight tension with Milbank's theological metaphysics.[52] Milbank is suspicious towards transcendental approaches, due to what he sees as its tendency "to 'formally distinguish' a realm of pure nature in concrete humanity:" or, in other words, the use of immanent "neutral," criterion as determining what is human.[53]

However, Taylor explicitly supports Milbank's account concerning the ramifications of Scotus' thought in terms of a "new 'univocal' understanding of being, predicated alike of God and of creatures, as the crucial shift from which other changes flow." [54] Furthermore, Taylor accounts in depth for a pre-modern moral order "organized around a notion of a hierarchy in society which expresses and corresponds to a hierarchy in the cosmos," to which he contrasts the "The Malaises of Modernity" with symptoms like "the fragility of meaning, the search for an over-arching significance," and "the utter flatness, emptiness of the ordinary."[55] In Taylor's account, the modern idea of moral order undoes this previous hierarchy in favor of a society which seeks to bring individuals together, based on a different metaphysical idea, or "ontic component." According to this new social order, the reciprocal actions of individuals are said to lead to mutual benefit by "the spread of free markets, liberal societies and democratic forms of rule" in a manner that will "ensure a golden age for humankind, promising universal peace and growing well-being for all."[56] For Taylor, something is lost in "the shift from hierarchical, mediated-access societies to horizontal, direct-access societies."[57] Taylor can here be understood as longing for certain aspects entailed in a metaphysically grounded hierarchy; or, at the very least, displaying nostalgia for an enchanted but lost world.[58] Taylor, however, does not identify with this critique, and links "nostalgia" to sympathy for a certain anti-modernism prevalent in some Roman Catholic circles in the period before the Second Vatican Council, to which Taylor claims to have "close to zero sympathy with."[59] Against charges of nostalgia, Taylor states that "times have irrevocably changed. Christendom is no longer compatible with diverse democracies."[60]

Having accounted for Taylor, Milbank, and Connolly's ontologies in terms of analogy and univocity of being, I will now address another aspect of metaphysics in which they differ: their accounts of transcendence.

6.2 Transcendence and immanence: an attempt at a typology

I want to suggest that it is possible to see the contours of three different post-secular ideal types based on the different accounts of the transcendent and the immanent encountered in Habermas, Milbank and Taylor, and Connolly. I further suggest that these ideal types could be labeled; "Protestant post-secularism," "French Catholic post-secularism," and "Deleuzian post-secularism." I would like to visualize the three ideal types as shown in Figure 6.1 below.

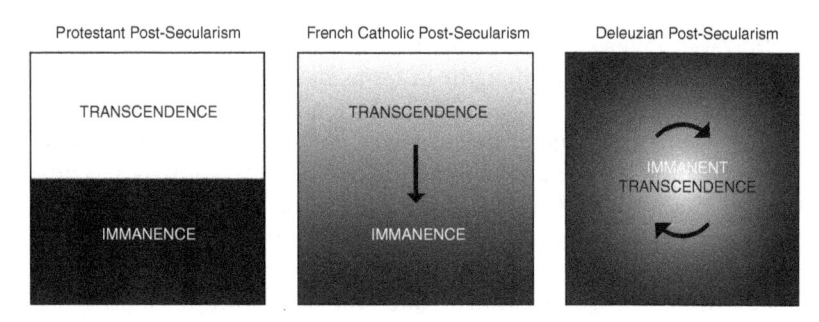

Figure 6.1 Construals of transcendence and immanence

Protestant post-secularism

The two first of these ideal types are related to the medieval distinction between *via antiqua* and *via moderna*. This is a distinction between two different positions on universals, which draws on two different ways of reading Aristotle. The *via antiqua*, the "old way," recognized the capacity of human reason to know the world apart from revelation and was famously propounded by Aquinas.[61] The *via moderna*, the "modern way," was originally propounded by William of Ockham and questioned the rationality of Christian belief, rejecting the philosophical approach of Aristotelian teleology which Aquinas had worked out.[62] The *via moderna* operated with an antithetical relationship between faith and reason which can be traced up to the present from Ockham via Luther.[63] Luther's construal of the relationship between faith and reason is clearly expressed in his writings against the Anabaptist.

> The anabaptist pretend that children, not as yet having reason, ought not receive baptism. I answer: That reason in no way contributes to faith. Nay, in that children are destitute of reason, they are all the

more fit and proper recipients of baptism. For reason is the greatest enemy that fait has: it never comes to the aid of spiritual things, but – more frequently than not – struggles against the Divine Word, treating with contempt all that emanates from God. If God can communicate the Holy Ghost to grown persons, he can *à fortiori*, communicate it to young children. Faith comes of the Word of God, when this is heard; little children hear that Word when they receive baptism, and therewith they receive faith.[64]

This antithetical relationship between faith and reason has further been traced to Kant, who from an early age was influenced by protestant pietism, and is sometimes referred to as "the philosopher of Protestantism."[65] I suggest that this stance is also valid for Habermas, who, affirming the link between the nominalism of *via moderna*, Protestantism, and Kant, writes: "the move from Duns Scotus to nominalism does not merely lead to the Protestant voluntarist deity [Willensgott] but also paves the way for modern natural science. Kant's transcendental turn leads not only to a critique of the proofs of God's existence but also to the concept of autonomy which first made possible our modern European understanding of law and democracy."[66] Accordingly Luther's rejection of reason's ability to grasp the mysteries of faith, and Kant's rejection of metaphysical speculation, both draw on the same sort of separation of faith and reason. So, as others have argued, in the same way that Luther claimed "reason is limited to our experience and 'not able to apply itself to invisible things', so likewise, a cornerstone of Transcendental Idealism is that knowledge is confined to the scope of possible experience."[67]

Religion is then, neither for Luther nor for Kant, an intellectual enterprise, but a matter of the heart. Kant can in this manner be understood to continue Luther's separation of "faith and reason" through his project to "deny knowledge in order to make room for faith:" that is, to block reason from engaging in rationalist metaphysics concerning the nature of the divine.[68] The *via moderna* furthermore sought to account for the relationship between God and humans "covenantally rather than ontologically:" that is, instead of perceiving the link between God and human in realist terms, it was explained symbolically.[69] So, rather than assuming a direct presence of grace – "something supernatural in the soul," – the *via moderna*, along with the reformers, understood the relationship between God and human more in contractual, or covenantal terms.[70]

This difference is related to theological disputes during the reformation between Catholic and Protestant theologians concerning the supernatural role of grace, and to differences in how the Eucharist is understood. Luther famously opposed Scholastic theology, and argued that: "righteousness is not essentially in us, as the Papists reason out of Aristotle, but without us in the grace of God only and in his imputation."[71] Accordingly, Protestant theology argued that the imputed righteousness by which humans are made acceptable to God, was "alien" and "instilled from without."[72] In a similar manner, the Kantian outlook delimits the noumenal from the phenomenal, and associates the supernatural with the supersensible, of which we can have no knowledge except by revelation. As I have already hinted, I want to suggest that a similar account of the relationship between the transcendent and the immanent can be seen in Habermas' strict distinction between "faith and reason," and between religious and secular speech. In a manner that echoes the ideas of the *via moderna*, Habermas claims that "[o]nce the boundary between faith and knowledge becomes porous, and once religious motives force their way into philosophy under false pretenses, reason loses its foothold and succumbs to irrational effusion."[73] So, just as Kant placed "Religion within the Limits of Reason," so does Habermas seek to uphold "The Boundary Between Faith and Knowledge."[74] Accordingly, I propose that the antithetical relationship between faith and reason, along with a strict distinction between transcendence and immanence is typical for what I would label a Protestant post-secularism, and can be traced from Habermas back to Kant, and further back to Luther and Ockham and Scotus. It could here be objected that a strict distinction between transcendence and immanence is that which is constitutive of secularity, and that this position does not deserve to be called post-secular. However, my claim is not that a strict distinction between transcendence and immanence is a sufficient condition for what I call a Protestant post-secularism. My rudimentary typology is just focused on the construal of the relationship between transcendence and immanence within post-secular theory. What, for example, constitutes Habermas' post-secularism is moreover, as we have seen, "the situation in which secular reason and a religious consciousness that has become reflexive engage in a relationship."[75] However, this is more of an epistemological point, as opposed to a metaphysical one, which seeks to point out of a certain lack of "self-awareness" in secular reason, and how the Enlightenment was "unenlightened about itself," but now is becoming aware of its own limits.[76]

French Catholic post-secularism

What I am calling a "French Catholic post-secularity" in my typology might be viewed as Roman Catholic in the sense that it understands the supernatural, not as totally distinct from the natural, but rather in continuity with nature according to Aquinas' claim that "grace perfects nature."[77] An influential theological school of thought in Catholic theology during the mid-twentieth century is called *Nouvelle Théologie*. This school, which is associated with the French theologians Maurice Blondel and Henri de Lubac, sought to counter modernist streams in the church by going back to the early Church fathers.[78] Of central importance is de Lubac's rejection of the neo-Thomistic idea of "pure nature" – that it is possible to account for "nature apart from any consideration of grace or of a supernatural end."[79] *Nouvelle Théologie* rejected any stark dualism between nature and the supernatural. Human beings were rather understood to exist only as oriented toward their creator: that is, with a "natural desire for the supernatural."[80] Milbank's integralist theology, which seeks to "supernaturalize the natural," draws heavily on *Nouvelle Théologie,* and he has even written a positive appraisal of de Lubac's theology.[81] Taylor has also named de Lubac as a source of inspiration, and sympathizes with "the scholarship which links the critique of mediaeval 'realism' (as with Aquinas), and the rise of nominalism, possibilism, and a more voluntarist theology in Scotus, Occam, and others with the thrust towards a secular world."[82] In line with this perspective Taylor argues that this philosophical turn has generated a "mechanical outlook which splits nature from supernature," and "generates the modern concept of the 'miracle'; a kind of punctual hole blown in the regular order of things from outside, that is, from the transcendent."[83]

So, given Milbank's and Taylor's *Nouvelle Théologie*-inspired account of the porous line between transcendence and immanence, I label them as representatives of a French Catholic post-secularity. However, it should be pointed out that their similarity, in terms of belonging to this ideal type, only concerns their account of the relation between transcendence and immanence. As we have seen, their practical application, in terms of political vision and stance towards liberal democracy, differs drastically.

Deleuzian post-secularism

Finally, my third ideal type, of which I see Connolly as a representative, I refer to as Deleuzian post-secularism. Central for this perspective is Deleuze's account of a "plane of immanence" of which he writes: "It is only when immanence is no longer immanence to anything other than itself that we can speak of a plane of immanence."[84] Deleuze here builds on Spinoza's metaphysics, which makes no distinction between God and nature. Spinoza's claim "God, or Nature" (*Deus sive natura*) thus makes everything immanent and both divinizes nature and naturalizes divinity. The account of immanence typical for the theorists I associate with this position has been described as an "immanent transcendence," which does not mean a wholesale rejection of transcendence, but rather its reconfiguration in immanent or materialist terms.[85]

As we have seen, Connolly's account of immanent materialism locates the transcendent to the continuing processes of becoming, which he perceives as constantly bringing forward new opportunities. Connolly describes this "mundane transcendence" as "enchanted in some ways, even if it does not express divine meanings."[86] Drawing on Merleau-Ponty's terminology, Connolly also refers to his perspective as "transcendence without the Transcendent."[87] Instead of representing a personal force beyond the universe, the transcendent is imagined to be always already present within reality. This stream of thought has close affinities with the "new materialism" movement where concepts like Luce Irigaray's "horizontal transcendence," Rosi Braidotti's "enchanted materialism," and Jane Bennett's "vibrant matter," are part of the characteristic terminology.[88]

As indicated in Figure 6.1, what unites the French Catholic post-secularism of Milbank and Taylor with the Deleuzian post-secularism of Connolly is the rejection of a strict distinction between transcendence and immanence (that one finds in the Protestant post-secularism of which I label Habermas a representative). However, it should be pointed out that the proposed unity around the theme of a porous boundary between the transcendent and the immanent can be questioned given their different understandings of transcendence. Milbank, Taylor and Connolly all see transcendence as operative in the realm of immanence; but, in contrast to the French Catholic account, Connolly and those influenced by Deleuze and the new materialism, tend to understand transcendence naturalistically. Connolly's account of transcendence is, as we have seen, focusing on what he refers to as the infrasensible (rather than supersensible) level, by which he means that which is operating below feeling and awareness and is "efficacious and inscrutable (to a certain degree)."[89] However, the purpose of my typology is not so much to account for the complex relation between different accounts of transcendence, but more the sketching of three main types of post-secularism with regard to the relation between transcendence and immanence.

6.3 Practical implications

Having focused on the ontological and theoretical aspects of Taylor, Milbank, and Connolly, I will now move on to the political and democratic implications of their metaphysics, as well as their attempts to formulate alternatives to secular liberalism. I will do so on the basis of four aspects: *Ontology and ethics*, *The terms of dialogue*, *The ethics of difference*, and *Post-secular visions*. In *Ontology and ethics* I will start by accounting for how Taylor, Milbank and Connolly, in stark opposition to the tradition of liberal secularism, seek to make ontology relevant for ethics and politics. In *The terms of dialogue* I intend to account for how Milbank, Connolly, and Taylor understand the possibilities of communication and a genuine understanding between differing perspectives and metaphysical outlooks. In *The ethics of difference* I focus on the metaphysical and political discussions concerning identity and difference, which entail the paradoxical notion of how difference is constitutive for identity, in the sense that a central part of what it means to be me is not being you. From a political perspective, this issue concerns the question of how one identity (e.g. being a Muslim) relates to the difference (of not being a Christian). But conversely, it can be questioned whether difference can exist in itself, or whether it needs a notion of identity or sameness in order to be conceived of as difference.

Ontology and ethics

Taylor, Milbank, and Connolly all agree that there is a connection between ontological commitments and ethico-political commitments.[90] But, what does this connection look like? Does ontology or ethics have primacy? Or, differently put, does a specific ontology or account for the basic structure of things commit you to certain ethical values, or do your ethical commitments implicate a certain ontology? As we shall see, Taylor, Milbank, and Connolly differ in how they construe the specific relation between the material and the immaterial, between ontology and ethics. However, Taylor, Milbank, and Connolly all emphasize that the dilemma of finding a satisfactory way of accounting for the relation between the material and the immaterial, or between mind and matter, is an ongoing task even in secular natural science. Thus, the question: If matter is "mind-less," how is it that mind is produced? – is, for them, an equally central question for both science and religions. Furthermore, their common assumption of a connection between ontology and ethics puts them all in stark opposition to central features of secularism as well as of liberalism in its Rawlsian form. To assume a connection between these domains is not uncontroversial, given that, during much of modernity ontology and ethics were considered to belong to different spheres. Central to this separation is Weber's distinction between "facts" (which concerned ontology) and "values" (which concerned ethics). In his own words "the capacity to distinguish between empirical knowledge and value-judgments, and the fulfillment of the scientific duty to see the factual truth as well as the practical duty to stand up for our own ideals constitute the program to which we wish to adhere with ever increasing firmness."[91] However, while propounding this distinction as an ideal, Weber also recognized that this distinction is subjective. Commenting on "the hair-line which separates science from faith," he argued that,

> The objective validity of all empirical knowledge rests exclusively upon the ordering of the given reality according to categories which are subjective in a specific sense, namely, in that they present the presuppositions of our knowledge and are based on the presupposition of the value of those truths which empirical knowledge alone is able to give us. [...] The belief which we, all have in some form or other, in the meta-empirical validity of ultimate and final values, in which the meaning of our existence is rooted, is not incompatible with the incessant changefulness of the concrete viewpoints, from which empirical reality gets its significance.[92]

It is in this sense, by emphasizing how "the ordering of the given reality" is dependent on subjective "faith," that Taylor, Milbank, and Connolly resist any sharp distinction between value and fact, along with distinctions between religious beliefs and self-sufficient reason.

The typical liberal democratic approach to religious and cultural difference has tended to rely on proceduralism, understood as the priority of constitutionally agreed-upon rules. Habermas is a good example of this, as far as he "focuses exclusively on the procedural aspects of the public use of reason and derives the system of rights from the idea of legally institutionalizing it [i.e., the public use of reason]."[93] In such an approach "the normative substance of basic liberal rights is already contained in the indispensable medium for the legal institutionalization of the public use of reason of sovereign citizens."[94] Milbank, Connolly, and Taylor have all argued at length that this kind of proceduralism is a central problem of secular liberalism. For example, Connolly argues that "procedure, reason, and neutrality are highly congenial to secular liberals who endorse individual rights and who believe there is a universal matrix of procedural reason drawing together people who diverge at other levels in their conceptions of the good life."[95] Taylor has in a similar way argued against the "disengaged reason" or "the view from nowhere" which he sees as a consequence of the attempt by certain Enlightenment thinkers to entertain an "ontologizing of rational procedure." By this he means an understanding in which "the proper procedures of rational thought were read into the very constitution of the mind, made part of its very structure."[96] Against such an account, Taylor emphasizes how difficult it is to distinguish neutral procedures from substantive goals. Taylor exemplifies this dilemma by comparing how *laïcité*, which is the French, supposedly neutral, principle of not favoring one religion over another, has dealt with the contemporary debate around religious symbols such as Muslim headscarves and Christian crosses. Taylor here points out that while headscarves were banned, crosses worn as "decorations" were unchallenged. This, Taylor argues, suggests that France is a "post-Christian society, following centuries of Christian culture," and asks "How can one expect to convince Muslims that this combination of rulings is neutral?"[97]

Milbank has, against Habermas, argued that "if one restricts reason to the formal and insists that it operates only within knowable boundaries, one will encourage entirely irrational and purely emotive political movements to take centre-stage by exploiting procedurally rational norms against the intentions of those who set up those norms in the first place."[98] Milbank exemplifies this bold claim with the Nazis' rise to power under the Weimar republic, a republic that Milbank describes as thoroughly "Kantian." Milbank here critiques the Kantian formal criterion of morality – the categorical imperative, which states that you should only act on that maxim that you can will as a universal law. Milbank's critical claim is that the categorical imperative is vulnerable to the fact that even immoral policies can be universalized. The Kantian dilemma, which Milbank seeks to point out, has elsewhere been eloquently formulated as "if the criterion is formal, it is empty; if it has content, it cannot demonstrate its rationality."[99] For Milbank, this dilemma points to the danger of a liberal politics that seeks to instill a sharp separation between "reason and faith," which through its claim that "faith" is non-rational, implies that it is "beyond the reach of any sort of argument."[100] Differently put, given that values can't be "scientific," but must draw on metaphysical sources, Milbank here argues that a strict separation between "reason and faith" leads either to nihilism or to purely emotive politics.

Despite the high level of agreement between Taylor, Milbank, and Connolly's critiques of liberal proceduralism, their metaphysical outlooks as well as their practical approaches with regards to the possibilities of dialogue differ dramatically, as I will now go on to point out. Charles Taylor distinguishes himself in an important way from Milbank and Connolly given his willingness to argue from the basis of common human experience, or in philosophical language, by his willingness to utilize transcendental arguments. In *Sources of the Self*, Taylor argues that there is an inherent relationship "between senses of the self and moral visions, between identity and the good."[101] Taylor in this way seeks to bring out the close connection between an understanding of "who I am" and "what I ought to do." But, what is it that constitutes this link between "who I am" and "what I ought to do?" To answer this question Taylor employs a transcendental anthropology. Transcendental arguments typically start with something that is self-evident, something that everyone can be sure of.[102] For Kant one such self-evident feature was the notion of conscious awareness, for Taylor, it is the notion that we are bodily creatures or "embodied beings."[103] Transcendental arguments then move on to identify the conditions that make this self-evident feature possible. For Taylor, this involves the claim that "our perception of the world as that of an embodied agent is not a contingent fact we might discover empirically; rather our sense of ourselves as embodied agents is constitutive of our experience."[104] In this sense, Taylor argues, we cannot separate our intellectual understanding of the world from our bodily experience of it. In summary, Taylor, in a manner typical of transcendental arguments, here establishes the stronger thesis that our experience is essentially that of embodied agents, on the allegedly self-evident claim that we are embodied beings. But, where does this philosophical exercise get Taylor? What can be derived from the claim that our thought and our experience must be described as essentially the thought or experience of embodied agents? Taylor is careful not to draw too far-reaching conclusions about how human thought and action should be explained. However, Taylor does argue that the claim that our existence as subjects should be described as essentially the experience of embodied agents, says something important about the nature of our lives as subjects, namely, that "we can't effectively exercise subjectivity, and be aware of a world without a sense of ourselves as embodied subjects; for this sense is constitutive of our awareness."[105]

Furthermore, Taylor suggests that despite differences between cultures, it is possible to vaguely identify what he calls human constants. Amongst these constants Taylor claims that humans are socially dependent animals, story-telling animals that make sense of existence through narratives, and perhaps most importantly, that we are "strong evaluators" in contact with moral sources.[106] As we have seen by "strong evaluators" Taylor means that we desire some desires above others, and are capable of pursuing moral and other strongly-valued goals, and by "moral sources" he means that which "constitutes the goodness" of our actions and motives.[107] Taylor further argues in *A Secular Age* and elsewhere, that "from my perspective, humans have an ineradicable bent to respond to something beyond life; denying this stifles."[108] The Australian political philosopher Ruth Abbey who has written extensively about Taylor, has here referred to Taylor's "fixed need for contact with the transcendent" as an "ontological property of selfhood."[109] In this sense, a "human constant" in Taylor's transcendental anthropology is that humans are also "religious animals" (homo religiosus).[110]

William Connolly stands in stark contrast to Taylor concerning the possibility of transcendental arguments grounded in common human features. Connolly follows Foucault, and in explicit contrast to Taylor, doubts that "any transcendental argument in the late-modern context can foreclose the terms of ontopolitical contestation."[111] Thus, Connolly is skeptical of approaches, such as transcendentalism, which seek a pure method by which to represent the world. A central part of Connolly's critique of secularism is, as we have seen, that it wrongly assumes that secular perspectives can escape the realm of ontopolitics, and thereby create a neutral platform from which unbiased dialogue would be possible. Rather than seeking to establish objective or self-evident criteria in order to make sense of the world, Connolly stresses that our understanding is discursively mediated. Against assertions of "human constants," Connolly instead stresses the "steady infiltration of ontopolitical presumptions into established cultural understandings."[112]

However, such a position raises questions regarding the possibilities of genuine dialogue across cultures and religions. Is there no core or constant in humanity that will function as a platform for such a conversation? Is all there is just different "ontopolitical interpretations," that is, interpretations that inevitably invoke different sets of fundaments about necessities and possibilities of human being?[113] For Connolly, the answer to the last question is "yes." Connolly argues that "no perspective has at its disposal a consensual, pastoral, or transcendental strategy capable of reducing competitors in this domain to a small set of friendly alternatives."[114] If from Connolly's theoretical horizon there is such a thing as general human condition (a suggestion that Connolly might reject as an illegitimate transcendental "human constant"), it might be described as the ever-changing nature of all things. Connolly emphasizes "the constitutive experience of uncertainty and instability in the will," which leads him to reject the notion of "a whole, secure, centered, transcendental way of being" in favor of an outlook on life on the person that is guided by "the awesome contingency of the human condition."[115] The notion of contingency is so central to Connolly that he claims to "revere" the "effervescent energies flowing through and over identity, the universal, and the real."[116] In this sense Connolly's position might be described by referencing Heraclitus' dictum that "the only thing that's constant is change."[117]

Regarding the question of the validity of transcendental arguments, John Milbank can be understood as siding with Connolly against Taylor. Milbank's critique concerns the allegedly neutral and seemingly self-evident character of such arguments. Milbank argues that Kantian transcendental arguments are "metaphysically dogmatic" rather than an "innocent, descriptive account of how things really are."[118] By this claim Milbank attacks Kant's construal of the metaphysical world as strictly separated from the phenomenal world (objects as the they appear to us). Milbank's point is here that it is only possible to draw such a line if one stands metaphysically above phenomena. Differently put, the one who seeks to draw a border must know at least something about what is on the other side of that border. Milbank here argues that the metaphysics underlying transcendental arguments in its Kantian form is dogmatic, and assumes an elevated cognitive position from where it can judge and set the limits for the immaterial and atemporal. Against such a position Milbank argues that even the claim to draw a boundary between the noumenal and the phenomenal is undergirded by a metaphysic, or constructed from within "our linguistic being-in-the-world." Accordingly, for Milbank, there is no transcendental "outside" of a narrative "no liberal enclave in which one can shelter;" instead, "the real cultural issue lies between this nihilism and theology."[119] Milbank's theology should therefore, according to him, be understood as "saving metaphysics" in the sense that it seeks to keep together the phenomenal and the noumenal, the natural and the supernatural. However, according to Milbank's theological metaphysics "being is not a transcendental framework that includes even the divine; rather being and God are identified as the transcendent source in which all else participates."[120]

Critics have argued that the choice between theology and nihilism that Milbank posits assumes a previous metanarrative which enables this very choice, and thereby points to a discourse outside his narrative.[121] Against this important critique, Milbank has conceded that "just as I can appeal to a certain inchoate current human preference for peace over violence that is both innate (from my metaphysical point of view) and a post-Christian residue, so also I can appeal to a certain bias towards reason rather than unreason (present for similar reasons)."[122] In this sense even Milbank, despite his claim of self-sufficiency of the theological narrative, assumes a thin anthropology common to all outside his theological narrative, which sees humans as rational and peace-seeking.

The terms of dialogue

Taylor, Milbank, and Connolly represent three different approaches with regards to the possibilities of dialogue between different religions and cultures. These differences, I will argue, are related to ontological assumptions that are directly related to their respective religions or existential creeds. As we have seen, Milbank understands the term "dialogue" in a fairly specific sense that denotes "a commonly recognized subject matter and certain truths that can be agreed about this subject matter by both (or all) participants."[123] Given this understanding of dialogue, paired with his rejection of neutral, tradition independent reason, a cross-cultural or inter-religious dialogue becomes close to impossible. The crux for Milbank is that he perceives religions in ontological terms, as different ways of accounting for "Being itself, or for 'what there is'."[124] As a consequence of this view, which denies the possibility of a neutral account of things, is that any encounter between two religions/cultures necessitates a struggle about whose language will be used to describe and position the other. In this sense "each religion has to reclassify other, incommensurable accounts" according to its own perspective.[125] Milbank furthermore argues that attempts to "respect the other" engage in an act of "imperializing reclassification," given that such a description seeks to impose its own account of "what there is," or what constitutes the other's otherness. That description will then shape the decision whether the differences that the Other embodies should be overcome or kept at distance. As we have seen, Milbank makes no secret of the fact that the only narrative he believes has the capacity to peacefully order and overcome difference is his metaphysical reading of Christian theology. He therefore, in an act of paradoxical imperialism, argues that "it is only through insisting on the finality of the Christian reading of 'what there is' that one can both fulfill respect for the other and complete and secure this otherness as pure neighborly difference."[126] What this means is that Milbank's peaceful reconciliation of difference is only attainable through a Christian account of society, which for him is manifested in the church. Accordingly, Milbank rejects the idea that inter-religious dialogue is a way to arrive at truth, and refers to any claim that attempts to seek a position outside a particular religion as "a profoundly ethnocentric illusion."[127] His *Theology and Social Theory* can in this sense be read as an attempt to "end" the dialogue between theology and sociology since no other perspective or narrative than theology is viable.[128] As a consequence, Milbank's vision entails a situation where theology resumes its role as "the queen of the sciences," as it had in scholastic thought during the High Middle Ages, or differently put, as the narrative that positions all other narratives. I will later return, under the section *Post-secular visions*, to what Milbank's vision of the church has to say to all of those who do not wish to be a part of that church, or sympathize with his vision.

William Connolly shares Milbank's critical stance towards attempts to establish "criteria of public dialogue or justice that are neutral between opposing conceptions of the good."[129] But Connolly is also critical of attempts to establish criteria of public dialogue that derive from one particular tradition. This is exemplified in his critique of Pope Benedict XVI, who in the encyclical *Deus Caritas Est* called for dialogue between the world religions. The problem with this call was, according to Connolly, that the Pope "was setting the Vatican understanding of the relation between reason and faith as the framework within which such discussions could proceed." Connolly sees this as a problematic example of a sort of dialogue that seeks to "define the fundaments of their own theory to set the authoritative context in which debates about legitimate and illegitimate diversity should be waged."[130] Rejecting the idea of a neutral and rational consensus, Connolly instead propounds the notion of "agonistic dialogue" in which a double perspective is applied.[131] This entails the project of bringing the fullness of one's identity along with one's conception of the good or divine into the dialogue/meeting, yet at the same time, deploying a readiness to continuously question your own convictions in the light of your opponents' critique. Connolly describes this project as "disclosing contingent elements in any specific identity; to politicize the ambiguity in human being."[132]

Taylor's view regarding the possibilities of dialogue is somewhat more hopeful compared to Milbank's, and perhaps also to that of Connolly's. An important reason for Taylor to engage in dialogue with other religions is that he understands his Catholic faith as "a calling to understand very different positions, particularly very different understandings of fullness."[133] For Taylor, what enables these dialogues across the boundaries of religions is a conviction that it is possible to build friendships "based on a real mutual sense, a powerful sense, of what moves the other person."[134] On the one hand, Taylor here finds himself in agreement with Connolly's agonistic approach in the sense that he does not seek to establish "a compromised solution or synthesis" but rather to build friendships that aren't conditioned upon agreement.[135] In a manner similar to Connolly, he also argues that we define our identity "always in dialogue with, sometimes in struggle against, the things our significant others want to see in us."[136] However, on the other hand, Taylor also claims to resonate with the romantic idea of "humanity as the orchestra, in which all the differences between human beings could ultimately sound together in harmony."[137] Taylor's hopeful account of the harmonious ordering of difference goes against Connolly's agonistic outlook.

Central to Taylor's approach to the issue of dialogue between different cultures and religions is, as we have seen, his reliance on Gadamer's "fusion of horizons."[138] Taylor here seeks to account for how we can move from the language, or horizon, from which we first encounter a new culture (from which we are always tempted to "ethnocentrically distort" the encountered culture), to a richer language that emerges in our active encounter with the new culture. It is Taylor's conviction that we cannot "carry out this process without allowing into our ontology something like alternative horizons or conceptual schemes:" that is, by opening ourselves up to alternative ways of seeing the world.[139] Such a renewed understanding has in Taylor's language "an identity cost," in the sense that a willingness to be transformed by different horizons also transforms the viewer – "no understanding the other without a changed understanding of self."[140] However, what prevents Taylor's approach from resulting in total relativism in the sense that every horizon, or way of understanding the world, would be equally valid, is that he also asserts a certain overlap between cultures and religions – an ontological common denominator of sorts – that remains the same across all cultures and religions. This overlap, which could be understood in the sense of a common humanity, makes it possible when encountering other cultures, in Taylor's Gadamerian language, to identify "that facet of our lives that their strange customs interpellate, challenge, and offer a notional alternative to."[141] Taylor thus argues that it is possible to overcome the perceived incommensurability between different religions and cultures, by identifying a starting point in common features, which will enable "an eventual fusion of horizons."[142] I will seek to explain this in more detail below.

Commenting on a famous article by British philosopher Peter Winch, *Understanding a Primitive Society*, Taylor addresses the dilemma concerning the issue of incommensurability of different cultures.[143]

Winch argues that the magical practices of the Azande people in Central Africa have their own internal standards of rationality, and that the Azande rituals are not simply different from our practices, they are incommensurable. Accordingly, claims Winch, we cannot assert the superiority of our scientific method over the Azande magic practices, given that the standard by which we measure is influenced by the way we live our lives and differences in activities: between their magical and pre-scientific world and our technological society. Against such a position, Taylor argues that a mutual feature can be identified between Azande magic and our scientific method, namely the struggle to achieve technological control "there is an inner connection between understanding the world and achieving technological control."[144] Taylor assumes that the universe exhibits a meaningful order, which he argues becomes clear if we view "understanding the universe and coming into attunement with it as inseparable activities."[145] So, somewhat paradoxically, Taylor argues that transcultural judgments of rationalities can arise precisely where there are differences such as those between the sets of beliefs underlying primitive magic as well as modern science. Differently put, Taylor argues that it is possible to identify distinct internal criteria of success – despite incommensurable cultural systems – which make it possible to transcend cultural particularities. Taylor has elsewhere addressed this dilemma in terms of "cultural overlaps," as exemplified by the historical encounter between the Conquistadors and the Aztecs, and how the Conquistadors identified the Aztecs' bloody sacrifices and ripping out of hearts with the worship of the devil. While affirming the Conquistadors' interpretation that the Aztec's ripping out of hearts referred to a "religious" or super-empirical reality, and thus to a common "spiritual reality," Taylor goes further and identifies a cultural overlap between what went on in the Aztec sacrifice and the Conquistadors' Catholic mass, in terms of the centrality of sacrifice. The central point is, according to Taylor, the possibility to identify that "we share the same humanness" which can be identified in our different ways of dealing with conditions which we share.[146] However, Taylor here acknowledges the danger of applying broad labels to denote such overlaps. Such labels are, according to Taylor, prone to displaying ethnocentric biases, and he exemplifies with how the term "religion" easily takes on board meanings that are specific to just one culture and thereby runs the risk of becoming imperialistic. Taylor's advice is here to avoid broad labels altogether, and argues that "the Mass and Aztec sacrifice belong to rival construals of a dimension of the human condition for which we have no stable, culture-transcendent name."[147]

Taylor's vision of a "dialogue society" in which "diversity is welcomed as richness and not feared as a prelude to division," stands in contrast to Milbank's vision.[148] Taylor's society would put "dialogue itself in the central position occupied in earlier societies by an established religion, and in totalitarian societies by an official ideology."[149] However, in order to achieve this, Taylor emphasizes the notion of commonality between people. Connolly is wary of formulating such commonalities, or categories of "sameness," given the risk of oppression that comes with such labels, which tend to impose sameness on difference. A central part of Connolly's *Why I Am Not a Secularist* entails a critique of the intellectualist reduction of deliberative democracy to pure argument, at the expense of bodily and culturally imbued aspects of politics. Connolly furthermore argues that the attempts to be postmetaphysical entail a certain secularism that depreciates the visceral and the embodied aspects of politics such as religions and rituals that refuse to be relegated to a private sphere, and thereby seek to achieve a notion of purity into politics.[150] Differently put, by critiquing a Kantian metaphysic that draws on a distinction between the supersensible and the sensible, or the transcendent and the immanent, Connolly seeks to employ the notion of the "infrasensible." By this term Connolly denotes the porous and complex interrelations between body and mind. Drawing on Nietzsche's quip that "we think with our stomachs," Connolly argues that images, desires and moods are only partly subject to direct overview and control, and that the infrasensible therefore is partly inscrutable.[151] Connolly is consequently critical of "intellectualist and deliberationist models of thinking that retain so much credibility in philosophy and the human sciences," given that they tend to underestimate the importance of the intricate networks that connect body, brain and culture.[152] Taylor also wants to take the visceral and the bodily aspects of politics seriously, but goes about it in a different manner. Where Taylor utilizes a transcendental anthropology that seeks to formulate a notion of universality based on our experiences as embodied creatures, Connolly fears that such an approach would fail to account for the diversity and richness of different ways of being. A transcendental approach is, in this sense, ill-fitted to a metaphysical outlook that emphasizes the continuously becoming universe. Connolly accordingly rejects the idea that we can discourse with one another from a point "above differences in metaphysical or religious orientation."[153] Milbank differs from Taylor and Connolly in that he is less interested in the physical body. While certainly showing an interest in the material, his account of the body more often denotes a certain view of community or politics, as in "corporality," or a "social body," which for Milbank is the Church or "the body of Christ" as "the new social body which can transgress every human boundary."[154]

Against Jürgen Habermas' view that a formal and content-neutral framework is required in order to facilitate arguments between seemingly incommensurable positions, Milbank claims that no argument is possible "outside a horizon of shared faith."[155] However, this should perhaps not be understood in quite as exclusivist terms as it might sound given that Milbank also states that "shared faith means something like 'common feeling'."[156] Milbank here draws on David Hume's account of feeling which Milbank argues posits an "empirical connection" to the "real" in the sense that our feelings (and not pure reason) is viewed as that which "truly reveals to us the real."[157] Hume held that moral distinctions are based on feelings, but this did not lead him to a position of moral relativism given that "the notion of morals implies some sentiment common to all mankind."[158] In this sense, Milbank understands inward "feeling" as able to provide an "'outwardness' of cognition and meaning" in a way that enables a relation to a common reality.[159] The notion of "outwardness" thus enables Milbank to escape the charges of idealism stemming from his strong emphasis on narrative accounts of reality. In fact, Milbank goes as far as to claim that feelings play a central role in shaping the way we perceive the world, and are "responsible for shaping the sedimented habits that then constitute the regular shape of the universe, and with which human 'culture' is in essential continuity."[160]

Milbank here seems to be assigning to "sympathy" (understood as "feeling together"), a capacity for mediation between "the clash of naturalistic and religious visions." Milbank sees in this "community of feeling" a supra-political space with affinities to both the "the Church" and "civil society."[161] However, Milbank's engagement with "feeling" is rather recent, and the further implications of this theme remain to be expounded. However, there are interesting affinities to be found between Milbank's recent focus on feelings and what Connolly refers to as the "visceral register" of politics (with which he seeks to account for the porous relation between body, brain and culture, or the "affective energy below the threshold of intellectual attention").[162] However, Taylor has more thoroughly developed the prospect of cross-cultural communication with regards to humanity's common embodiedness. Judging from these comparisons regarding feelings and affective moods, the notion of a transcendental sphere seems to exist with all three theorists. I will explore this common theme in the end of this chapter, but first I will turn to the issue of pluralism and difference.

The ethics of difference

Milbank, Connolly, and Taylor are in broad agreement regarding what they perceive as the weaknesses of liberal pluralism and have in various ways raised the issue of whether liberalism truly recognizes diversity, and in particular religious difference. Rejecting the idea that mere rational consensus is able to reconcile moral differences, they all seek to formulate alternative accounts of pluralism which aim to take different ways of being in the world seriously in a way that don't exclude religions.

Milbank has perhaps formulated the harshest critique against liberal pluralism, and portrayed it as imperialistic in the sense that it displays the "arrogance of locality," and ends up with a fossilized notion of freedom and justice.[163] What Milbank means is that liberal pluralism seeks to overcome the seemingly incommensurable differences between different religions and cultures through a procedural neutrality that doesn't take the different claims of particular religions seriously. In this sense, Milbank argues, liberal pluralism does not respect the "otherness of the other." He is critical of what he perceives to be a contradictory attitude within liberalism towards difference: where, on the one hand, differences are claimed to be valued for their own sake, or in themselves; while, on the other hand, differences are obliterated under broad universal categories. Milbank describes this as a situation where "postmodern terrorism of the particular and the different feeds off modernist terror of the formally universal and vice-versa."[164] Instead, Milbank suggests that "differences are not valid as such," but rather are to be understood as parts of "an elusive universal."[165] Milbank explains this "elusive universal" as entailing transcendence, and likens it to a cosmic community, which for Milbank is the Catholic universal church. According to Milbank, Christianity from the beginning pursued "a universalism which tried to subsume rather than merely abolish difference: Christians could remain in their many different cities, languages, and cultures, yet still belong to one eternal city ruled by Christ in whom all 'humanity' was fulfilled."[166] Liberalism is therefore, in Milbank's opinion, to be challenged by a metaphysically informed Christianity that he sees as capable of ordering difference harmoniously, without doing violence to it.

Taylor and Connolly, while subtler in their formulations, share much of Milbank's critique with regards to the need for a more generous account of pluralism that does not exclude religious difference. However, their constructive solutions differ radically. Connolly propounds his "multidimensional pluralism," in which he seeks to incorporate a "'deep plurality of religious/metaphysical perspectives' into public discourses."[167] Furthermore, as we have seen, Connolly also calls for the need to "acknowledge the comparative contestability of the fundamental perspectives" that one brings into public engagements "while working hard not to convert that acknowledgment into a stolid or angry stance of existential resentment."[168]

Taylor seeks to find agreement between different groups or existential outlooks in society based on moral convergence. One example of this is his three-cornered conflict between secular humanists, contemporary neo-Nietzscheans (to which he counts Foucault, Derrida and William Connolly),[169] and "those who acknowledge some good beyond life" (by which Taylor means acknowledgers of transcendence).[170] In analogy with the convergence between neo-Nietzscheans and acknowledgers of transcendence in Taylor's setup, Milbank, Connolly, and Taylor are in agreement "in their absence of surprise at the continued disappointments of secular humanism" regarding its hope that a purely "rational" worldview would bring peace and prosperity for all, and also in the sense that they perceive secular humanism to lack a dimension of life. While Taylor labels Connolly as neo-Nietzschean, he positions himself, along with Milbank (although not explicitly), in the "acknowledgers of transcendence" corner of the triangle. However, Taylor goes on to introduce a fourth possible position in the setup by arguing that the acknowledgers of transcendence are divided between those who argue that "the whole move to secular humanism was just a mistake, which needs to be undone," and those who (like himself) are more positive with regards to the benefits of the secularizing ethos of the Enlightenment, suggesting that its "practical primacy of life" has been a "great gain for human kind."[171] With this addition to the setup, Taylor separates himself from the views propounded by Milbank according to which there is strict distinction between "the Christian perspective" and "the secular one."

Milbank's vision for how we are to live peacefully together in a pluralist society is grounded in his unapologetic theological metaphysics. As we have seen, Milbank draws on a Platonic metaphysic that posits a hierarchical ordering of the universe in the sense of "a vertical sequence up which each individual can contemplatively and actively rise."[172] This hierarchical ordering, which for Milbank is central in order to challenge what he sees as liberal pluralism's indifference to difference, is enabled by an ontology where everything is imagined to participate in God. It is this "participatory ontology," which sees an analogy in everything that exists (even between God and man), that for Milbank makes it possible to reconcile difference without obliterating it or reducing it to sameness.

William Connolly propounds an alternative view of difference and pluralism; a view that is equally critical of Milbank's hierarchical or "corporatist" pluralism, as well as the liberal pluralism which he argues fails to affirm "the irreducible plurality of sacred objects in late modern life." Instead, Connolly propounds a "deep pluralism," which "seeks to come to terms with a culture in which people honor different existential faiths and final sources of morality."[173] Connolly rejects Milbank's Platonic ontology as being too tree-like, or "arboreal," in its structure. For Connolly, such metaphysics are too bound up with hierarchical and oppressive structures that have been used politically to impose a fixed societal order. Connolly is therefore critical of metaphysics that attempt to order difference as if diversity could be viewed "as limbs branching out from a common trunk, fed by a taproot," in which "the trunk might be Christianity or Kantian morality or the history of a unified nation or secular reason."[174] Against such a hierarchical and arboreal ordering, Connolly employs the notion of a rhizomatic pluralism in which the imagery of grass without a central stem is invoked. Connolly's account of pluralism in this sense seeks to foster "a general ethos of generosity and forbearance" that refrains from ordering difference. Connolly here argues that his ethics aims to draw on "multiple sources rather than from a single, exclusionary" one.[175] However, this leaves Connolly with the question of whether there is anything in common that humans can share? Or differently put, what is the basis of "deep pluralism?" According to Connolly, what enables broad collaboration around something, despite our differences, is the experience of contingency; by which Connolly seeks to highlight "the notion of diverse, uncertain, and contingent forces that enter into the constitution of every self."[176] It is in a paradoxical sense by the realization of the randomness of existence, the realization that we as humans are "much more the result of contingent historical arrangements [...] than of civilizational necessities," that we according to Connolly "glimpse the outlines of a more rhizomatic pluralism."[177] And, conversely, Connolly holds that it is the notion of fixed and solid identities which threatens the possibility of a truly inclusive pluralism. It is in this sense, he argues, when "constituencies insist upon sinking deep, exclusionary roots," that truly democratic pluralism is threatened.[178]

Thus it becomes clear that Connolly differs from Taylor and Milbank with regard to their views of cultural roots and embeddedness, as well as how they understand contingency. Whereas (as we have seen) Connolly employs the rhizomatic ideal of pluralism and identity, Taylor, and to an even greater extent Milbank, emphasize the importance of deep roots. However, whereas Milbank argues the need to be rooted in one particular tradition/religion, Taylor seeks for "something midway" between a "homogenizing demand for recognition of equal worth, on the one hand, and the self-immurement within ethnocentric standards, on the other."[179] Their differences with regard to the issue of contingency center around the question: Contingent on what? For Connolly, our existence is contingent on fluctuating and interconnected "force fields" that interact and enter into the constitution of every self, and shape the world. By contrast, for Milbank and Taylor, the world is ultimately contingent on God, and the creator–creation distinction. Accordingly, the moral framework, along with its "strong qualitative discriminations," which is central to Taylor's philosophy "is not meant just as a contingently true psychological fact about human beings," but as "constitutive of human agency" and as an unchanging feature of personhood.[180] Milbank, for whom the notion "gift" and "gift-giving" is a central theological theme in his account of grace, views God as a non-contingent "gift-giver."[181]

Taylor, Milbank, and Connolly are in agreement concerning the problems related to the project of seeking to delimit a fundamental common human nature from a sphere of particular cultures, given their claim that all our knowledge is culturally mediated. Their rejection of a strict distinction between nature and culture is thus a central theme in the writings of all three theorists. This "blurring" of the nature/culture dichotomy is related to the blurring of another important philosophical distinction: that between subject and object. This distinction has been central to Western philosophy since Descartes introduced it, and posits that "the radical gap between what is inside the mind and what is outside in the world must be mediated in order for a subject to have knowledge of the world."[182] Against such a position Taylor, Milbank, and Connolly all share the conviction that the mind and the body are deeply interconnected, and they hence reject the idea of a detached knowing subject. What such a position implies is a different understanding of the relation between the physical and the mental, and furthermore between nature and culture. If the human body, (the physical) and the human mind or soul (the mental), are not distinct and differentiated phenomena, then, Taylor, Milbank, and Connolly would argue that this also breaks down any firm border between nature and culture. Following the French phenomenologist Maurice Merleau-Ponty, Taylor, Milbank, and Connolly reject Descartes' sharp distinction, along with the notion that we perceive reality in terms of mental images. Descartes famously held that mind and body were distinct substances and once declared himself to be "certain that I can have no knowledge of what is outside me except by means of the ideas I have within me."[183]

By contrast, Taylor, Milbank, and Connolly argue for a different account of mediation: one that seeks to ascribe more importance to the body. Rejecting the idea that we know the outer world by having it mediated by inner, mental representations or ideas, Taylor instead seeks to account for our knowledge of the outer world through our interaction with it: "the most primordial and unavoidable significances of things are, or are connected to, those involved in our bodily existence in the world."[184] Taylor here claims that Merleau-Ponty, more than anyone else, has shown what it means to understand ourselves as embodied agents.[185] In a similar way, Milbank argues that "our mind is not an ego looking through our body at what it sees. Rather, it is first of all our body itself which sees and touches."[186] The body has in this sense an ontological status given that it itself is tangible, and is at the same time something which senses other things. Connolly agrees with Milbank and Taylor and also draws on Merleau-Ponty to develop his account of the entanglement, or as he put it, the "multi-layered" conception of the brain and body that accounts for "how nature is mixed into every layer of culture."[187]

As mentioned, a rejection of a strict dichotomy between the experiencing subject and the object of experience has important implications for how the relation between nature and culture is perceived. As we have seen, Connolly argues that every conception of culture, identity, ethics or thinking contains an image of nature within it; conversely, even hardcore realists in physics presuppose "a cultural conception of how scientific cognition proceeds," given that we all presuppose that "human capacities for cognition can be brought into correspondence with the way of the world separate from those capacities."[188] Connolly here refers to Nietzsche's claim that such an (implicit) worldview preserves the remains of a forgotten theology as it presupposes that the world has an unchanging structure available to our cognition.[189] Connolly here suggests that such a view of the world would appear "improbable in a culture in which faith in a world created by a universal, omniscient God had not had a long run," and that "creationists and realists," insofar as they subscribe to this worldview, are "closer to each other in their assumptions and hubris than either acknowledges."[190] Rejecting Kant's idea that nature can only be comprehended by one authoritative, transcendental model, Connolly instead affirms a blend between Nietzschean philosophy of nature and modern physics, as put forward by Ilya Prigogine (a Nobel prize winner in chemistry and the inventor of complexity theory), and argues that "every cultural interpretation expresses an idea of nature; but because the partisans of each interpretation are themselves sunk in nature and culture" they "lack a position above this field from which to reach definitive judgments about it."[191] Such a position rejects the idea that "the world is governed by eternal laws discernible to a science properly organized," and instead seeks to affirm a description "in which there is room for both the laws of nature and novelty and creativity."[192] These sources lead Connolly to the radical conclusion that "it is not only in 'culture' that perception, interpretation, unpredictability, and history occur," but also in non-human processes.[193] Accordingly, Connolly seeks to incorporate biology into political and cultural theories, while still rejecting reductionist accounts of sociobiology, so that "nature is mixed into every layer of culture."[194]

Connolly distinguishes himself from Milbank and Taylor in his attempt to link natural science, such as complexity theory, to culture. However, Taylor is in agreement with Connolly in the sense that he sees "a big watershed in our intellectual world" between "those who hope to anchor an account of human nature below the level of culture, such that cultural variation, where it is not trivial and negligible, can be explained from this more basic account," and those who perceive this to be "an evasion of the most important explananda in human life, which are to be found at this level of cultural difference."[195] Against the Cartesian subject/object ontology, where the subject is viewed as a self-sufficient mind which relates to the objects in the world by way of internal mental states, Taylor argues that "[w]hatever we might identify as a fundamental common human nature, the possible object of an ultimate experience-transcending science, is always and everywhere mediated in human life through culture, self-understanding, and language."[196] Taylor's *A Secular Age* can be read as an attempt to explain the emergence and effects of a Cartesian worldview in which the border between what is inside the mind and what is outside in the world is constitutive for the distinction between nature and culture. As we have seen, a central part of Taylor's secularization narrative concerns the shift from what he refers to as the "porous self" to the "buffered self." Taylor and Connolly are here in agreement over what they see as the negative aspects of modern philosophy, following Descartes and Kant, in terms of rigid borders between nature and culture. But where Connolly to some extent follows Nietzsche in blaming Christianity for such an understanding, Taylor suggests that this development has more complex historical roots that are better understood as a distortion of Christianity. For Taylor, an important aspect of this development – what he refers to as the modern moral order – is the emergence of an anthropology in which humans are seen as agents endowed with self-evident rights "who through disengaged, disciplined action can reform their own lives, as well as the larger social order. They are buffered, disciplined selves."[197]

Milbank agrees with Taylor; but where Taylor focuses on how the West, through reform, became a disciplinary society and how "the ethical replaced the religious," Milbank seeks to trace the theological differences which he argues are to blame for the emergence of secular modernity.[198] Milbank, as we have seen, traces the central ideas behind Descartes' philosophy to medieval scholasticism, and in particular to Duns Scotus and William of Ockham. A central aspect of Milbank's theology concerns the rejection of a realm of "pure nature" in humanity: that is, a sphere separated from the transcendent, or in Milbank's theological language, from supernatural grace.[199] However, Milbank argues that "our perceptions of nature and culture seem to be merging" even outside theology as seen in modern physics and biology.[200] Milbank exemplifies this claim with recent scientific theories which, rather than using the terminology of "natural laws," talks in terms of "irreversible temporal processes" and "relatively fixed habits;" and, furthermore, of how biologists describe nature in terms of "codes" and "codings." In a similar way, Milbank argues that "human mental life is increasingly thought of as an embodied life," subject to manipulation by drugs and physical activities. All this, Milbank argues, testifies to the "the blurring of the boundary between nature and culture."[201] But to claim that the borders between nature and culture are blurred is merely a philosophical presupposition for Taylor, Milbank, and Connolly. It is when we apply this philosophical position to the domain of religion, politics, and the secular, that important questions and differences start to emerge. If nature and culture are entangled, and secular science is unable to give a metaphysically unbiased account of reality, are we then not trapped inside culture, or imprisoned in our own outlook? Is this entanglement of nature and culture best described in immanent terms, or is there a need for some notion of transcendence? And if transcendence exists, how is the mediation between transcendence and immanence (or between mind and matter) envisioned? As we have seen, Taylor, Milbank, and Connolly differ in how they answer these questions, as well as in the manner by which they seek to gain knowledge and say something about the underlying structure of the intertwined reality of nature/culture.

Taylor engages the nature/culture entanglement through a hermeneutical approach. Different cultures are seen as parts, or incomplete accounts, of an underlying reality that he believes are possible to harmonize. However, Taylor acknowledges that "the really difficult thing is distinguishing the human universals from the historical constellations and not eliding the second into the first so that our particular way seems somehow inescapable for humans as such."[202] In fact, Taylor suggests that this might be "the greatest intellectual problem of human culture," to which he suspects "no satisfactory general formula can be found."[203] Taylor, drawing on Gadamer, here suggests that our cultural horizon can change and expand as we encounter other cultures.

Milbank is more skeptical of the Gadamerian notion of the fusion of horizons (*Horizontverschmelzung*). For Milbank, language and narration have the ability to convey the metaphysical ordering of nature, but compared to Taylor, he is quicker to point out the incommensurability between different metaphysical accounts. Milbank argues that "narration – of events, structures, institutions, tendencies as well as of lives – is the final mode of comprehension of human society."[204] Put more simply, for Milbank, it is culture that reveals what nature, or reality, is like. Milbank here equals reality with "the true order of things," and claims that any such account "must be mediated by particular human relations and practices." The reason for this is, Milbank argues, is that culture can be "neither merely arbitrary nor totally opposed to nature, since it is what truly discloses the latter."[205] Milbank is not here referring to any culture, but rather to culture in a qualified sense – as that which has the ability to reveal the true nature of things. More specifically, he is arguing for a metaphysically informed culture/theology inspired by Plato and Augustine. Central to this theology is the hierarchical structuring of desires and cultural idioms, which "sees nature as 'contrived' and human culture as part of a divine, and so natural, 'contrivance'." Milbank here emphasizes the importance of seeing the universe as ordered and "created *ex nihilo*," since this position "rejects any ontological region of chaos."[206]

Interestingly, Connolly also addresses this cosmological creed of *ex nihilo*. Connolly, however, takes a different position and instead emphasizes the randomness and chaos of creation. Connolly here refers to the American theologian Catherine Keller, who rejects the idea of creation *ex nihilo*. She argues that this concept reflects belief in an omnipotent Creator who upholds transcendent power structures in a manner she finds inconsistent with the complexity of the world.[207] Connolly here agrees to what he sees as the malignant effects of an understanding where the universe is created *ex nihilo*, and argues that "if a perfect God created the world from nothing, all worldly imperfection is either introduced by us through free will or a veil of appearances to be torn away in the future."[208] Instead, Connolly emphasizes the process of becoming and understands culture and nature as permeating each other in a chaotic fashion. However, Connolly argues, a scientific exploration into the complex relations between thinking, culture, brains, and bodies can help us gain knowledge about the basic structure of reality. But, against what he sees as the "contemporary guardians of determinism, reductionism, and the sufficiency of lawlike knowledge," Connolly sides with those who "project an element of unpredictability and historical development into the most complex systems of nature." It is with this latter scientific approach, which he sees represented in Nietzsche, as well as the physical chemist Ilya Prigogine, and the philosopher of science Isabelle Stengers, through which he seeks to explore the metaphysical relations between "thinking, culture, brains, and bodies."[209] Connolly in this sense blends metaphysics, science, and affective and existential dispositions into a layered account of being.

What emerges from these discussions about the relation between nature and culture are three different methods of accounting for the underlying structure of reality: Milbank's theological metaphysics in narrative form, Taylor's philosophical anthropology in phenomenological form, and Connolly's metaphysics of becoming paired with complexity theory. Common to all is the conviction that culture has the capacity to reveal nature in a way that exceeds the ability of reductive science. In Milbank's case, this is seen in the way he understands religion as a vehicle that can mediate an account of reality (as the true order of things), which he links to the "divine:" "the divine is never directly available, religion must instead be about how the divine is indirectly manifest."[210] For Taylor, human behavior, and in particular what he sees as our capacity to be moral evaluators, points to a reality laden with values. But, where Taylor construes this revealing capacity in terms of a hermeneutics approached from the bottom-up – or, differently put, through a process of interpretation and engagement with different cultures – Milbank can be understood as starting from the top by employing his theological metaphysics.

With the term "world-disclosure," Heidegger argued that our access to the world is structured by language.[211] Employing this term, one might say that Taylor locates the world-disclosing function in his transcendental account of the body, while Milbank locates the world-disclosing function in his theological narrative, by which he argues that the particular event of the incarnation discloses universal humanity and values. Connolly attributes a world-disclosing capacity to the science of complex systems theory and neurology, a capacity he claims reveals a becoming and contingent character of the world. However, against a theorist such as Habermas who, in his essay *Excursus On Leveling the Genre Distinction between Philosophy and Literature*, separates "problem-solving" and argumentation from "world-disclosure" and narrative, Taylor, Milbank, and Connolly all refuse such a distinction.[212] For them, it is not really possible to separate reality from our existentially infused narratives or "ontopolitical interpretations," and they claim that even scientific language displays elements of world disclosure. Where Habermas would place religion in the same sphere as literature and poetry, separated from the sphere of philosophy and science, Taylor, Milbank, and Connolly reject the secularism implicit in this division of spheres. For them, world disclosure is at the heart also of scientific language.

While united in their rejection of a neutral, detached or non-metaphysical account of reality, the central difference between Taylor, Milbank, and Connolly concerns the metaphysical reality they profess. As we have seen, Milbank's and Taylor's metaphysics of hierarchy and moral order, stand in contrast to Connolly's metaphysic of becoming which emphasize the temporal and process-character of being. However, such an account begs the question of whether there is a core or something persisting in subjectivity. Against traditional accounts of the human subject, Connolly attempts to find a middle ground that rejects both a recent post-humanist trend in philosophy that seeks to "erase the human subject," as well as what he sees as anthropocentric attempts to restrict subjectivity entirely "to human beings and/or God."[213] Connolly here seeks to construe an account of subjectivity that affirms a notion of the self that is open to influence and formation (be it cultural, bacterial, or climatic), and on the other hand rejects an understanding of the self in which "everything is always in radical flux."[214]

On a span between a Parmenidean account of existence – as timeless, uniform, and unchanging, and a Heraclitean insistence on ever-present change in the universe, Connolly would no doubt position his philosophy of becoming closer to Heraclitus, while at the same time seeking to avoid an account a position that involves total and constant flux. Milbank, on the other hand, given his preference for Plato's metaphysics, would position himself closer to Parmenides, while at the same time seeking to avoid a singlehanded emphasis on being over becoming, given his claim that "a renewed metaphysics should not seek to suppress the primacy of becoming and the event either in nature or culture."[215] Against Connolly's emphasis on the importance of affirming the contingent nature of our identities and the absence of anything fixed (his ontology of becoming), Taylor argues that cultures which have "articulated their sense of the good, the holy, the admirable" over a long period of time "are almost certain to have something that deserves our admiration and respect."[216] Thus, Taylor can be understood as being more conservative in his view of history and change, especially with regard to his remarks that some of the most powerful moral stories and imageries "have their roots in religious and philosophical doctrines which many moderns have abandoned."[217]

Seeking to resist the label "cultural relativist," Connolly emphasizes "how violent it is to treat cross-cultural differences as if they were different 'values' painted on the surface of the same acts and identities."[218] Connolly here seeks to formulate what he sees as the porous boundary between brain, body and culture, or between meaning and matter, by constructing new terms such as "neurocultural" and "biocultural."[219] Connolly's point is that we humans are shaped by "experiences of exploitation or reciprocity, injury or gratification, degradation or respect, naturalness or disorder" to an extent which makes it valid to talk about a "corporealization of culture." By this term Connolly seeks to address what he sees as the complex relation between cultural norms and corporeal experience. Connolly exemplifies this with how sex between Catholic priests and adolescent boys is perceived very differently today, compared to how sex between aristocratic adult men and adolescent boys was perceived in classical Greece. Connolly suggests that part of the difference can be explained in terms of how different conceptions of what constitute a natural order have been corporealized by the parties involved. Given the complex interrelation between nature and culture, we are therefore, according to Connolly "never in a perfect epistemological position" to draw strict ethical boundaries. He admits that he would place, for example, clitoridectomy "on the injurious side" of that boundary, but he hastens to add that "other established judgments in this domain will eventually undergo reassessment in response to reflective experiences opened up by new drives to pluralization."[220] Connolly is here somewhat vague concerning how far he thinks that such "reassessments" of ethical boundaries can go. Most people would probably agree that ethical boundaries vary with time and culture to some extent, but few would hesitate to condemn the practice of beheading members of different religions as universally evil. Seeking to navigate this dilemma, the ethics which flow out of Connolly's ontology of becoming and which underlie his pluralism "strive to cultivate wisdom about a world that is neither designed for our benefit nor plastic enough to be putty in our hands."[221]

While Connolly in this sense maintains a radical openness to the plurality of traditions, Taylor's account of ontology and notion of common goods has by critics been argued to be "singular in its focus" and leaving "little room for reasonable divergence."[222] Other commentators have argued that Taylor's Catholic faith comes to the forefront in the way in which he seeks to re-order how different ideas of what is good should be valued. According to Taylor's terminology "constitutive goods" enable us to define what a good action is, or what constitutes the goodness of our actions or motives.[223] However, as we have seen, Taylor tends to refrain from explicitly metaphysical language, but nevertheless entertains a moral philosophy that puts primacy on the notion of the good as opposed to which procedures should be considered to be right. That is, rather than attempting to resolve ethical dilemmas by focusing on the process by which conflicting views and practices can be resolved (such as applying general maxims or rules for conduct based on disengaged reason in order to make specific decisions), Taylor seeks to start from the question of what it is that makes a good action good. He further argues that our understanding of what is good is intimately linked with our identity and our frameworks for orienting ourselves in this world. Identity, ontology and ethics are thus closely related for Taylor insofar as "to know who you are is to be oriented in moral space, a space in which questions arise about what is good or bad, what is worth doing and what not, what has meaning and importance for you and what is trivial and secondary."[224] In his critique of liberal philosophers who tend to leave "the good" unspecified or irrelevant, Taylor here follows the British moral philosopher Iris Murdoch and in particular her work *The Sovereignty of Good*. Taylor, however, eschews Murdoch's Platonist language and instead, as discussed above, develops an anthropology based on transcendental arguments. Central to this argument is the idea that humans inevitably operate with constitutive goods, or some idea of an overarching good which orients our actions and motives as higher.[225]

So rather than utilizing Milbank's theological language, or Connolly's Deleuzian metaphysics, Taylor instead focuses on his philosophical anthropology that posits that there are "human constants," empowering images, and stories that function as moral sources of inspiration in any culture. Taylor's approach does not seek to replace more explicitly religious or metaphysical beliefs, but can, according to Taylor "go on pointing to something which remains for us a moral source, something the contemplation, respect, or love of which enables us to get closer to what is good."[226] Taylor applies, in a somewhat pragmatic manner, the strategy of overlapping consensus in order to reach limited moral agreements between different religions; but then, in a second step, continues to ask questions about the moral source which grounds any ethical account. In opposition to Milbank, who starts from his particular theological account about the transcendent source of morality, Taylor starts from the general by asking what different religious accounts have in common, and then moves on to an inquiry about what he argues points to a transcendent source for morality.

While Milbank rejects a foundationalist grounding for his ethics, and has critiqued what he sees as Habermas' attempt to defend a "reasonable humanism" on "neutral, secular ground," it is possible to detect a slight change in his more recent approach.[227] However, as previously mentioned, Milbank employs a revisionist reading of David Hume and in a romantic fashion argues that "faith" and reason are mediated by feeling. Milbank here blames Habermas' strict separation between faith and reason for an "increasing sundering of reason from the emotive and the aesthetic, and a corresponding sundering between reason and a will increasingly viewed as pure 'choice' and 'decision'."[228] So, against earlier accounts of his outlook as being based strictly on narrative, Milbank now argues that "it is necessary to insist, in a 'romantic' fashion, upon the embedding of reason in the emotive, the aesthetic, the linguistic, the social, the historic and the natural."[229] It is here worth noting that Taylor is skeptical of feelings of sympathy as a way of grounding morality. Against the notion of Humean sympathy and the "alleged extension of sympathy with civilizational development," Taylor argues that, it fails to account for "our sense that there is something higher, nobler, more fully human about universal sympathy."[230] Taylor is here critical of attempts to anchor morality in vague notions of human dignity, or in terms of "natural" human sentiment. A central reason for Taylor's critique concerns what he sees as the inability of naturalist philosophies to account of what is "higher," and the inability of the scientific method of explanation to generate value judgments. Instead, Taylor stresses the importance of the question of what kind of ontology is needed to make sense of our ethical or moral lives. While acknowledging that the issue of "what lies behind," our sense of moral obligation is an unresolved issue, Taylor has his "own – theistic – hunches."[231]

We have now established that Taylor's, Milbank's, and Connolly's different approaches to social difference are anchored in distinct metaphysical construals. In the next section we will focus on the broader political visions that underlie Taylor, Milbank and Connolly's post-secularisms.

6.4 Three post-secular visions

My opening question in the introductory chapter concerned alternative ways to construe the relation between religions and secularity in the wake of various critiques of the typical Enlightenment narrative. If human history is not to be understood as a straightforward and stadial progression from religion to reason, culminating in secular modernity, and, if "religion" is not easily identified, separated, and legitimately relegated to a "private sphere," what alternative accounts are available? These questions are made relevant following critique that has deconstructed and historicized the concepts of "religion" and "secular," along with the epistemological foundations of Enlightenment. In particular, this critique has challenged the status and function of "the secular as a transcendental regulator," which consequently has implications for how religious and cultural differences are to be solved in a democratic society.[232] Specifically, if the idea of secular reason – that is, reason that doesn't reflect the commitments or agendas of any particular religion, morality, or ideology, have been seriously criticized – how should we then negotiate our differences? How can people of diverse religious and cultural identities live together peacefully if secular reason is no longer trusted to be the neutral and ultimate adjudicator of religious difference?

Taylor, Milbank, and Connolly have all proposed alternative accounts for how to construe, not only the relation between "religion" and "the secular," but also how cultural and religious differences should be negotiated in pluralistic societies. Taylor, Milbank, and Connolly argue that any attempt to negotiate difference will always display metaphysics, implicitly or explicitly. However, their engagements with metaphysics have very different political implications. Milbank argues that only an orthodox Christian metaphysical account of analogy, which sustains his notion of Christendom, is able to reconcile and peacefully order difference. He propounds a "corporative" pluralism linked to a metaphysical understanding where difference is able to find its proper place in relation to a larger body, which for Milbank is the Church.[233] Connolly, on the other hand, propounds a rhizomatic and non-hierarchical pluralism, analogous to his account of a pluralistic and "messy" universe of becoming. Connolly here relies heavily on the assumption that the "abundance of being," displayed in his metaphysics of the becoming universe, will evoke a sense of gratitude that spills over in the form of generosity. A generosity that, Connolly argues, should affect the way we construe our identities and perceive differences. Finally, Taylor, who argues that secularism has less to do with the relation of the state and religion and everything to do with the (correct) response of the democratic state to diversity, is arguing for an overlapping consensus – a least common denominator of sorts that, in contrast to John Rawls' version, doesn't seek to strain out metaphysics. Taylor seeks to replace an understanding in which secularism is mainly concerned with controlling religion, with a version of secularism that seeks to manage the metaphysical diversity of views that also include non- and anti-religious outlooks. Accordingly, for Taylor, religious difference does not constitute a special case – "the state can be neither Christian nor Muslim nor Jewish, but, by the same token, it should also be neither Marxist, nor Kantian, nor utilitarian."[234] So, Taylor's modified secularism implicates the position that the state must refrain from favoring any of the "deeper" or motivating reasons for its ethic, and treat religions just as any secular worldview.

I suggest that Milbank, Connolly and Taylor can be understood as representing three different post-secularisms that might be presented as constituting three different democracy ideals – all of which differ from secular liberalism. While running the risk of oversimplification, I propose naming these three alternatives: democratic theocracy, agonism, and overlapping consensus. As we have seen, each of these "post-secularisms" is grounded in different ontological accounts, resulting in three distinct approaches to the challenges of dialogue and pluralism. However, as we have also seen, these post-secularisms bring with them new difficulties and dilemmas with regards to what they implicate ethically and politically. These differences I would now like to discuss further.

As we have seen, Connolly's and Taylor's appraisals of modernity and liberal democracy are considerably more positive compared with Milbank's account of "democratic theocracy." However, it should be made clear that, when Milbank talks enthusiastically about monarchism, he is not referring to "any dogmatic literal 'monarchism'," which he admits is an "absurdity."[235] Rather, what Milbank finds attractive in monarchism is the conservative effects of the institution, which he claims enables the safeguarding of a particular understanding of the common good. The hidden premise here is that the will of a monarch is deemed more stable over time compared to fluctuating opinions of the people, and that the monarch is able to represent the true will of the people. Milbank in this way envisions politics as "a 'permanent' power of interest of the general will across time" by which he claims that the notion of an eternal God is central to secure justice on earth and to "protect the interests, responsibilities and valid rights of individuals and corporate bodies against the tyranny of mass opinion."[236] Accordingly,

Milbank's approach to seek a unity-in-plurality has been perceived by many critics as displaying totalitarian tendencies, given his wish to reinstate theology as the master narrative. From a liberal democratic standpoint, a central problem with Milbank's post-secularism is its neglect for each individual's right to live out his or her account of the good life. Milbank, however, argues that it is liberalism that is totalitarian, in the sense that it attempts to achieve societal peace in the midst of diversity by excluding metaphysical accounts of the good; a strategy that Milbank sees as nihilistic: "it acknowledges no supra-human power beyond itself by which it might be measured and limited."[237] Milbank has elsewhere critiqued this approach as seeking to "draw boundaries around 'the same', and exclude 'the other'."[238] Against such an approach Milbank claims that "Christianity should not draw boundaries," and the Church should instead be understood as a "nomad city" that includes even that which is different.[239] Accordingly, Milbank's alternative to a polity based on secular reason is the church. However, the contour of this church remains rather abstract. On the one hand Milbank describes the church in sacramental terms as "the continued event of the ingestion of the body of Christ," and he further describes this church as a "universal society," distinct from the polis.[240] On the other hand, he suggests that the apostle Paul, when speaking about the church "proposes a new sort of polis which can counteract and even eventually subsume the Roman empire."[241] In his vision of the church, Milbank seeks to counter both construals where the Church is "narrowly defined as a cure of souls," and construals where the Church sees itself as having a particular sphere of interest which "will mimic the procedures of political sovereignty, and invent a kind of bureaucratic management of believers."[242] Accordingly, Milbank's vision entails an "extremely hazy," border between Church and state with "many complex and interlocking powers," so that a "sovereign state, or a statically hierarchical Church" can both be avoided.[243] However, as the American scholar of religion Jeffrey Stout, has pointed out, Milbank's theology tends to "reinforce the sort of boundary-drawing it officially opposes" by its very rejection of the existing public sphere's inability to subsume under Christendom.[244]

Given the centrality Milbank puts on both Platonism and Christianity, questions emerge regarding how those who do not subscribe to those perspectives are viewed in his political vision. Do we all have to adopt an analogical or participatory metaphysics? Does everyone have to become Christian? Hence, those less sympathetic of Milbank's account of Christian Platonism would not be without reason to feel subsumed into Christendom.

Furthermore, Milbank's flat-out depiction of secular reason as "either deviancy or falsehood," rejects any possibility of cooperation or notion of a neutral public sphere.[245] Consequently, Milbank's post-secularism seems to imply the paradoxical idea of having an overarching narrative imposed in order to have your difference recognized.

William Connolly's agonistic post-secularism in many ways constitutes a stark contrast to Milbank's vision of Christendom, specifically in the sense that it doesn't seek to establish a "thick" particular tradition at the political center. Instead, central to Connolly's post-secularism is his call for pluralization, understood as a goal rather than as a state of the present order. Key to Connolly's political vision is what he sees as the "inability of contending parties, to date, to demonstrate the truth of one faith over other live candidates."[246] From this claim, he makes contestability and generosity central in the sense that you should be willing to have your own philosophical outlook (religious or secular) called into question, and show respect towards others' creeds. This outlook flows naturally from his ontology of becoming which rejects the notion of any transcendent ordering mechanism above all, and leads to the position that the best we can do in the midst of diversity is to respect each other's different creeds. But the critical question regarding relativism arises as to what it is that should make us respect the Other, beyond Connolly's mere admonition. And furthermore, are not the lines which he actually draws, in order to protect pluralism against Unitarian movements, just as contingent as anything else? Rejecting both the notion of a *telos*, in the sense of a guiding moral purpose to human life, as well as a Kantian categorical imperative, Connolly is pressed for questions concerning the foundation and motivation behind his ethics.

Connolly's emphasis on processes of becoming and lack of any overriding logic or design in the universe associates him with a certain "post-humanist" or "new materialist" strand in philosophy. Matter is here viewed as "lively," or as displaying agency. This opens up political and ethical questions to the extent that matter is perceived in terms of processes from which humans can't be separated. Such a perspective gives rise to a number of difficult questions: If everything is constantly changing, how is it possible to sustain a personal identity over time? And, if a unified conception of the self is ultimately illusory, how is ethical accountability possible? However, these important themes remain underdeveloped in Connolly's writing, as does the more basic philosophical question: If everything changes all the time, how can we even talk about change?

Connolly's post-secular agonism emphasizes the importance of an ethos of generosity and engagement. However, ethical dilemmas rarely concern *if* we should be generous in general, but rather: with whom we are to empathize, or to whom we are to show generosity. Furthermore, it is not entirely clear how this ethos should be instilled amongst the broad population. Connolly argues that "more of us must cultivate gratitude [...] seeking to infuse care for the future into the families, schools, companies, churches, and spiritual assemblies to which we belong."[247] However, given that Connolly's ethical framework, due to its ontological grounding in a world of becoming, lacks a "thick" ethic or a more elaborated particular moral tradition, it is not immediately clear from where he can draw motivating and sustaining resources. Specific traditions tend to have particular ways in which they embody what Connolly refers to as gratitude for the abundance of being: ways that may or may not be open to construe openness to difference in the same way as Connolly sees it. For example, it is not clear how "gratitude for the abundance of being" leads you to agree with Connolly's support of gay rights and medically assisted suicide. Connolly's ethics in this sense seems to imply that gratitude will lead us in a certain ethical and political direction. This assumption can also be seen in Connolly's political vision, or what he refers to as "interim futures," which for him entails a visualization of Copenhagen, a city with "wide bike lanes, considerable bus traffic, [...] where poverty and crime are present but not rampant."[248] What might be perceived as a certain flatness in this political vision might be attributed to what he himself concedes as "our inability in a world of becoming to imagine constructively beyond an interim horizon...."[249]

Here, it might be possible, against Connolly, to ask Taylor's question, whether "we are not living beyond our moral means in continuing allegiance to our standards of justice and benevolence."[250] Taylor's critique, which he originally directed at the Enlightenment naturalism, suggested that its secular ethics was "parasitic" in the sense that "the original model for its universal benevolence" is a Christian understanding of love (*agape*).[251] Connolly, however, argues that his ethic of cultivation "is not entirely reducible to subjectivity or intersubjectivity," but instead of, like Taylor, grounding his ethic in a theistic account, Connolly confesses the "abundance of being over identity that can exceed and energize us."[252] However, given Connolly's hesitancy to anchor his ethics in a particular tradition, the more precise meaning of terms such as "evil," "undeserved human suffering," and "noble," remains unclear. There also exist important differences between, what Connolly refers to as, Taylor's "teleo-communitarian morality," which acknowledges transcendent moral sources embedded in social practices and traditions, and Connolly's own "agono-pluralistic ethic."[253] For example, where Taylor would talk about "a moral force" and "a purposive god," Connolly would rather talk in terms of "ethical sensibility" and "the abundance of life."[254] However, Connolly shares with Taylor the emphasis on the importance of sources for morality. But, Connolly is critical of Taylor's talk about better and worse sources, and more specifically, his talk about transcendent sources of morality as higher sources. Connolly has furthermore critiqued Taylor for his way of describing and contrasting philosophies of pure immanence as "closed," with those that acknowledge transcendence as "open." The problem with this terminology is, according to Connolly, that it portrays a limited understanding of transcendence in which Connolly's own immanent naturalism is deemed "closed." Against such a description, Connolly refers to his mundane transcendence as projecting "an open temporal horizon exceeding human mastery that is irreducible to both closed naturalism and radical transcendence."[255] Differently put, Connolly understands his account of transcendence in temporal, rather than spatial terms, in the sense of being open to time as becoming or process, rather than as a realm beyond. Taylor recognizes the moral attraction of a worldview grounded in immanence and materialism, and especially points out the idea that "we are in an order of 'nature', in which we are part of this greater whole, arise from it, and don't escape or transcend it, even though we rise above everything else in it."[256] However, as we have seen, Taylor argues against the immanent worldview that it is unable to "make sense of our moral experience."[257]

Against critics who argue that Taylor has left philosophy behind, given his Christian beliefs, Connolly defends him and argues that "philosophy and faith are interwoven," and that "so far no philosophy known to me has established itself authoritatively by argument alone."[258] But where Taylor confesses faith in a transcendent God, Connolly confesses his belief in "a reserve or virtual field below articulation without intrinsic purpose or salvational promise."[259] Connolly describes the difference between him and Taylor as "the dicey disparity between an appeal to the whisper of transcendence and an inspiration drawn from the fugitive well of immanence."[260] Nevertheless, Connolly is critical of Taylor's lack of respect for nontheistic sources of the good, and argues that "it is only when he encounters nontheistic faiths inside the historic territories of Christendom that his generosity sometimes falters."[261] However, Connolly assumes his own attitude of "agonistic respect" towards Taylor and argues that his own stance actually is able to practice a more all-encompassing respect, given that it acknowledges the deep contestability implicit in every human account of being. Accordingly, Connolly argues that an agonistic respect "strengthens rather than weakens" the relation between people given that it recognizes the conditions of fragility and contingency which he sees as escaping intellectual or more systematic formulation, and in this sense "does not require a positive fund of commonality as its only base."[262]

What emerges in the discussion between Taylor and Connolly might be seen as an updated version of the political philosophy debate between communitarians and liberals in the 1980s. That debate concerned the question whether it is possible to define and defend rights without presupposing any particular conception of the good life. Taylor, then as well as now, argues for the priority of the good over the right, and claims that a democratic society needs some commonly recognized definition of the good life. Connolly, while rejecting Kantian and Rawlsian beliefs in the ability of supposedly neutral and universal reason to resolve conflicts in a procedural fashion, pursuits the possibility of a universal respect that avoids being rooted in a particular tradition. Taylor, in an attempt to give depth to the liberal-communitarian debate beyond the notion of two monolithic opposing camps, made a distinction between the ontological aspects and the advocacy aspects of the debate. Taylor's point is that an ontological position (such as the choice between atomism and holism) does not necessarily entail a choice of moral norms and public policies (such as the choice between a collectivist or an individualist society). Accordingly, there are not only atomist individualists (such as the American libertarian philosopher Robert Nozick according to which the individual stands as the sole measure of right) and holist collectivists (such as Karl Marx), but also holist individualists and even atomist collectivists. Taylor argues, with regards to the category of holist collectivists that "they represent a trend of thought that is fully aware of the (ontological) social embedding of human agents, but at the same time prizes liberty and individual differences very highly."[263] In the light of these distinctions, I take it that Taylor (who exemplifies this position in company with the Romantic German philosopher and naturalist Alexander von Humboldt), would label Connolly as a holist individualist, given Connolly's common emphasis on holism in terms of the interrelation of all physical sciences – such as the conjoining of biology, meteorology and geology, as well as his emphasis on individual difference.

Charles Taylor's vision of a post-secularism of overlapping consensus might be perceived as taking a middle position between Milbank's Christian vision, and Connolly's dialogical engagement with the Other. Taylor steers away from Milbank's explicitly theological language, as well as Connolly's metaphysics of becoming, and seeks, through a phenomenological method that posits an ontology of embodiment, to find common ground between different cultures and religions. This transcendental approach has been criticized by both Milbank and Connolly, where the former rejects the notion of neutrality implicit in the method, and the latter points out the oppression that transcendental accounts of "the human" historically have fallen prey to given the tendency of each constituency "to construe its ultimate standards to be natural, rational, established by common sense, a series of binding transcendental arguments."[264]

While it is easy to see Connolly agreeing with Taylor's position that "there can never be a total fusion of the faith and any particular society; and the attempt to achieve it is dangerous for the faith," it is somewhat harder to see Milbank doing so given his enthusiasm for an exclusive reading of Catholic Christendom.[265] Taylor describes his reading of Catholicism in terms of "reconciliation between human beings, and it doesn't simply mean within the Church, and it doesn't mean that it's conditioned on being within the Church," and depicts in romanticist terms "humanity as the orchestra, in which all the differences between human beings could ultimately sound together in harmony."[266] Milbank, on the other hand, gives a different account of the conditions for reconciliation between different cultures, which is related to his view of problems related to dialogue. According to Milbank, each tradition or religion "has to reclassify other, incommensurable accounts when it encounters them, according to its own perspective."[267] Thus, Milbank argues, if the multitude of preferences, desires and values propounded by different religions and philosophies reject to be ordered by a single transcendent good, this will only amount to "a 'secular' peace of temporarily suspended violence or regulated competition."[268] As opposed to such a "temporary settlement," Milbank argues that "an ultimate organising logic...cannot be wished away," and for him, this logic is best displayed in Catholic Christianity.[269] As we have seen, Milbank's harmony is not achieved through dialogue with different religions, but rather when "it is in the hands of those acquainted with the true 'art of government', which means those who understand how what is different can be combined, because they have a vision of their common, superordinate origin."[270] Milbank's Christianity thus implies a universalism which tries to "subsume rather than merely abolish difference." While neither Taylor, nor Connolly seek to "abolish difference," they, in contrast to Milbank, do not seek "to make of all these differential additions a harmony, 'in the body of Christ'."[271] Furthermore, against Milbank's negative view of secular modernity due to its dismantling of

Christendom, Taylor paradoxically sees modern culture as, through its secularizing effect on Christian culture, to have enabled the spread of Christianity. Taylor here argues that modern culture "in breaking with the structures and beliefs of Christendom, also carried certain facets of Christian life further than they ever were taken or could have been taken within Christendom."[272]

While differing over Christendom, Milbank and Connolly in some sense share an agonistic outlook on politics as the arena where different visions have to compete with each other without the prospect of a consensus solution. However, where Connolly's political center is empty and continuously contested, Milbank seeks to re-establish one particular tradition at the ruling center. Taylor's position in this sense constitutes an alternative to both Milbank's and Connolly's views through his belief in the prospect of state neutrality, and the possibility of an overlapping consensus as a process for providing a least common denominator for basic values to build a political community around. However, this alternative secularism entails a tension with regards to the concept of neutrality. On the one hand, Taylor critiques the philosophical notion of value neutrality as an unattainable ideal and rejects the possibility of a "view from nowhere." But at an institutional level, on the other hand, he favors state neutrality and argues that a state's decisions shouldn't be "framed in a way that gives special recognition to any particular [...] views." Taylor recognizes the difficulty of combining these positions, but instead of engaging this tension further, he rhetorically asks "what better alternative is there for diverse democracies?."[273]

So, where Milbank conditions his political harmony on whether "the reality of God is properly attended to," Taylor and Connolly have considerably more faith in the discursive and affective capacities of people with different religions to find mutual respect.[274] Where Taylor, in a Gadamerian fashion, seems to suggest that reconciliation between human beings occurs through a fusion of horizons and through mutual willingness to learn from the differences between human beings, Milbank's horizon is non-negotiable, orthodox Christianity. Milbank argues that the distinctiveness of Christianity lies in its "reconciliation of virtue with difference," but unlike Gadamer he does not accept that this is achieved through interpretation. Instead, Milbank's vision is to secure a peace that is "subordinate to a pastoral concern for developing a true desire."[275] Milbank's distinction between "true" and "false" here draws on an Augustinian understanding of virtue with the aim of a "rightly ordered love," or differently put, where a particular theological vision orders the societal diversity at hand.[276]

7
Conclusion

7.1 Transcending the secular

I started out accounting for what Jürgen Habermas has depicted as the paradoxical return of both naturalistic worldviews and religious orthodoxies. The dilemma at hand concerned the mediation of "uncritical faith in science" and religious traditions critical of "the liberal assumptions of the Enlightenment:" that is, between scientism and fundamentalism.[1] Habermas has, in an essay titled *The Boundary Between Faith and Knowledge* (2008), described the inability of pure reason to generate values which can sustain a liberal democracy by claiming that "pure practical reason can no longer be so confident in its ability to counteract a modernization spinning out of control armed solely with the insights of a theory of justice."[2] Habermas' "solution" involves the idea of context-transcendent validity claims accessible through a discursive and postmetaphysical procedure.[3] It is on this discursive account of reason that Habermas bases his strict distinction between faith and reason, a distinction central to his well-known account of the post-secular.[4] Thus, Habermas does not actively engage with metaphysical questions since he chooses to draw a strict distinction between religion and the secular, between the transcendent and the immanent.

Against Habermas, each of the theorists at the center of my study has engaged with these questions, arguing that metaphysics is an inescapable aspect of any philosophical or religious account. Instead of taking a postmetaphysical stance and emphasizing "the difference that exists between faith and knowledge," Taylor, Milbank and Connolly have each actively engaged with ontological questions and emphasized what they perceive to be a blurred line between religion and the secular, belief and knowledge.[5] However, such a position remains a controversial one, and particularly so within religious studies. Where academic religious studies traditionally have been defined in opposition to religious thinking about religion, and have erected a clear boundary between, on the one hand, religion, and on the other hand, the secular study of religion, Taylor, Milbank and Connolly reject this distinction. According to the shared post-secular stance of Taylor, Milbank and Connolly, the idea of non-confessional standpoints is an illusion.

My study has presented three theorists who, each in different ways, have engaged in "religious thinking about religion." As we have seen, the post-secular approaches taken by Taylor, Milbank and Connolly, are skeptical regarding the prospect of finding value neutral analytical concepts. Rather than seeking objectivity from a supposedly neutral point of view, they emphasize the tradition-based nature of all reasoning, and seek to think "with religion" rather than at a distance from it. In this sense, Taylor, Milbank and Connolly are, in Jonathan Z. Smith's terminology, less interested in "processes of proof" and more in "rhetorics of persuasion."[6] However, a central theme in Taylor, Milbank and Connolly's thought is that they all question the very possibility of making a clear distinction between "proof" and "rhethoric," and instead emphasize that reason and fact-making are dependent on language and tradition. In this sense they are all following Johann Georg Hamann who, in his response to Kant's *Critique of Pure Reason*, argued against what he saw as flawed attempts to treat reason as a purified object detached from culture and religion.[7]

Instead of seeking to de-link the connection between religion and the secular, Taylor, Milbank and Connolly, have approached the emergence of the secular as related social and historical processes. Perhaps this comes across most starkly in their genealogies of secular consciousness, in which all three theorists highlight the theological disputes during the scholastic period. Such an approach stands in traditional tension with attempts to explain secularization as resulting from non-religious forces such as modern science, or more material conditions of human existence that seek to instrumentalize a religious cosmology.[8] Instead, what stands at the center of their respective approaches is the refusal of any strict distinction between ideas and the material conditions of reality, between nature and culture, in a way that seeks to highlight how beliefs and practices are inseparable from any account of the world.

Connolly accounts for this refusal of any strict distinction between nature and culture in terms of the affective, unconscious, and visceral elements of belief systems. Taylor addresses the same theme through his terminology of the "conditions" of belief and the "pre-ontological" context: that is, the unfocused and unformulated background to our thinking. For Taylor "'ideas' always come in history wrapped up in certain practices."[9] Taylor's interest in the material can also be noted in his phenomenological critique of cognitivism, in which the embedding of the body in the world plays a central role. Differently put, against a disengaged understanding in which the outside world is perceived and represented as ideas in our head, Taylor has emphasized how our bodies are crucial in the interpretative interaction of experiencing the world. Milbank, who remains within the framework of his Christian narrative, has also engaged with the issue of how to account for material reality, but has done so by seeking to overcome the nature/culture duality through a theological account of materialism.[10] The distinctive feature of Milbank's theological materialism is displayed in his integralist approach that seeks to "supernaturalize the natural" and rejects a dualist account where matter is separated from the soul.

The specific blend of materialism and transcendence displayed in the work of Taylor, Milbank and Connolly, brings to mind John Caputo's quip that "Materialism just isn't what it used to be. Nowadays everyone wants to be a materialist, even the theologians, while the materialists want to look like they lead a spiritual life."[11] In this sense, Taylor, Milbank and Connolly can be viewed as part of a broader trend within religious studies and theology that has become increasingly integrated with findings in cognitive science, evolutionary biology, and "new materialism."[12] However, oftentimes when "religion" has been studied by researchers in the fields of cognition and neuroscience, the approach has been to "explain away" religion by boiling it down to certain non-religious causes by use of a certain reductive approach. For example, it has been argued that "religion exploits the brain's hardwired imperative to wield beliefs for personal and social advantage," and "religious belief" viewed "as a kind of 'placebo effect' – a beneficial psychological outcome arising from faith in the potency of chosen supernatural agents."[13]

Taylor, Milbank and Connolly reject such a view for reasons related to both methodology and ontology. As we have seen, they have critiqued the essentialist understanding of "religion" underlying this project which assumes that "religion" can be reduced to a utilitarian need. In this sense they are in agreement with the religious studies scholars William Edward Arnal and Russell T. McCutcheon, who argue that "'religion' will never be capable of successful reduction, simply because the category is made up of wholly heterogeneous elements. It seems to us that the only possibility for an ultimate reduction (and thus intellectually acceptable understanding) of 'religion' would require a thorough redefinition, or even rejection, of the term as currently understood."[14] Taylor, Milbank and Connolly furthermore reject the Cartesian metaphysical dualism which separates body from mind, and facilitates the position that "religious" beliefs (and in fact any belief, along with consciousness), is reducible to neurons in the brain. Against such a position, Taylor, Milbank and Connolly argue that mind and body are interpenetrated and thus take an "embodied" approach to the study of culture and religion.[15] Accordingly, Taylor, Milbank and Connolly represent a form of materialism, which rejects the view that everything in the universe, including us, can ultimately be understood through its physical properties, and instead claims that there is more to reality than empirical science can account for. In this, they exemplify the kind of "religious belief" that the British theologian Graham Ward has described as "a way of responding to the world that recognises and valorizes the invisible operative within what is materially visible of that world."[16]

However, their accounts remain controversial, primarily due to their rejection of the idea of a neutral secular outlook, as well as their engagements with metaphysics. Yet, religious studies scholars Marcus Dressler and Arvind Mandair have here suggested that scholarship which seeks to rethink the categories of religion and the secular have also "by implication," helped to rethink "the academic study of religion."[17] Despite the relatively diverse group of scholars engaged in post-secular scholarship, Dressler and Mandair identify three different strands: (1) the sociopolitical of philosophy of liberal secularism, (2) a "postmodernist" strand with "critiques of ontotheological metaphysics by radical theologians and Continental philosophers that have helped to revive the discourse of 'political theology'", and (3) those who, following Foucault, employ discourse analysis focusing on genealogies of power, which Dressler and Mandair exemplify with the work of Talal Asad.[18]

Seeking to locate our three theorists within these groups, I concur with their explicit assignment of Taylor to the first group, given his active attempt to accommodate religion in liberal democracies. In the second group, I would place John Milbank, due to his critique of ontotheological metaphysics, which for him means metaphysics independent of theology. William Connolly seems to straddle the border between the second and the third groups. His preoccupation with Deleuzian metaphysics might place him in the second group, but his numerous references to Foucault makes him more at home in the third. Acknowledging that Taylor, Milbank and Connolly in this sense represent three different accounts of post-secular scholarship, I want to argue that they in another sense can be viewed as constituting a common stream of post-secular thought, separate from the post-secularism proposed by Habermas.

7.2 A metaphysical post-secularity

In his book *The Wisdom of the World*, the French historian of philosophy Rémi Brague has explored different historical civilizations' conceptions of the cosmos, and in particular, the ethical ideas these entail. According to Brague, when the ancient Greeks looked up into the heavens, they saw not just the sun and the moon, stars and planets, but a complete, coherent universe, and a model of the good that could serve as a guide to a better life.[19] There existed, according to Brague, an ontological dimension of the political – an interaction between the order of nature and the political order. Such pre-modern visions of the cosmos constitute a stark contrast to the modern universe, as exemplified by Kant. According to Brague, morality for Kant is only postulated, and remains in the domain of hope and belief; whereas, for men and women of ancient and medieval times, the sovereignty of the good was already given in the cosmic harmony. Kant famously claimed that "two things fill the mind with ever new and increasing admiration and reverence, the more frequently and persistently one's meditation deals with them: the starry sky above me and the moral law within me."[20] Brague's point here is that, in the wake of Kant, the connection between the outer universe and the inner moral feeling was relegated to the domain of private belief. The moral law is "within," rather than "without," subjective not objective. With Kant, Brague claims "the world can no longer be the object of an experience, only of a thought."[21]

I want to suggest that Taylor, Milbank and Connolly should be read as scholars who attempt to re-establish the link between metaphysics (understood as an account of the basic structure of reality itself) and political morality; or, differently put, as seeking to establish an ontological dimension of the political. In this sense, they give a different account of the post-secular compared to the postmetaphysical approach suggested by Habermas. Whereas Habermas, who stands in the Kantian tradition "refrains from making ontological pronouncements on the constitution of being as such," Taylor, Milbank and Connolly have all made ontology central to their projects.[22] Furthermore, Habermas asserts that it is possible to reason independently of one's deepest ontological and ethical commitments, and holds that a procedural approach to politics will grant agreement in questions regarding the common good.[23] Accordingly, Habermas' post-secularism entails a bracketing of that which cannot be shared (such as particular languages and cultural or religious expressions) and a desire to stay in the realm of what he argues *can* be shared: secular reason.[24] Consequently, Habermas' postmetaphysical post-secularity tends to make questions regarding cosmology, worldview, or religion of secondary importance, and relegate them to an area of "private beliefs."

Against such a view, Taylor, Milbank and Connolly have all rejected the idea of a place outside culture from which it is possible to separate secular reason from religion (or faith and reason). Instead, for them, to be human is to be always already entangled with nature and culture through what they describe as the layered constitution of human beings. It is, from their perspectives, impossible to postpone claims about the ethical and the political until one has sorted out one's metaphysics. Instead, they argue that one has to recognize that every attempt to structure the ethical and the political presupposes metaphysical claims. We are thus always already working with metaphysics.

Religious beliefs are in this sense, not understood as constituting a separate epistemic category, but as indistinguishable from other ways of accounting for our being in the world. Such an account challenges more traditional approaches to religion, as seen in the natural science inspired method of Donald Wiebe, which draws on a distinction between cognitive and existential inquiries, where thinking is supposed to be unaffected by existential experiences and "religious studies must be purely cognitive, committed to the advancement of objective and neutral knowledge about religion and religions."[25] Furthermore, it also challenges the study of religion as detached from metaphysical assumption: seen, for example, in Russel McCutcheon's distinction between myth-making and explanation. McCutcheon employs a strict fact/value distinction by claiming that "'facts of life' (i.e., events in the natural world) in themselves are neither bitter nor sweet – they just are."[26] As we have seen, Taylor, Milbank and Connolly would oppose such an approach, and argue the socially constructed nature of facts.[27] In this sense, they echo the Scottish philosopher Alasdair MacIntyre's claim that "Facts, like telescopes and wigs for gentlemen, were a seventeenth-century invention."[28]

In propounding this perspective Taylor, Milbank and Connolly are challenging what might be understood, in Foucault's terminology, to constitute a secular "regime of truth:" that is, the hegemonic status of secular science in describing and ordering the world.[29] They do so both in the sense that they refuse to let their positions be bracketed and/or limited to an alleged "religious" sphere, but also by rejecting a sharp distinction between belief and knowledge. In contrast to Habermas, who primarily uses "post-secular" in a sociological or an epistemological sense, Milbank, Connolly and Taylor, suggest that attempts to make delimitation between "religion" and "secular," between transcendent and immanent, have to do with metaphysics – with the underlying structure of reality. However, Taylor, Milbank and Connolly do not engage in the debate about religions and secularization in an empirical or analytical way, but rather through a *meta* approach which seeks to ask more fundamental questions about what we really talk about when we talk about religion. Central to this issue is the metaphysical discussion of the relation between transcendence and immanence, or the natural and the supernatural. As has been suggested by the Irish philosopher William Desmond, *meta* in metaphysics can be understood both in terms of "beyond" and "in the midst." Desmond argues that this double meaning requires "both ontological exploration of the immanent between of finitude and metaphysical transcending to what cannot be determined in entirely finite terms."[30] Differently put, Desmond argues that metaphysics includes not only the study of the transcendent beyond, but also that within the material realm, which seems to evade our explanation in immanent terms. Accordingly, he seeks to identify a "being in between" – a *metaxu* – in order to mediate Platonic attempts to leave immanence behind, and Nietzschean attempts to desert transcendence. In this vein, I would suggest that Taylor, Milbank and Connolly share a "metaxological" outlook in their metaphysics: that is, an attempt to account for what they take to be a blurred or porous line between transcendence and immanence.[31]

While united by their critique of a strict distinction between immanence and transcendence, the natural and the supernatural, and between faith and reason, important differences remain among Taylor, Milbank and Connolly. These differences primarily concern their metaphysics and how they describe reality in terms of transcendence and immanence; and, secondly, the means by which they hold it possible to say something about the basic structure of reality: or, more specifically, how the transcendent and the immanent are thought to be related. Instead of seeking to approach religion in general, as a fixed phenomenon or pure essence, Taylor, Milbank and Connolly each suggests, in different ways, that there is a blurred line, not only between religion and the secular, but also between the immanent and the transcendent, the natural and the supernatural. The interesting difference for them is not between "religion" and "the secular" – instead, their focus lies in seeking to formulate alternative socio-political accounts to liberal secularism. In doing so they engage with metaphysical questions in ways that challenge the postmetaphysical separation between the immanent and the transcendent. But, by what means is it possible to say something about this underlying reality that supposedly entails a blurring between immanence and transcendence? Taylor, Milbank and Connolly utilize different approaches in order to answer this question.

Broadly speaking, Milbank and Taylor operate here with a similar ontology, in terms of their shared Christian confession of a triune God who is both transcendent and immanent. Sociologically, Taylor seeks to describe the social imaginary of the modern West as an "immanent frame" – an area sealed off from transcendence. His own ontology, however, implies, much in the same way as Milbank's ontology, that immanence and transcendence intersect and are ultimately inseparable. It should be noted that all three theorists, in so far as they talk about religion in a general sense, do so from an outlook which is shaped by, and addresses, Christianity: Taylor's account of secularization in *A Secular Age*, addresses "Latin Christendom" or "North Atlantic civilization;"[32] Milbank's account of the prospect of religious dialogue is made from within his account of Orthodox Christianity;[33] and Connolly's critique of religion mainly targets Christianity (and does so in part through an engagement with Christian theology).[34]

A central idea in Milbank's project is that the very notion of a sphere free of religion is an ideological construction; or, in his theological language, a heresy. Milbank seeks to counter the idea of the secular with a "metanarrative realism:" that is, the idea that all political outlooks, religions, or philosophies should be perceived as rival narratives that compete for hegemonic status. The world is, according to Milbank's theological metanarrative, situated within the Christian story. This story stands in conflict with the liberal metanarrative that seeks to position the Christian narrative as one story amongst many in the secular world. Milbank's theology can be viewed as metaphysics in narrative form, which seek to affirm how the transcendent, in the form of God "supernaturalizes the natural," in the sense that the divine permeates everything.[35] Given that Milbank rejects the notion of secular or neutral criteria outside his theological meta-narrative, Milbank's account of reality is primarily to be preferred for reasons related to what he argues concerns "literary taste," in the sense that Christianity supposedly offers a "better" story. However, in order to enable a choice between rival narratives, Milbank concedes the existence of certain transcendental criteria, which exist outside his metanarrative in the form of "human preference for peace over violence that is both innate," as well as "a certain bias towards reason rather than unreason."[36] Accordingly, Milbank's metaphysic isn't entirely story-based, but asserts a limited realist anthropology.

Taylor takes a different approach: rejecting explicit metaphysical language, he instead pursues a phenomenological path which focuses on practices of moral evaluation, debate, and understanding. According to Taylor "we cannot understand ourselves, or each other, cannot make sense of our lives or determine what to do, without accepting a richer ontology than naturalism allows, without thinking in terms of strong evaluation."[37] For Taylor, the morally neutral universe presented by natural science is unable to provide the necessary criteria for human self-understanding. For him, the notion of transcendence trickles through even into what he calls the "immanent frame," and makes many people feel "a sense of malaise at the disenchanted world," that is, a sense of it as flat, empty, which makes people search for something that could "compensate for the meaning lost with transcendence."[38]

Connolly's ontology, on the other hand, does not recognize any transcendent teleological purpose, but is one of "immanent naturalism." Drawing inspiration from Spinoza and Deleuze, Connolly's immanent naturalism can be understood as a "plane of immanence" that includes everything there is – even that which has not yet come into being, but has the potentiality to do so. Connolly positions his immanent naturalism in contrast to eliminative naturalism, which he construes as "a metaphysical faith that reduces the experience of consciousness to nonconscious processes,"[39] and mechanical naturalism, which "denies any role to a supersensible field while finding both the world of non-human nature and the structure of the human brain to be amenable 'in principle' to precise representation and complete explanation."[40] Connolly's immanent naturalism, in this sense, does not just concern empirically knowable and existing objects, but seeks to account for the world as a process of becoming. Connolly thus rejects a separation between natural and supernatural, visible and invisible, knowable and unknowable, given that everything is part of the same world. In fact "the very point of his immanent naturalism," has been described as "to blur the stark division between immanence and transcendence."[41] From the perspective of a more traditional understanding of transcendence as "vertical," or as a supernatural dimension above the mundane reality, this appears somewhat paradoxical. Thus, Connolly refers to his account of transcendence as "mundane transcendence," which can be described as a "horizontal," or immanent, account of transcendence. Connolly further claims that recent developments in biochemistry, evolutionary theory, and neuroscience (which evade reductive or mechanical science) make it possible, at least to some degree, to account for this immanent transcendence. While Connolly claims that complexity theory in several sciences break with the dominant views of science, he "do[es] not think that they put us in a position to adopt, say immanent transcendence as a proven or incontestable philosophy." Rather he suggests that complexity theory can help to pursue immanent transcendence as a philosophy that can be advanced and defended in public life, where "the old secular/transcendence debates did not leave much room for this orientation to find any expression."[42] In this vein Connolly describes his immanent naturalism as seeking to "naturalize a place for mystery."[43]

7.3 Differing accounts of difference

My opening question in the introductory chapter concerned alternative ways to construe the relation between religions and secularity in the wake of various critiques of the typical Enlightenment narrative. If human history is not to be understood as a straightforward and stadial progression from religion to reason, culminating in secular modernity, and, if "religion" is not easily identified, separated, and legitimately relegated to a "private sphere," what alternative accounts are available? These questions are made relevant following critique that has deconstructed and historicized the concepts of "religion" and "secular," along with the epistemological foundations of Enlightenment. In particular, this critique has challenged the status and function of "the secular as a transcendental regulator," which consequently has implications for how religious and cultural differences are to be solved in a democratic society.[44] Specifically, if the idea of secular reason – that is, reason that doesn't reflect the commitments or agendas of any particular religion, morality, or ideology – has been seriously criticized, how should we then negotiate our differences? How can people of diverse religious and cultural identities live together peacefully if secular reason is no longer trusted to be the neutral and ultimate adjudicator of religious difference?

Taylor, Milbank and Connolly have all proposed alternative accounts for how to construe, not only the relation between "religion" and "the secular," but also for how cultural and religious differences should negotiated in pluralistic societies. Taylor, Milbank and Connolly argue that any attempt to negotiate difference will always display metaphysics, implicitly or explicitly. However, their engagements with metaphysics have very different political implications. Milbank argues that only an orthodox Christian metaphysical account of analogy, which sustains his notion of Christendom, is able to reconcile and peacefully order difference. He propounds a "corporatist", organic, pluralism linked to a metaphysical understanding where difference is able to find its proper place in relation to a larger body, which for Milbank is the Church.[45] Connolly, on the other hand, propounds a rhizomatic and non-hierarchical pluralism, analogous to his account of a pluralistic and "messy" universe of becoming. Connolly here relies heavily on the assumption that the "abundance of being," displayed in his metaphysics of the becoming universe, will evoke a sense of gratitude that spills over in the form of generosity. A generosity that, Connolly argues, should affect the way we construe our identities and perceive differences. Finally, Taylor, who argues that secularism has less to do with the relation of the state and religion and everything to do with the (correct) response of the democratic state to diversity, is arguing for an overlapping consensus – a least common denominator of sorts that, in contrast to John Rawls' version, doesn't seek to strain out metaphysics. Taylor seeks to replace an understanding in which secularism is mainly concerned with controlling religion, with a version of secularism that seeks to manage the metaphysical diversity of views that also include non- and anti-religious outlooks. Accordingly, for Taylor, religious difference does not constitute a special case – "the state can be neither Christian nor Muslim nor Jewish, but, by the same token, it should also be neither Marxist, nor Kantian, nor utilitarian."[46] So, Taylor's modified secularism implicates the position that the state must refrain from favoring any of the "deeper" or motivating reasons for its ethic, and treat religions just as any secular worldview.

I have argued that Taylor, Milbank and Connolly represent a similar strain of post-secular metaphysics in terms of their mutual rejection of any strict distinction between transcendence and immanence (what I typologically refer to as "Protestant post-secularism"). However, where Taylor and Milbank construe this relation in terms of a porous line which allows the transcendent to influence the immanent ("French Catholic post-secularism"), Connolly's metaphysics is one of immanent transcendence, which rejects the idea of a God who creates, informs, and governs, along with the idea of a *telos* or any intrinsic purpose, and instead seeks to reconfigure the transcendent in immanent terms ("Deleuzian post-secularism").

I have furthermore argued that Taylor, Milbank and Connolly display three distinctive approaches to difference; each grounded in their specific metaphysics, and linked to a particular political vision. Milbank's theological metaphysics points in the direction of a "democratized theocracy."[47] Connolly's metaphysics of becoming implies an agonistic account of democracy, or perhaps a "radical democracy."[48] Taylor's phenomenology of the transcendent takes more of a middle position between Milbank and Connolly. Although based in transcendental argumentation, which takes its starting point in a supposedly common human experience, it is closer to a traditional, although post-secular, liberal democracy, that doesn't discriminate between religious and secular outlooks. However, Connolly and Taylor's political visions would be possible to reconcile to the extent that they favor the ideal of institutional neutrality of the liberal state. Milbank's political vision seems, on the other hand, hard to reconcile with any other perspective given its unwillingness to subsume itself under a rival narrative.

At the heart of Taylor's, Milbank's and Connolly's post-secular critique against the postmetaphysical search for a neutral point of objectivity, lies the conviction that the there is, in Thomas Nagel's words "no view from nowhere," or in Žižek's words no "absent center of political ontology."[49] Instead, they suggest that we are all, secular and religious alike, always already invested in some venture of faith. Instead of taking a postmetaphysical stance, and like Habermas emphasizing "the difference that exists between faith and knowledge," Taylor, Milbank and Connolly actively engage ontological questions and emphasize what they perceive to be the porous line between religion and the secular, belief and knowledge, transcendence and immanence.[50] Their brand of metaphysical post-secularism not only differs fundamentally from ontologies grounded on reductive materialism, but also the kind of post-secular construal of the relation between religion and the secular as distinct spheres, formulated by Habermas. In particular, the metaphysical engagements exemplified by Taylor, Milbank and Connolly seek to provide alternative ways to account for difference than those traditionally associated with postmetaphysical liberalism. It remains to be seen whether such conscious metaphysical engagements will be able to facilitate a more fruitful strategy for the peaceful accommodation of religious and cultural difference in increasingly pluralistic societies.

Notes

1 Introduction: Between Scientism and Fundamentalism

1. John Rawls, *Political Liberalism* (Columbia University Press, 2005); Jürgen Habermas, *The Theory of Communicative Action, Vol 1: Reason & the Rationalization of Society* (Beacon Press, 1985); Robert Audi "Liberal Democracy and the Place of Religion in Politics," in Robert Audi and Nicholas Wolterstorff, *Religion in the Public Square: The Place of Religious Convictions in Political Debate* (Rowman & Littlefield Publishers, 2000), 1–66.
2. See, Michael Hoelzl and Graham Ward, *The New Visibility of Religion: Studies in Religion and Cultural Hermeneutics* (Continuum, 2008); Peter L. Berger, *The Desecularization of the World: Resurgent Religion and World Politics* (Wm. B. Eerdmans Publishing, 1999).
3. Gianni Vattimo "The Trace of the Trace" Jacques Derrida and Gianni Vattimo, *Religion* (Stanford University Press, 1998), 81.
4. See, Slavoj Žižek, *The Fragile Absolute Or, Why Is the Christian Legacy Worth Fighting For?* (Verso, 2001); Alain Badiou, *Saint Paul: The Foundation of Universalism* (Stanford University Press, 1997); Giorgio Agamben, *The Kingdom and the Glory: For a Theological Genealogy of Economy and Government* (Meridian: Crossing Aesthetics, 2011).
5. For an ambitious account of new approaches towards "religion," see: Hent de Vries, *Religion: Beyond a Concept* (Fordham University Press, 2007).
6. See for example: Hans Blumenberg, *The Legitimacy of the Modern Age* (MIT Press, 1985); Karl Löwith, *Meaning in History: The Theological Implications of the Philosophy of History* (University of Chicago Press, 1957); John Milbank, *Theology and Social Theory: Beyond Secular Reason* (Wiley-Blackwell, 2006); Talal Asad, *Formations of the Secular: Christianity, Islam, Modernity* (Stanford University Press, 2003); Charles Taylor, *A Secular Age* (Belknap Press, 2007).
7. Jürgen Habermas, *Glauben Und Wissen* (Suhrkamp Verlag, 2001). For an English translation, see: http://socialpolicy.ucc.ie/Habermas_Faith_and_knowledge_Ev07-4_En.htm.
8. Hent de Vries and Lawrence Eugene Sullivan, *Political Theologies: Public Religions in a Post-Secular World* (Fordham University Press, 2006); Arie Molendijk, Justin Beaumont, and Christoph Jedan, eds, *Exploring the Postsecular* (Brill, 2010); Peter Nynäs, Mika Lassander, and Terhi Utriainen, *Post-Secular Society* (Transaction Publishers, 2012); Philip Gorski, *The Post-Secular in Question : Religion in Contemporary Society* (New York University Press, 2012); José Casanova "Exploring the Postsecular" in Craig Calhoun, Mendieta Eduardo, and Jonathan VanAntwerpen, *Habermas and Religion* (Cambridge: Polity, 2013), 27.
9. Jürgen Habermas, *Between Naturalism and Religion: Philosophical Essays* (Polity, 2008), 1.
10. Ibid., 140–141.

11. Audi and Wolterstorff, *Religion in the Public Square*, 105; cited in Habermas, *Between Naturalism and Religion*, 141, note 48.
12. Habermas, *Between Naturalism and Religion*, 3.
13. Jürgen Habermas "Notes on Post-Secular Society," *New Perspectives Quarterly* 25, no. 4 (2008): 21.
14. Jürgen Habermas "Religious Pluralism and Civic Solidarity" in Habermas, *Between Naturalism and Religion*, 141.
15. Jürgen Habermas "Religious Pluralism and Civic Solidarity" in ibid.
16. Jürgen Habermas "The Boundary Between Faith and Knowledge" in ibid., 211.
17. Quoted in Jürgen Habermas "Pre-political Foundations of the Democratic Constitutional State?" in Jürgen Habermas and Joseph Ratzinger, *The Dialectics of Secularization: On Reason and Religion* (Ignatius Press, 2006), 21.
18. Habermas "Notes on Post-Secular Society," 28.
19. Jürgen Habermas "Pre-political Foundations of the Democratic Constitutional State?" in Habermas and Ratzinger, *The Dialectics of Secularization*, 30; See also, Michael Reder and Josef Schmidt "Habermas and Religion" in Jürgen Habermas, Michael Reder, and Josef Schmidt, S.J., *An Awareness of What Is Missing: Faith and Reason in a Post-Secular Age* (Polity, 2010), 10.
20. Habermas, Reder, and Schmidt, *An Awareness of What Is Missing*, 18.
21. H. Tristram Engelhardt Jr and Terry P. Pinkard, *Hegel Reconsidered: Beyond Metaphysics and the Authoritarian State* (Springer, 1994), 7, 64.
22. Jürgen Habermas, *Postmetaphysical Thinking: Philosophical Essays* (MIT Press, 1994), vii.
23. Jürgen Habermas "Religion in the Public Sphere," *European Journal of Philosophy* 14, no. 1 (2006): 16.
24. Ibid., 15.
25. Jürgen Habermas "A Postsecular World Society? On the Philosophical Significance of Postsecular Consciousness and the Multicultural World Society," *The Immanent Frame*, February 3, 2010, http://blogs.ssrc.org/tif/wp-content/uploads/2010/02/A-Postsecular-World-Society-TIF.pdf.
26. Jürgen Habermas, *The Holberg Prize Seminar 2005 "Religion in the Public Sphere"* (University of Bergen, 2005), 17.
27. Habermas and Ratzinger, *The Dialectics of Secularization*.
28. Joseph Ratzinger "That Which Holds the World Together" in Jürgen Habermas and Joseph Ratzinger, *The Dialectics of Secularism: On Reason and Religion* (Ignatius Press, 2006), 77–78.
29. Jürgen Habermas "Communicative Action and the Detranscendentalized 'Use of Reason'" in Habermas, *Between Naturalism and Religion*, 24–77.
30. Immanuel Kant, *Critique of Pure Reason* (Cambridge University Press, 1999), sec. A 299.
31. Jürgen Habermas "Communicative Action and the Detranscendentalized 'Use of Reason'" in Habermas, *Between Naturalism and Religion*, 25.
32. For an account of how Habermas utilize Kant and Hegel, see: Jürgen Habermas "From Kant to Hegel and Back Again – The Move Towards Detranscendentalization," *European Journal of Philosophy* 7, no. 2 (August 1, 1999): 129–157.
33. Ibid., 134.

34. Jürgen Habermas "The Boundary between Faith and Knowledge: On the Reception and Contemporary Importance of Kant's Philosophy of Religion" in Habermas, *Between Naturalism and Religion*, 211.
35. Jürgen Habermas "On the Architectonics of Discursive Differentiation: A Brief Response to a Major Controversy" in ibid., 79.
36. Habermas has in his later writings admitted that "postmetaphysical thinking cannot cope on its own with the defeatism concerning reason which we encounter today both in the postmodern radicalization of the 'dialectic of the Enlightenment' and in the naturalism founded on a naive faith in science" in Habermas, and Schmidt, *An Awareness of What Is Missing*, 18.
37. Ruth Groff, *Ontology Revisited: Metaphysics in Social and Political Philosophy* (Routledge, 2012), xiii, 1.
38. Austin Harrington "Habermas and the 'Post-Secular Society'," *European Journal of Social Theory* 10, no. 4 (November 1, 2007): 557.
39. Habermas, *Between Naturalism and Religion*, 113.
40. Derek McGhee "Moderate Secularism in Liberal Societies?" in Gavin D'Costa et al., *Religion in a Liberal State* (Cambridge University Press, 2013), 131.
41. Michelle Dillon "Jürgen Habermas and the Post-Secular Appropriation of Religion: A Sociological Critique" in Gorski, *The Post-Secular in Question,*, 250.
42. Antoon Braeckman "Habermas and Gauchet on Religion in Postsecular Society. A Critical Assessment," *Continental Philosophy Review* 42, no. 3 (2009): 280.
43. Andrew F. March "Rethinking Religious Reasons in Public Justification," *American Political Science Review* 107, no. 3 (2013): 523–539. For other examples, see: Romand Coles, *Beyond Gated Politics: Reflections for the Possibility of Democracy* (Minneapolis, MN: Univ Of Minnesota Press, 2005); Jeremy Waldron "Secularism and the Limits of Community" in George Rupp, *Globalization Challenged: Conviction, Conflict, Community* (Columbia University Press, 2013), 52–67; Michael Walzer "Drawing the Line: Religion and Politics," *Soziale Welt* 49, no. 3 (January 1, 1998): 295–307.
44. March "Rethinking Religious Reasons in Public Justification," 424.
45. Bryan Garsten, *Saving Persuasion: A Defense of Rhetoric and Judgment* (Cambridge, Mass.; London: Harvard University Press, 2009), 191.
46. Ibid.
47. Romand Coles, *Rethinking Generosity: Critical Theory and the Politics of Caritas* (Cornell University Press, 1997), 35.

2 Whose Religion, Which Secular?

1. Immanuel Kant, *Critique of the Power of Judgment* (Cambridge University Press, 2000), 343.
2. Friedrich Schleiermacher, *Schleiermacher: On Religion: Speeches to Its Cultured Despisers* (Cambridge University Press, 1996), 22.
3. Wayne Proudfoot, *Religious Experience* (University of California Press, 1987), xii.
4. For contemporary developments of this approach, see: Jürgen Habermas et al., *The Power of Religion in the Public Sphere* (Columbia University Press,

2011), 65–68; John Rawls "Justice as Fairness: Political Not Metaphysical," *Philosophy & Public Affairs* 14, no. 3 (n.d.): 223–251, accessed May 17, 2012.
5. Habermas "Religion in the Public Sphere," 17; In the light of such claims it has been argued that "Habermas has come to see that religious meanings may be sui generis, irreducible to any secular substitute," in D.Z. Phillips "Introduction" in D.Z. Phillips and Timothy Tessin, *Philosophy of Religion in the twenty first Century* (Palgrave Macmillan, 2002), xiii.
6. José Casanova "The Secular, Secularizations, and Secularism" in Craig Calhoun, Mark Juergensmeyer, and Jonathan VanAntwerpen, *Rethinking Secularism* (New York: Oxford University Press, 2011), 56.
7. Asad, *Formations of the Secular*, 192; See also, José Casanova "The Secular, Secularizations, and Secularism" in Calhoun, Juergensmeyer, and VanAntwerpen, *Rethinking Secularism*, 2011, 56; For an extended discussion of profane and sacred times, see Taylor, *A Secular Age*, 54–61.
8. Jim Stone "A Theory of Religion Revised," *Religious Studies* 37, no. 2 (2001): 181.
9. Caroline Schaffalitzky de Muckadell "On Essentialism and Real Definitions of Religion," *Journal of the American Academy of Religion* 82, no. 2 (2014): 508.
10. Allen Verhey, *Nature and Altering It* (Wm. B. Eerdmans Publishing, 2010), 107; See also: Nicholas Lash, *The Beginning and the End of "Religion"* (Cambridge University Press, 1996), 168.
11. Timothy Fitzgerald, *The Ideology of Religious Studies* (Oxford University Press, 2003), 16.
12. Ibid.; An alternative to the use of "supernatural" has been suggested by religious studies scholar Christian Smith, who instead has argued for the term "superempirical." The reason for this is that "the supernatural implies that the unseen order, the "spiritual," is not a part of nature, and that nature consists only of physical matter." Christian Smith, *Moral, Believing Animals: Human Personhood and Culture* (Oxford University Press, 2003), 98.
13. See, Talal Asad, *Genealogies of Religion. Discipline and Reasons of Power in Christianity and Islam* (Baltimore: The John Hopkins University Press, 1993); Timothy Fitzgerald, *Discourse on Civility and Barbarity* (Oxford University Press, 2007); Russell McCutcheon, *Manufacturing Religion* (New York: Oxford University Press, 1997); Daniel Dubuisson, *The Western Construction of Religion. Myths, Knowledge, and Ideology* (Baltimore: The John Hopkins University Press, 2007); Russell T. McCutcheon, *Manufacturing Religion: The Discourse on Sui Generis Religion and the Politics of Nostalgia* (Oxford University Press, 2003), 3.
14. Asad, *Formations of the Secular*, 183.
15. Ibid., 200.
16. See, for example, Stathis Gourgouris' "Detranscendentalizing the Secular," *Public Culture* 20, no. 3 (September 21, 2008): 437–445.
17. See for example: Jürgen Habermas' "Habermas on Faith, Knowledge and 9–11" (Paulskirche, Frankfurt, Germany, October 14, 2001), http://www.nettime.org/Lists-Archives/nettime-l-0111/msg00100.html; Habermas "Religion in the Public Sphere;" Habermas, Reder, and Schmidt, S.J., *An Awareness of What Is Missing*; However, for an earlier use of the term "post-secular," see: Phillip Blond, ed., *Post-Secular Philosophy: Between Philosophy and Theology* (Routledge, 1998).

18. José Casanova "Are We Still Secular? Explorations on the Secular and the Post-Secular" in Peter Nynäs, Mika Lassander, and Terhi Utriainen, *Post-Secular Society*, 27.
19. José Casanova "Exploring the Postsecular" in Calhoun, Eduardo, and Van Antwerpen, *Habermas and Religion*, 28–29.
20. Taylor describes the "Immanent frame" as: "the different structures we live in: scientific, social, technological, and so on, constitute such a frame in that they are part of a 'natural', or 'this-worldly' order which can be understood in its own terms, without reference to the 'supernatural' or 'transcendent'" in Taylor, *A Secular Age*, 594.
21. José Casanova "Are We Still Secular? Explorations on the Secular and the Post-Secular" in Nynäs, Lassander, and Utriainen, *Post-Secular Society*, 32.
22. José Casanova "Are We Still Secular? Explorations on the Secular and the Post-Secular" in ibid., 44.
23. For an ambitious overview of different post-secular streams, see James A Beckford "SSSR Presidential Address Public Religions and the Postsecular: Critical Reflections," *Journal for the Scientific Study of Religion* 51, no. 1 (March 1, 2012): 1–19; See also, Gorski, *The Post-Secular in Question*; and, Gregor McLennan "The Postsecular Turn," *Theory, Culture & Society* 27, no. 4 (July 1, 2010): 3–20.
24. I acknowledge that Žižek has rejected a certain brand of post-secular thought (what he labels as "soft" postmodern theology and associates with Jacques Derrida, Gianni Vattimo and John Caputo) but I here focus on his claim that "the counter-posing of formal Enlightenment values to fundamental-substantial beliefs is false, amounting to an untenable ideologico-existential position" in Slavoj Žižek, *Living in the End Times* (Verso, 2011), 252; See also, Slavoj Žižek, John Milbank, and Creston Davis, *The Monstrosity of Christ: Paradox or Dialectic?* (MIT Press, 2009), 254–260.
25. Habermas, Reder, and Schmidt, S.J., *An Awareness of What Is Missing*, 18.
26. Jürgen Habermas "A Postsecular World Society? On the Philosophical Significance of Postsecular Consciousness and the Multicultural World Society," *Monthly Review*, (March 21, 2010), http://mrzine.monthlyreview.org/2010/habermas210310p.html.
27. Hent de Vries "Global Religion and the Postsecular Challenge" in Calhoun, Eduardo, and VanAntwerpen, *Habermas and Religion*, 204.
28. Eduardo Mendieta "Spiritual Politics and Post-Secular Authenticity" in Gorski, *The Post-Secular in Question*, 311.
29. Ola Sigurdson "Beyond Secularism? Towards a Post-secular Political Theology," *Modern Theology* 26, no. 2 (April 1, 2010): 177–196.
30. Craig Calhoun "Secularism, Citizenship, and the Public Sphere" in Calhoun, Juergensmeyer, and Van Antwerpen, *Rethinking Secularism* (Oxford University Press, 2011), 79.
31. Habermas, Reder, and Schmidt, S.J., *An Awareness of What Is Missing*, 19.
32. Steven Douglas Smith, *The Disenchantment of Secular Discourse* (Harvard University Press, 2010), 16.
33. Beckford "SSSR Presidential Address Public Religions and the Postsecular," 7.
34. Beckford "SSSR Presidential Address Public Religions and the Postsecular," 7.
35. Clayton Crockett, *Radical Political Theology: Religion and Politics After Liberalism* (Columbia University Press, 2011), 2.

36. Ibid., 27.
37. Ibid., 2.
38. Elizabeth Shakman Hurd "A Suspension of (Dis)Belief: The Secular-Religious Binary and the Study of International Relations" in Calhoun, Juergensmeyer, and VanAntwerpen, *Rethinking Secularism*, 2011, 181.
39. Elizabeth Shakman Hurd "A Suspension of (Dis)Belief: The Secular-Religious Binary and the Study of International Relations" in ibid., 172.
40. James K. A. Smith "Secular Liturgies and the Prospects for a 'Post-Secular' Sociology of Religion" in Gorski, *The Post-Secular in Question*, 163.
41. Craig Calhoun. "Secularism, Citizenship, and the Public Sphere" in Calhoun, Juergensmeyer, and VanAntwerpen, *Rethinking Secularism*, 2011, 75.
42. Plato, *Timaeus and Critias* (Oxford University Press, 2008), 16; For an interesting account of this distinction see, Robert Bolton "Plato's Distinction between Being and Becoming," *The Review of Metaphysics* 29, no. 1 (September 1, 1975): 66–95.
43. S. Marc Cohen "Aristotle's Metaphysics," in *The Stanford Encyclopedia of Philosophy*, Edward N. Zalta, Summer 2014, 2014, http://plato.stanford.edu/archives/sum2014/entries/aristotle-metaphysics/.
44. Michael Loux, *Metaphysics: A Contemporary Introduction* (Routledge, 2013), 4–5.
45. Adrian Pabst, *Metaphysics: The Creation of Hierarchy* (Wm. B. Eerdmans Publishing Company, 2012), xxix.
46. Philip Tonner, *Heidegger, Metaphysics and the Univocity of Being* (Continuum International Publishing Group, 2010), 18.
47. Richard Cross, *Duns Scotus* (Oxford University Press, USA, 1999), 33.
48. See for example, Tonner, *Heidegger, Metaphysics and the Univocity of Being*; Nathan Widder "John Duns Scotus" in Graham Jones and Jon Roffe, *Deleuze's Philosophical Lineage* (Edinburgh University Press, 2005), 27–43.
49. Tonner, *Heidegger, Metaphysics and the Univocity of Being*, 2.
50. Brad S. Gregory, *The Unintended Reformation: How a Religious Revolution Secularized Society* (Harvard University Press, 2012), 36–38.
51. Ibid., 37–38, 43; For an interesting account of Scotus and the rise of nominalism, see: Amos Funkenstein, *Theology and the Scientific Imagination: From the Middle Ages to the Seventeenth Century* (Princeton University Press, 1986), 57 ff.
52. Loux, *Metaphysics*, 1–2.
53. Ibid., 1.
54. Johann Georg Hamann, *Hamann: Writings on Philosophy and Language* (Cambridge University Press, 2007), xvii.
55. For an interesting account of Hamann as a precursor of post-secular thought, see John R. Betz, *After Enlightenment: The Post-Secular Vision of J. G. Hamann* (John Wiley & Sons, 2012).
56. Martin Paleček and Mark Risjord "Relativism and the Ontological Turn within Anthropology," *Philosophy of the Social Sciences* 43, no. 1 (March 1, 2013): 5.
57. Stephen K. White, *Sustaining Affirmation: The Strengths of Weak Ontology in Political Theory* (Princeton University Press, 2000), 4.
58. Kristen Deede Johnson, *Theology, Political Theory, and Pluralism: Beyond Tolerance and Difference* (Cambridge University Press, 2007), 20–21.

59. E.J. Lowe, *An Introduction to the Philosophy of Mind* (Cambridge University Press, 2000), 4.
60. Sandra Harding and Merrill B. Hintikka, *Discovering Reality: Feminist Perspectives on Epistemology, Metaphysics, Methodology, and Philosophy of Science* (Springer, 2003), xv.
61. Kathryn Pyne Addelson "The Man of Professional Wisdom" in ibid., 165–186.
62. Sandra Harding "Secularism, Multiculturalism, and Democracy: Philosophy of Science Issues" (Lecture, University of Lethbridge, Canada, September 19, 2013), http://www.lethbridgeliving.com/events/sandra-harding-qsecularism-multiculturalism-and-democracyq; Sandra Harding, *Objectivity and Diversity*, forthcoming.
63. Kathryn Pyne Addelson "The Man of Professional Wisdom" in Harding and Hintikka, *Discovering Reality: Feminist Perspectives on Epistemology, Metaphysics, Methodology, and Philosophy of Science*, 167, 170.
64. Slavoj Žižek "Only a Suffering God Can Save Us," accessed March 17, 2015, http://www.lacan.com/zizshadowplay.html.
65. Paul W. Franks, *All Or Nothing: Systematicity, Transcendental Arguments, and Skepticism in German Idealism* (Harvard University Press, 2005), 20.
66. Christopher Ben Simpson, *Religion, Metaphysics, and the Postmodern: William Desmond and John D. Caputo* (Indiana University Press, 2009), 1.
67. See for example, John D. Caputo, Gianni Vattimo, and Jeffrey W. Robbins, *After the Death of God* (Columbia University Press, 2009); Professor Richard Rorty, Gianni Vattimo, and Professor Santiago Zabala, *The Future of Religion* (Columbia University Press, 2005).
68. See, for example: Anthony Paul Smith, Pamela Sue Anderson, and Daniel Whistler, eds, *After the Postsecular and the Postmodern: New Essays in Continental Philosophy of Religion* (Cambridge Scholars Publisher, 2011); Clayton Crockett, B. Keith Putt, and Jeffrey W. Robbins, eds, *The Future of Continental Philosophy of Religion* (Bloomington: Indiana University Press, 2014).
69. For an introduction to this stream of thought, see: Levi Bryant, Nick Srnicek, and Graham Harman, *The Speculative Turn: Continental Materialism and Realism* (re.press, 2011).
70. Quentin Meillassoux and Ray Brassier, *After Finitude: An Essay on the Necessity of Contingency* (Continuum International Publishing Group, 2010), 46.
71. Quentin Meillassoux "The Immanence of the World Beyond" in Peter M. Candler, Jr. and Conor Cunningham, *The Grandeur of Reason: Religion, Tradition and Universalism* (SCM Press, 2010), 445.
72. Bruno Latour, *On the Modern Cult of the Factish Gods* (Duke University Press, 2010), 46–47.
73. Bruno Latour "Gifford Lectures: Facing Gaia. Six Lectures on the Political Theology of Nature.," February 18, 2013, http://www.ed.ac.uk/about/video/lecture-series/gifford-lectures.
74. Loux, *Metaphysics*, 6–7.
75. Iris Marion Young, *Justice and the Politics of Difference* (Princeton University Press, 2011), 156–191.
76. For an influential work concerning the ontological primacy of difference, see: Gilles Deleuze, *Difference and Repetition* (Continuum International Publishing Group, 2004); For an engagement with the concept of difference in relation to religion, see: Jonathan Z. Smith "What a Difference a Difference Makes" in

Jonathan Z. Smith, *Relating Religion: Essays in the Study of Religion* (University of Chicago Press, 2004), 251–302.
77. Jonathan Z. Smith "What a Difference a Difference Makes" in Smith, *Relating Religion*, 252.
78. John Gray, *Two Faces of Liberalism* (Polity Press, 2000), 1.
79. John Gray, *Enlightenment's Wake: Politics and Culture at the Close of the Modern Age* (Routledge, 2007), 102–106.
80. Joseph Cardinal Ratzinger "'Le Pluralisme: Problème posé à l'Église et à la théologie'," in Studia Moralia 24 (1986): 307; cited in Vries and Sullivan, *Political Theologies*, 51.
81. Bruce Lincoln "Bush's God Talk" in ibid., 275.
82. Bruce Lincoln, *Religion, Empire, and Torture: The Case of Achaemenian Persia, with a Postscript on Abu Ghraib* (University of Chicago Press, 2010), 97.
83. Vries and Sullivan, *Political Theologies*, 52; See also, Phillip Blond and Adrian Pabst "The Twisted Religion of Blair and Bush – The New York Times," accessed March 20, 2014, http://www.nytimes.com/2006/03/10/opinion/10iht-edpabst.html?_r=1&.
84. The European Court of Human Rights, *French Ban on the Wearing in Public of Clothing Designed to Conceal One's Face Does Not Breach the Convention*, Press Release, (July 1, 2014), http://hudoc.echr.coe.int/sites/eng-press/pages/search.aspx?i=003-4809142-5861661#{%22itemid%22:[%22003-4809142-5861661%22]}.
85. Kwame Anthony Appia "Causes of Quarrel: What's Special about Religious Disputes?" in Thomas Banchoff's, *Religious Pluralism, Globalization, and World Politics* (Oxford University Press, 2008), 58.
86. Charles T. Mathewes, *A Theology of Public Life* (Cambridge University Press, 2007), 112.
87. Writing under the header of "Tyranny of the Majority" Tocqueville famously argued "For what is a majority taken collectively if not an individual with opinions and, more often than not, interests contrary to those of another individual known as the minority? Now, if you are willing to concede that a man to whom omnipotence has been granted can abuse it to detriment of his adversaries, why will you not concede that the same may be true of a majority?" in Alexis de Tocqueville, *Democracy in America* (Library of America, 2004), 288–289.

3 Phenomenology and Overlapping Consensus

1. Robert Meynell, *Canadian Idealism and the Philosophy of Freedom: C.B. Macpherson, George Grant, and Charles Taylor* (McGill-Queen's University Press, 2011), 9–10.
2. Charles Taylor, *Sources of the Self: The Making of the Modern Identity* (Harvard University Press, 1989), 203–204.
3. By the term practices Taylor means "any stable configuration of shared activity, whose shape is defined by a certain pattern of dos and don'ts, can be a practice for my purpose." Ibid., 204.
4. Ibid.
5. Taylor, *A Secular Age*, 29.
6. For Taylor's account of Hegel, see: Charles Taylor, *Hegel* (Cambridge University Press, 1989); See also: Charles Taylor, *Hegel and Modern Society* (Cambridge University Press, 1977).

7. See Taylor's contributions in: Habermas et al., *The Power of Religion in the Public Sphere*; Jocelyn Maclure and Charles Taylor, *Secularism and Freedom of Conscience* (Harvard University Press, 2011); Sarah Coakley, *Faith, Rationality and the Passions* (John Wiley & Sons, 2012); Alfred Stepan and Charles Taylor, eds, *Boundaries of Toleration* (Columbia University Press, 2014); See also, Part III in Charles Taylor, *Dilemmas and Connections: Selected Essays* (Harvard University Press, 2011).
8. Taylor, *Hegel and Modern Society*, 85.
9. See Taylor's contributions in: Habermas et al., *The Power of Religion in the Public Sphere*; Maclure and Taylor, *Secularism and Freedom of Conscience*; Coakley, *Faith, Rationality and the Passions*; Stepan and Taylor, eds, *Boundaries of Toleration*; See also, Part III in Taylor, *Dilemmas and Connections: Selected Essays*.
10. Nicholas H. Smith, *Charles Taylor: Meaning, Morals and Modernity* (John Wiley & Sons, 2013), 199.
11. Taylor, *A Secular Age*, 371.
12. Charles Taylor "Two Theories of Modernity," *Hastings Center Report* 25, no. 2 (1995): 24, doi: 10.2307/3562863.
13. Ibid.
14. Charles Taylor, *The Ethics of Authenticity* (Harvard University Press, 1991), 23.
15. Charles Taylor, *A Catholic Modernity?: Charles Taylor's Marianist Award Lecture, with Responses by William M. Shea, Rosemary Luling Haughton, George Marsden, Jean Bethke Elshtain* (Oxford University Press, 1999), 36–37.
16. Ibid., 30.
17. Ibid., 31.
18. Taylor, *Sources of the Self*, 508.
19. Taylor, *A Catholic Modernity?*, 35.
20. Charles Taylor "Reason, Faith, and Meaning" in Coakley, *Faith, Rationality and the Passions*, 13–28.
21. Charles Taylor "Die Blosse Vernunft" in Taylor, *Dilemmas and Connections*, 328.
22. Charles Taylor "Reason, Faith, and Meaning" in Coakley, *Faith, Rationality and the Passions*, 13–14.
23. Charles Taylor "Reason, Faith, and Meaning" in ibid., 14.
24. Taylor, *Dilemmas and Connections*, 324, 328.
25. Ibid., 328.
26. Ibid., 327.
27. Ibid., 329.
28. Taylor, *A Secular Age*, 565.
29. Charles Taylor "Reason, Faith, and Meaning" in Coakley, *Faith, Rationality and the Passions*, 16.
30. Taylor, *A Secular Age*, 835, note 27 Quote attributed to Joseph Renan (1823–1892), French philosopher and expert of Middle East ancient languages and civilizations.
31. Ibid., 12.
32. Ibid., 574; The quote is attributed to Ernest Renan and translated by Taylor from, Sylvette Denèfle, *Sociologie de la Secularisation: Être sans-religion en France à la fin du XXe siècle* (Editions L'Harmattan, 1997), 93–94.
33. Taylor, *A Secular Age*, 425–426.

34. Taylor here follows José Casanova: "we are witnessing the 'deprivatization' of religion. ... Religious traditions throughout the world are refusing to accept the marginal and privatized role which theories of modernity as well as theories of secularization had reserved for them." in José Casanova, *Public Religions in the Modern World* (University of Chicago Press, 1994), 5, 20, 211.
35. Taylor, *A Secular Age*, 253.
36. Ibid., 22.
37. Ibid., 3.
38. Charles Taylor "Afterword" in Michael Warner, Jonathan VanAntwerpen, and Craig J. Calhoun, *Varieties of Secularism in a Secular Age* (Harvard University Press, 2010), 304.
39. Taylor, *A Secular Age*, 542.
40. Ibid., 549.
41. Ibid., 22.
42. Ibid., 561, 562.
43. Ibid., 77.
44. Charles Taylor, *Varieties of Religion Today: William James Revisited* (Harvard University Press, 2003), 26.
45. Ibid., 24.
46. Taylor, *A Secular Age*, 4–5.
47. Ibid., 430.
48. Ibid., 15.
49. Ibid., 16.
50. Ibid., 20.
51. Ibid.
52. Ibid., 18.
53. Charles Taylor, *Modern Social Imaginaries* (Duke University Press, 2003), 92.
54. Taylor, *A Secular Age*, 60.
55. Taylor, *Modern Social Imaginaries*, 93.
56. Ibid.
57. Ibid., 94.
58. Ibid., 206, note 14.
59. Taylor, *A Secular Age*, 164.
60. Ibid., 168.
61. Ibid., 571.
62. Charles Taylor "The Meaning of 'Post-Secular'" (Normative orders, Goethe University, Frankfurt am Main, 2011), http://www.normativeorders.net/de/veranstaltungen/ringvorlesungen/38-veranstaltungen/ringvorlesungen/925-mittwoch-15-juni-2011-18-uhr.
63. Taylor, *A Secular Age*, 534.
64. Ibid., 291.
65. Ibid., 427–428.
66. Taylor "The Meaning of 'Post-Secular'."
67. Charles Taylor "The Politics of Recognition" in Charles Taylor and Amy Gutmann, *Multiculturalism: Examining the Politics of Recognition* (Princeton University Press, 1994), 25.
68. Taylor, *A Secular Age*, 558.
69. Charles Taylor, *Multiculturalism: Examining the Politics of Recognition*, ed. Gutmann, 62.

Notes 173

70. Ruth Abbey, ed., *Charles Taylor* (Cambridge University Press, 2004), 14.
71. Maclure and Taylor, *Secularism and Freedom of Conscience*, 21.
72. Charles Taylor, *Philosophical Papers: Volume 1, Human Agency and Language* (Cambridge University Press, 1985), 85.
73. White, *Sustaining Affirmation*, 42.
74. Taylor, *Sources of the Self*, 8.
75. Arto Laitinen, *Strong Evaluation without Moral Sources: On Charles Taylor's Philosophical Anthropology and Ethics* (Walter de Gruyter, 2008), v.
76. Taylor, *A Secular Age*, 164, 256.
77. Ibid., 164.
78. Ibid., 165.
79. Ibid., 187.
80. Ibid., 196.
81. Ibid., 164.
82. Ibid., 177.
83. Ibid., 4–5.
84. Ibid., 549.
85. Taylor, *Sources of the Self*, 7.
86. Taylor, *A Secular Age*, 510.
87. Ibid., 16.
88. Ibid., 18.
89. Ibid., 8.
90. Ibid., 769.
91. Taylor, *Sources of the Self*, 92.
92. Ibid., 516.
93. Taylor, *A Secular Age*, 605–606.
94. Ibid., 609.
95. Ibid.
96. Ibid., 607.
97. Charles Taylor "What is Secularism?" in Geoffrey Brahm Levey and Tariq Modood, *Secularism, Religion and Multicultural Citizenship* (Cambridge University Press, 2009), xi.
98. Charles Taylor "Why We Need a Radical Redefinition of Secularism" in Habermas et al., *The Power of Religion in the Public Sphere*, 34.
99. Charles Taylor "Why We Need a Radical Redefinition of Secularism" in ibid., 35–36.
100. Charles Taylor "What is Secularism?" in Levey and Modood, *Secularism, Religion and Multicultural Citizenship*, xxii.
101. Charles Taylor "Gadamer on the Human Sciences" in Robert J. Dostal, *The Cambridge Companion to Gadamer* (Cambridge University Press, 2002), 126.
102. For an interesting comparison of Taylor's concept "deep diversity" and Habermas' idea of "constitutional patriotism," see John Erik Fossum "Deep Diversity versus Constitutional Patriotism Taylor, Habermas and the Canadian Constitutional Crisis," *Ethnicities* 1, no. 2 (June 1, 2001): 179–206.
103. Charles Taylor "Gadamer on the Human Sciences" in Dostal, *The Cambridge Companion to Gadamer*, 132.
104. Charles Taylor "Understanding the Other: A Gadamerian View on Conceptual Schemes" in Taylor, *Dilemmas and Connections*, 37.

105. Susan Hekman "From Epistemology to Ontology: Gadamer's Hermeneutics and Wittgensteinian Social Science," *Human Studies* 6, no. 1 (December 1, 1983): 207.
106. Taylor, *Multiculturalism*, 63.
107. Maclure and Taylor, *Secularism and Freedom of Conscience*, 19.
108. Ibid., 21.
109. Ibid., 16.
110. Ibid., 11.
111. Ibid.
112. John Rawls, *A Theory of Justice* (Harvard University Press, 2009), 340; See also, John Rawls "The Idea of an Overlapping Consensus," *Oxford Journal of Legal Studies*, 1987, 1–25.
113. Maclure and Taylor, *Secularism and Freedom of Conscience*, 11–12.
114. Ibid., 15.
115. Charles Taylor "Modes of Secularism" in Rajeev Bhargava, *Secularism and Its Critics* (Oxford University Press, 1998), 51.
116. Charles Taylor "Modes of Secularism" in ibid., 52.
117. Taylor, *Multiculturalism*, 61.
118. Charles Taylor "Modes of Secularism" in Bhargava, *Secularism and Its Critics*, 53.
119. Gérard Bouchard and Charles Taylor, *Building the Future, a Time for Reconciliation: Abridged Report* (Commission de consultation sur les pratiques d'accomodement reliées aux différences culturelles, 2008), 23.
120. Ibid., 37.
121. Ibid., 43.
122. Ibid., 45.
123. Ibid., 41.
124. Ibid., 47.
125. Ibid., 49.
126. Ibid., 58.
127. Taylor, *Sources of the Self*, 521.
128. Taylor, *A Catholic Modernity?*, 12.
129. Ibid., 18.
130. Charles Taylor "Modes of Secularism" in Bhargava, *Secularism and Its Critics*, 46.
131. Charles Taylor "Why We Need a Radical Redefinition of Secularism" in Habermas et al., *The Power of Religion in the Public Sphere*, 56.
132. Charles Taylor "Why We Need a Radical Redefinition of Secularism" in ibid., 36.
133. Taylor, *Multiculturalism*, 62.
134. Taylor, *A Secular Age*, 428.
135. Charles Taylor "Why We Need a Radical Redefinition of Secularism" in Habermas et al., *The Power of Religion in the Public Sphere*, 51.

4 Analogy and Corporatist Pluralism

1. Milbank, *Theology and Social Theory*, 9.
2. Ibid.

3. Ibid., 1.
4. John Milbank, *The Word Made Strange: Theology, Language, Culture* (Wiley-Blackwell, 1997), 250.
5. Milbank, *Theology and Social Theory*, 331.
6. Ibid., 25.
7. John Milbank "The End of Dialogue" in Gavin D'Costa, *Christian Uniqueness Reconsidered: The Myth of a Pluralistic Theology of Religions* (Orbis Books, 1990), 177–178.
8. John Milbank "The End of Dialogue" in ibid., 182.
9. Milbank, *Theology and Social Theory*, xiv.
10. Milbank's references to Catholic Christianity should not be understood as denominational or ecclesial label (Milbank is a member of the Anglican church, and is not a Roman Catholic), but rather as a creedal remark concerning his emphasis on the historical continuity of Christian faith and practice as a tradition with roots in the first millennium. The emphasis on Catholic Christianity can be understood in contrast to Protestantism, which tends to rely solely on the Bible (and not on tradition).
11. Jennifer A. Herdt, "The Endless Construction of Charity: On Milbank's Critique of Political Economy," *Journal of Religious Ethics* 32, no. 2 (2004): 301; I am indebted to Jennifer A. Herdt for the suggested alternative title as a clever play on Blumenberg, *The Legitimacy of the Modern Age*.
12. John Milbank, *Being Reconciled: Ontology and Pardon* (Routledge, 2003), 121.
13. Milbank, *Theology and Social Theory*, 1.
14. Ibid., 4.
15. Ibid., 22–23.
16. John Milbank "Without Heaven There Is Only Hell on Earth: 15 Verdicts on Zizek's Response," *Political Theology* 11, no. 1 (2009): 127.
17. John Milbank, Graham Ward and Catherine Pickstock "Suspending the Material: The Turn of Radical Orthodoxy" in John Milbank, Catherine Pickstock, and Graham Ward, *Radical Orthodoxy: A New Theology* (Routledge, 2002), 3–4.
18. Milbank, *Theology and Social Theory*, 206.
19. Milbank, *Being Reconciled: Ontology and Pardon*, 122.
20. Milbank, Pickstock, and Ward, *Radical Orthodoxy*, 24.
21. John Milbank, Slavoj Žižek, and Creston Davis, *Paul's New Moment: Continental Philosophy and the Future of Christian Theology* (Brazos Press, 2010), 10. For an account of Taylor's subtraction theory, see; Taylor, *A Secular Age*, 22, 245.
22. Milbank, *Theology and Social Theory*, 9.
23. John Milbank "The Conflict of the Faculties" in John Milbank, *The Future of Love: Essays in Political Theology* (Hymns Ancient & Modern Ltd, 2009), 307–312.
24. John Milbank "Stanton Lecture 1: The Return of Metaphysics in the 21st Century," item, (January 28, 2011), http://www.abc.net.au/religion/articles/2011/01/28/3123584.htm?topic1=home&topic2.
25. Milbank, Pickstock, and Ward, *Radical Orthodoxy*, 6.
26. For a conflicting account of Scotus' importance as facilitator of modernity as well as the interpretation of the univocity of being, see: Richard Cross "'Where Angels Fear to Tread': Duns Scotus and Radical Orthodoxy," *Antonianum* 76, no. 1 (n.d.): 7–41, accessed November 25, 2012; Richard Cross "Duns Scotus

176 *Notes*

      and Suárez at the Origins of Modernity" in Wayne J. Hankey and Douglas Hedley, *Deconstructing Radical Orthodoxy: Postmodern Theology, Rhetoric And Truth* (Ashgate Publishing, Ltd., 2005), 65–80.
27. Milbank, *Theology and Social Theory*, 10.
28. John Milbank "A Closer Walk on the Wild Side" in Warner, VanAntwerpen, and Calhoun, *Varieties of Secularism in a Secular Age*, 62–63.
29. John Milbank "A Closer Walk on the Wild Side" in ibid.
30. John Milbank "A Closer Walk on the Wild Side" in ibid., 64.
31. John Milbank "A Closer Walk on the Wild Side" in ibid., 65.
32. John Milbank "A Closer Walk on the Wild Side" in ibid., 71.
33. For an account of the various reforms, see the chapter "The Bulwarks of Belief" in Taylor, *A Secular Age*.
34. John Milbank "A Closer Walk on the Wild Side" in Warner, VanAntwerpen, and Calhoun, *Varieties of Secularism in a Secular Age*, 71.
35. John Milbank "A Closer Walk on the Wild Side" in ibid., 77.
36. John D. Caputo, *On Religion* (London, 2001), 62; Ingolf Dalferth U. "Post-Secular Society: Christianity and the Dialectics of the Secular," *Journal of the American Academy of Religion* 78, no. 2 (2010): 317; Beckford "SSSR Presidential Address Public Religions and the Postsecular," 8.
37. Wayne Hudson "Schelling's Berlin Lectures" in Paolo Diego Bubbio and Paul Redding, *Religion After Kant: God and Culture in the Idealist Era* (Cambridge Scholars Publisher, 2012), 139.
38. John Milbank "The End of Dialogue" in Milbank, *The Future of Love*, 282–283.
39. Milbank, *Theology and Social Theory*, 279–280.
40. Ibid., 3.
41. John Milbank "The End of Dialogue" in Milbank, *The Future of Love*, 288.
42. John Milbank "The End of Dialogue" in ibid., 292.
43. Milbank, *Being Reconciled: Ontology and Pardon*, 5.
44. Milbank, *Theology and Social Theory*, xxii.
45. Milbank "Stanton Lecture 1."
46. Milbank, *Theology and Social Theory*, 15.
47. John Milbank "Knowledge. The Theological Critique of Philosophy in Hamann and Jacobi" in Milbank, Pickstock, and Ward, *Radical Orthodoxy*, 23–24.
48. Cross, *Duns Scotus*, 39; See also, Peter King "Scotus on Metaphysics" in Thomas Williams, *The Cambridge Companion to Duns Scotus* (Cambridge University Press, 2003), 18–21.
49. For an introduction to the philosophical debates related to Heidegger's critique of onto-theology, see: Jeffrey W. Robbins "The Problem of Ontotheology: Complicating the Divide Between Philosophy and Theology," *Heythrop Journal* 43, no. 2 (April 2002): 141.
50. John Milbank "Only Theology Saves Metaphysics: On the Modalities of Terror" in Conor Cunningham and Peter M. Candler, *Belief and Metaphysics* (SCM Press, 2007), 452.
51. John Milbank "Only Theology Overcomes Metaphysics: On the Modalities of Terror" in ibid., 493.
52. John Milbank "Only Theology saves Metaphysics: On the Modalities of Terror" in ibid., 452.

53. D. Stephen Long "Radical Orthodoxy" in Kevin J. Vanhoozer, *The Cambridge Companion to Postmodern Theology* (Cambridge University Press, 2003), 127.
54. Milbank, *Theology and Social Theory*, 382.
55. John Milbank "Only Theology saves Metaphysics" in Cunningham and Candler, *Belief and Metaphysics*, 495.
56. Milbank, *Theology and Social Theory*, 382.
57. Ibid.
58. Ibid., 260–261.
59. Ibid., 261.
60. Ibid., 328.
61. Ibid.
62. Ibid., 275.
63. Ibid., 281.
64. Ibid., 4.
65. Ibid., 410.
66. Ibid., 327.
67. Ibid.
68. Ibid., 328–329.
69. Ibid., 392.
70. Ibid., 5.
71. Ibid., 290.
72. Ibid., 332.
73. Ibid., 377.
74. Ibid., 423.
75. Ibid., 381.
76. Ibid., 307 It should be pointed out that evil according to the Augustinian understanding on which Milbank draws are thought to be an absence of the good, and thus having no being. Consequently Milbank argues that "only Catholic Christianity can be completely 'positivist', since it understands all evil and violence in their negativity to be privation." (xvi).
77. Ibid., 383.
78. Ibid., 331.
79. Gavin Hyman "John Milbank and Nihilism: A Metaphysical (mis) Reading?," *Literature and Theology* 14, no. 4 (2000): 432.
80. Milbank, *Theology and Social Theory*, xvi.
81. Ibid., xxi.
82. John Milbank "Liberality versus Liberalism" in Milbank, *The Future of Love*, 242.
83. John Milbank "Liberality versus Liberalism" in ibid., 242–243.
84. John Milbank "Liberality versus Liberalism" in ibid., 243–244.
85. Milbank, *Theology and Social Theory*, 30–31.
86. John Milbank "Liberality versus Liberalism" in Milbank, *The Future of Love*, 244.
87. Milbank, *The Word Made Strange*, 275.
88. John Milbank "Liberality versus Liberalism" in Milbank, *The Future of Love*, 248; According to the principle of subsidiarity "a community of a higher order should not interfere in the internal life of a community of a lower order, depriving the latter of its functions, but rather should support it in case of need and help to coordinate its activity with the activities of

the rest of society, always with a view to the common good." Pope John Paul II "Centesimus Annus, Encyclical Letter," May 1, 1991, para. 48 § 4, http://www.vatican.va/holy_father/john_paul_ii/encyclicals/documents/hf_jp-il_enc_01051991_centesimus-annus_En.html.
89. Milbank, *The Future of Love*, 245.
90. Milbank, *The Word Made Strange*, 279.
91. Milbank's political project is perhaps best described as non-statist socialism, rather than "the limited Christian democracy of so-called Christian-Democratic parties." John Milbank "The Gift of Ruling: Secularization and Political Authority," *New Blackfriars* 85, no. 996 (2004): 231.
92. John Milbank "Liberality versus Liberalism" in Milbank, *The Future of Love*, 245.
93. John Milbank "How Democracy Devolves into Tyranny," *ABC Religion & Ethics (Australian Broadcasting Corporation)*, accessed March 13, 2013, http://www.abc.net.au/religion/articles/2010/07/20/2959228.htm.
94. See for example: Jeffrey Stout, *Democracy and Tradition* (Princeton University Press, 2005), 115, 298; Nico Vorster "The Secular and the Sacred in the Thinking of John Milbank: A Critical Evaluation," *Journal for the Study of Religions and Ideologies* 11, no. 32 (June 25, 2012): 109–131; Herdt "The Endless Construction of Charity."
95. John Milbank and Ben Surino "Theology and Capitalism: An Interview with John Milbank," *The Other Journal*, April 4, 2005, http://theotherjournal.com/2005/04/04/theology-and-capitalism-an-interview-with-john-milbank/.
96. Ibid.
97. Milbank, *Being Reconciled: Ontology and Pardon*, 175.
98. Milbank, *Theology and Social Theory*, 412.
99. John Milbank "Shari'a and the True Basis of Group Rights" in Rex Ahdar and Nicholas Aroney, *Shari'a in the West* (Oxford University Press, 2010), 155.
100. Milbank, *Theology and Social Theory*, 382.
101. Ibid.
102. John Milbank "Red Toryism Is the Best Hope of a New Progressive Politics," *The Guardian*, May 22, 2008, http://www.theguardian.com/politics/2008/may/22/2; Red Toryism is a conservative ideological stream within British politics that seeks to promote communitarianism, localism, and the devolution of powers from the central governments to local communities. See Phillip Blond "Rise of the Red Tories," *Prospect Magazine* 155 (2009), https://www.prospectmagazine.co.uk/magazine/riseoftheredtories/; Milbank also supports "Blue Labour" which is a political tendency within the British Labour Party that advocates the belief that working class voters will be won back to Labour through socially conservative ideas. See, John Milbank "Blue Labour, One-Nation Labour and Postliberalism: A Christian Socialist Reading" (Centre of Theology and Philosophy, Nottingham, November 9, 2012), http://theologyphilosophycentre.co.uk/papers/Milbank_BlueLabour OneNationLabourAndPostliberalism.pdf.
103. Milbank "Red Toryism Is the Best Hope of a New Progressive Politics."
104. John Milbank "Multiculturalism in Britain and the Political Identity of Europe," *International Journal for the Study of the Christian Church* 9, no. 4 (2009): 275.

105. John Milbank "Shari'a and the True Basis of Group Rights" in Ahdar and Aroney, *Shari'a in the West*, 144–145.
106. John Milbank "Shari'a and the True Basis of Group Rights" in ibid., 143.
107. John Milbank "Shari'a and the True Basis of Group Rights" in ibid., 144.
108. John Milbank "Shari'a and the True Basis of Group Rights" in ibid., 154.
109. John Milbank "Shari'a and the True Basis of Group Rights" in ibid., 136.
110. John Milbank "Shari'a and the True Basis of Group Rights" in ibid.
111. John Milbank "Shari'a and the True Basis of Group Rights" in ibid.
112. John Milbank "Shari'a and the True Basis of Group Rights" in ibid., 135.
113. John Milbank "Shari'a and the True Basis of Group Rights" in ibid., 139.
114. John Milbank "Shari'a and the True Basis of Group Rights" in ibid.
115. John Milbank "Shari'a and the True Basis of Group Rights" in ibid., 140.
116. Milbank, *Theology and Social Theory*, xxii.
117. John Milbank "Shari'a and the True Basis of Group Rights" in Ahdar and Aroney, *Shari'a in the West*, 147.
118. John Milbank "Liberality versus Liberalism" in Milbank, *The Future of Love*, 243.
119. John Milbank "Shari'a and the True Basis of Group Rights" in Ahdar and Aroney, *Shari'a in the West*, 147.

5 Becoming and Rhizomatic Pluralism

1. Alan Finlayson, ed., *Democracy and Pluralism: The Political Thought of William E. Connolly* (Taylor & Francis, 2010), 14.
2. William E. Connolly "The Challenge to Pluralist Theory" in Samuel A. Chambers and Terrell Carver, eds., *William E. Connolly: Democracy, Pluralism and Political Theory*, 1st ed. (Routledge, 2007), 24.
3. William E. Connolly, *Identity/Difference: Democratic Negotiations of Political Paradox, Expanded Edition*, Revised (University of Minnesota Press, 2002), xiv.
4. Ibid., 93.
5. William E. Connolly, *The Ethos of Pluralization* (University of Minnesota Press, 1995), 40.
6. Chantal Mouffe, *The Democratic Paradox* (Verso, 2000), 104.
7. William E. Connolly, *Pluralism* (Duke University Press, 2005), 64.
8. Ibid., 123.
9. Ibid., 71–72.
10. Ibid., 73.
11. Ibid., 43.
12. Patrice Haynes, *Immanent Transcendence: Reconfiguring Materialism in Continental Philosophy* (Continuum, 2012).
13. Alan Finlayson, ed., *Democracy and Pluralism: The Political Thought of William E. Connolly*, 1st ed. (T & F Books UK, 2009), 27.
14. Connolly, *A World of Becoming*, 18.
15. Ibid., 19.
16. William E. Connolly "Metaphysics, Method and Faith" (Problems and Methods in the Study of Politics, Yale University, Department of Political Science, December 6, 2002), 12, http://www.yale.edu/probmeth/Connolly.rtf.
17. Connolly, *A World of Becoming*, 17.

18. William E. Connolly, *The Augustinian Imperative: A Reflection on the Politics of Morality* (Rowman & Littlefield, 2002), 1.
19. William E. Connolly, *Capitalism and Christianity, American Style* (Duke University Press, 2008), 69.
20. William E. Connolly, *Why I Am Not a Secularist* (University of Minnesota Press, 1999), 52.
21. Connolly, *The Ethos of Pluralization*, 2.
22. Ibid., 3.
23. Connolly, *Pluralism*, 27.
24. William E. Connolly "Catholicism and Philosophy" in Ruth Abbey, *Charles Taylor* (Cambridge University Press, 2004), 171.
25. William E. Connolly "Catholicism and Philosophy" in ibid.
26. William E. Connolly "Catholicism and Philosophy" in ibid.
27. Connolly, *Capitalism and Christianity, American Style*, 71.
28. Ibid.
29. Ibid., 78.
30. Connolly, *A World of Becoming*, 111.
31. William E. Connolly "Some Theses on Secularism," *ABC Religion & Ethics (Australian Broadcasting Corporation)*, April 7, 2011, http://www.abc.net.au/religion/articles/2011/04/04/3181942.htm.
32. Connolly, *Why I Am Not a Secularist*, 10.
33. Connolly, *Pluralism*, 58.
34. Connolly, *Why I Am Not a Secularist*, 6.
35. Jane Bennett and William E. Connolly "Contesting Nature/Culture: The Creative Character of Thinking," *The Journal of Nietzsche Studies* 24, no. 1 (2002): 148.
36. Ibid.
37. Ibid., 149.
38. Connolly, *Why I Am Not a Secularist*, 20.
39. Connolly, *The Augustinian Imperative*, xix.
40. Connolly, *Why I Am Not a Secularist*, 21.
41. Ibid., 58.
42. Ibid., 19.
43. Ibid., 5.
44. Ibid., 157.
45. Connolly, *Pluralism*, 46.
46. Connolly, *Capitalism and Christianity, American Style*, 77.
47. David Campbell and Morton Schoolman, eds., *The New Pluralism: William Connolly and the Contemporary Global Condition* (Duke University Press Books, 2008), 318.
48. Connolly, *Why I Am Not a Secularist*, 20.
49. Ibid., 6.
50. Ibid., 6–7.
51. Ibid., 19.
52. Ibid., 158.
53. Ibid., 55.
54. Ibid.
55. Connolly, *Why I Am Not a Secularist*, 55.
56. Ibid., 16.

57. Connolly, *Pluralism*, 64.
58. Connolly, *Identity/Difference*, 155.
59. Ibid.
60. Connolly, *The Ethos of Pluralization*, 183.
61. Connolly, *Identity/Difference*, xxix.
62. Connolly, *Why I Am Not a Secularist*, 54.
63. Ibid., 39.
64. Ibid., 184.
65. Ibid., 52.
66. Connolly, *The Ethos of Pluralization*, 5.
67. Ibid., 8.
68. Connolly, *Why I Am Not a Secularist*, 9–10.
69. Ibid., 30.
70. Ibid., 31.
71. Ibid., 32.
72. Ibid., 174.
73. William E. Connolly "White Noise" in Chambers and Carver, *William E. Connolly*, 303.
74. Connolly, *Why I Am Not a Secularist*, 15.
75. Connolly, *The Ethos of Pluralization*, 1.
76. Ibid.
77. William E. Connolly "Beyond Good and Evil: The Ethical Sensibility of Michel Foucault," *Political Theory* 21, no. 3 (August 1, 1993): 377.
78. Connolly, *Identity\Difference*, ix–x.
79. See for example, Diana Coole and Samantha Frost, eds., *New Materialisms: Ontology, Agency, and Politics* (Duke University Press, 2010); Rick Dolphijn and Iris van der Tuin, eds., *New Materialism: Interviews & Cartographies* (Open Humanities Press, 2012); Jane Bennett, *Vibrant Matter: A Political Ecology of Things* (Duke University Press, 2009).
80. Coole and Frost, *New Materialisms*, 7.
81. Ibid., 9.
82. Clayton Crockett and Jeffrey W. Robbins, *Religion, Politics, and the Earth: The New Materialism* (Palgrave Macmillan, 2012), xx.
83. Coole and Frost, *New Materialisms*, 7.
84. William E. Connolly, *The Fragility of Things: Self-Organizing Processes, Neoliberal Fantasies, and Democratic Activism* (Duke University Press, 2013), 7–8.
85. Ibid., 141.
86. Mark Wenman "William E. Connolly: Pluralism without Transcendence," *The British Journal of Politics & International Relations* 10, no. 2 (May 1, 2008): 157.
87. Connolly, *The Fragility of Things*, 169–170.
88. William E. Connolly, *Neuropolitics: Thinking, Culture, Speed* (University of Minnesota Press, 2002), 2.
89. Ibid., 85.
90. Connolly, *A World of Becoming*, 9.
91. Connolly, *Neuropolitics*, xii.
92. Connolly, *A World of Becoming*, 17.
93. Ibid., 70.
94. Ibid., 71–72.

95. Ibid., 71–72.
96. Ibid., 80.
97. Ibid., 43.
98. Ibid., 74–75.
99. Ibid.
100. Ibid., 70.
101. Ibid.
102. Connolly, *The Fragility of Things*, 149–150.
103. William E. Connolly "White Noise" in Chambers and Carver, *William E. Connolly*, 303.
104. William E. Connolly "White noise" in ibid., 304.
105. William E. Connolly "Some Theses on Secularism," *Cultural Anthropology* 26, no. 4 (2011): 649.
106. Connolly, *The Fragility of Things*, 179.
107. Ibid., 172.
108. Connolly, *The Augustinian Imperative*, 149.
109. Connolly, *Capitalism and Christianity, American Style*.
110. William E. Connolly "The Evangelical-Capitalist Resonance Machine," *Political Theory* 33, no. 6 (December 1, 2005): 872.
111. Connolly, *Identity\Difference*, 74.
112. Ibid.
113. Ibid.
114. Connolly, *Why I Am Not a Secularist*, 19.
115. Schoolman and Campbell "Introduction: Pluralism 'Old' and 'New'" in Campbell and Schoolman, *The New Pluralism*, 1.
116. Rawls, *Political Liberalism*.
117. Connolly, *The Ethos of Pluralization*, xiii.
118. Ibid., 4.
119. Ibid., 8.
120. Connolly, *Why I Am Not a Secularist*, 92.
121. Ibid.
122. Ibid.
123. Asad, *Formations of the Secular*, 177.
124. See "Introduction: Rhizome" in Gilles Deleuze and Félix Guattari, *A Thousand Plateaus* (Continuum, 2004), 3–25.
125. Connolly, *Why I Am Not a Secularist*, 185.
126. Connolly, *Pluralism*, 64.
127. Ibid., 65.
128. Connolly, *Why I Am Not a Secularist*, 65.
129. Connolly, *Pluralism*, 41.
130. William E. Connolly "Pluralism and Faith" in Vries and Sullivan, *Political Theologies*, 281.
131. William E. Connolly "Pluralism and Faith" in Vries and Sullivan, *Political Theologies: Public Religions in a Post-Secular World*, 281.
132. Connolly, *Pluralism*, 147.
133. Connolly, *The Augustinian Imperative*, xxiii.
134. Connolly, *The Ethos of Pluralization*, 190.
135. Connolly, *Identity/Difference*, 93.
136. Connolly, *The Fragility of Things*, 133.
137. Connolly, *Identity/Difference*, 180.

138. William E. Connolly "An Interview with William Connolly" in Campbell and Schoolman, *The New Pluralism*, 310.
139. Connolly, *The Ethos of Pluralization*, 190.
140. Connolly, *Identity/Difference*, 82.
141. Connolly, *The Ethos of Pluralization*, 189–191.
142. Connolly, *Pluralism*, 123.
143. Connolly, *Why I Am Not a Secularist*, 39.
144. Connolly, *The Ethos of Pluralization*, 93.
145. Connolly "Some Theses on Secularism," 2011, 652.
146. Connolly, *A World of Becoming*, 40–41.
147. Ibid., 41.
148. Connolly, *Pluralism*, 127.
149. Ibid., 26.
150. Ibid., 70.

6 Post-Secular Visions

1. Jürgen Habermas, *Between Naturalism and Religion: Philosophical Essays*, 2.
2. Jürgen Habermas "The Boundary Between Faith and Knowledge" in ibid., 211.
3. Habermas explains this mechanism as follows: "The theory of communicative action detranscendentalises the noumenal realm only to have the idealizing force of context-transcending anticipations settle in the unavoidable pragmatic presuppositions of speech acts, and hence in the heart of ordinary, everyday communicative practice." in Jürgen Habermas, *Between Facts and Norms: Contributions to a Discourse Theory of Law and Democracy* (MIT Press, 1998), 19; For a critique of Habermas account of context-transcendence in relation to the notion of situated rationality, see: Amy Allen "Having One's Cake and Eating It Too" in Calhoun, Eduardo, and VanAntwerpen, *Habermas and Religion* (Cambridge: Polity, 2013).
4. Jürgen Habermas "A Postsecular World Society? On the Philosophical Significance of Postsecular Consciousness and the Multicultural World Society," *The Immanent Frame*, February 3, 2010, 4, http://blogs.ssrc.org/tif/wp-content/uploads/2010/02/A-Postsecular-World-Society-TIF.pdf.
5. Jonathan Z. Smith "Connections" in Jonathan Z. Smith, *On Teaching Religion: Essays by Jonathan Z. Smith* (Oxford University Press, 2013), 54.
6. Hamann argues that "The first purification of reason consisted in the partly misunderstood, partly failed attempt to make reason independent of all tradition and custom and belief in them. The second is even more transcendent and comes to nothing less than independence from experience and its everyday induction [...] The third, highest, and, as it were, empirical purism is therefore concerned with language, the only, first, and last organon and criterion of reason, with no credentials but tradition and usage." Johan George Hamann "Metacritique on the Purism of Reason" in Hamann, *Hamann: Writings on Philosophy and Language*, 207.
7. For an interesting account of idealism and materialism in relation to secularization, see: Wendy Brown "Idealism, Materialism, Secularism?," *The Immanent Frame*, accessed May 16, 2014, http://blogs.ssrc.org/tif/2007/10/22/idealism-materialism-secularism/.

8. See for examples, Connolly, *Pluralism*, 140–141; Connolly, *Capitalism and Christianity, American Style*, 17–18; Taylor, *A Secular Age*, 773; Milbank, *Theology and Social Theory: Beyond Secular Reason*, 305–306; Also, for an interesting account of the theological roots of secularization, see: Gregory, *The Unintended Reformation: How a Religious Revolution Secularized Society*, 25–73; See also, Larry Siedentop, *Inventing the Individual: The Origins of Western Liberalism* (Penguin Books, 2015), 349–363.
9. Luke Bretherton "Sovereignty" in Nicholas Adams, George Pattison, and Graham Ward, *The Oxford Handbook of Theology and Modern European Thought* (Oxford University Press, 2013), 257.
10. A.M Fairwhether, ed., *Nature and Grace: Selections from the Summa Theologica of Thomas Aquinas* (Westminster John Knox Press, 1954), 8; "Grace does not destroy nature but perfects it." – Summa Theologica, Part 1, 1:8.
11. Ibid., 22.
12. For an interesting account of Descartes' nominalism and his assertion that "God could invalidate the most basic mathematical operations, for example, 2 + 1 = 3," see: Funkenstein, *Theology and the Scientific Imagination: From the Middle Ages to the Seventeenth Century*, 117.
13. Connolly, *Capitalism and Christianity, American Style*, 17.
14. Connolly, *Pluralism*, 141.
15. Connolly, *Why I Am Not a Secularist*, 21.
16. Connolly, *Pluralism*, 141.
17. Ibid.
18. Ibid.
19. Ibid., 145.
20. William Connolly "Twilight of the Idols" in Chambers and Carver, *William E. Connolly: Democracy, Pluralism and Political Theory*, 316.
21. William Connolly "Twilight of the Idols" in ibid., 318.
22. William Connolly "Twilight of the Idols" in ibid.
23. Connolly, *Why I Am Not a Secularist*, 187.
24. Taylor, *A Secular Age*, 773.
25. Ibid.
26. Ibid., 317.
27. Ibid., 329.
28. Ibid., 195.
29. "The Theological Construction of Secular Politics" in Milbank, *Theology and Social Theory*, 13–18.
30. Mayra Rivera Rivera "Radical Transcendence? Divine and Human Otherness in Radical Orthodoxy and Liberation Theology" in Rosemary Radford Ruether and Marion Grau, *Interpreting the Postmodern: Responses to "Radical Orthodoxy"* (Continuum International Publishing Group, 2006), 121.
31. Brian Davies and Eleonore Stump, *The Oxford Handbook of Aquinas* (Oxford University Press, 2012), 391.
32. Deleuze argues that "There has only ever been one ontological proposition: Being is univocal. There has only ever been one ontology, that of Duns Scotus, which gave being a single voice. We say Duns Scotus because he was the one who elevated univocal being to the highest point of subtlety, albeit at the price of abstraction." in Deleuze, *Difference and Repetition*, 35.
33. Connolly, *Capitalism and Christianity, American Style*, 132; The notion of "difference in itself" plays a central role for Connolly's account of democracy

and agonism "democracy is a medium through which difference can establish space for itself as alter-identity." in Connolly, *Identity/Difference: Democratic Negotiations of Political Paradox, Expanded Edition*, x.
34. David R. Howarth "Pluralizing methods" in Finlayson, *Democracy and Pluralism: The Political Thought of William E. Connolly*, 24.
35. Giorgio Pini "Univocity in Scotus's Quaestiones Super Metaphysicam: The Solution to a Riddle," *Medioevo* 30 (2005): 2; For an account of the importance of Scotus' concept "univocity of being," see: Gregory, *The Unintended Reformation*, 25–73; For the thesis that this concept was central to the origins of modernity, see: Michael Allen Gillespie, *The Theological Origins of Modernity* (University of Chicago Press, 2008); But cf. "Duns Scotus and Suárez at the Origins of Modernity" in Hankey and Hedley, *Deconstructing Radical Orthodoxy: Postmodern Theology, Rhetoric And Truth*, 65–80.
36. Stephen D. Dumont "Transcendental Being: Scotus and Scotists," *Topoi* 11, no. 2 (1992): 135.
37. Deleuze, *Difference and Repetition*, 37.
38. For an account of Deluzes indebtedness to Scotus, see Nathan Widder "John Duns Scotus" in Graham Jones and Jon Roffe, *Deleuze's Philosophical Lineage* (Edinburgh University Press, 2005).
39. Deleuze, *Difference and Repetition*, 41.
40. Connolly, *Why I Am Not a Secularist*, 160.
41. Connolly, *Identity/Difference*, 65–66.
42. The British philosopher Gavin Hyman argues that "the theological shifts enacted by Duns Scotus and his successors had wide-ranging ramifications, which were felt far beyond the bounds of theology" in Gavin Hyman, *A Short History of Atheism* (I.B. Tauris, 2010), 77; For an account of the philosophical implications of shifts in scholastic thought for modernity, see: Thomas Pfau, *Minding the Modern: Human Agency, Intellectual Traditions, and Responsible Knowledge*, 2013, 133–159; For an account of Scotus that is decidedly more hesitant of linking him to major philosophical shifts connected to modernity, and sharply critical of Radical Orthodoxy's reading, see: Richard Cross "'Where Angels Fear to Tread': Duns Scotus and Radical Orthodoxy," *Antonianum* 76, no. 1 (n.d.): 7–41, accessed November 25, 2012.
43. William E. Connolly "The order of modernity" in Chambers and Carver, *William E. Connolly*, 289.
44. Deleuze, *Difference and Repetition*, 83–84.
45. Milbank, *Theology and Social Theory*, 279.
46. Ibid., 301; Deleuze develops the notion of "difference in itself" along with his homage to Scotus in Chapter 1 in Deleuze, *Difference and Repetition*.
47. Milbank, *Theology and Social Theory*, 308.
48. Connolly, *Capitalism and Christianity, American Style*, 132.
49. Paul Patton, *Deleuze and the Political* (Routledge, 2002), 32.
50. Taylor, *The Ethics of Authenticity*, 51–52; See also Charles Taylor "The Politics of Recognition" in Taylor, *Multiculturalism: Examining the Politics of Recognition*.
51. Taylor, *The Ethics of Authenticity*, 51–52.
52. Taylor explains: "a good test for whether an evaluation is 'strong' in my sense is whether it can be the basis for attitudes of admiration and contempt." in Taylor, *Sources of the Self: The Making of the Modern Identity*, 523, note 2.
53. Milbank, *Theology and Social Theory*, 208–209.
54. Taylor, *A Secular Age*, 774.

55. Ibid., 163, 309.
56. Ibid., 690.
57. Ibid., 713.
58. See for example, Kieran Flanagan "A Secular Age: An Exercise in Breach-Mending," *New Blackfriars* 91, no. 1036 (2010): 699–721; Nicholas H. Smith "Taylor and the Hermeneutic Tradition" in Abbey, *Charles Taylor*.
59. Charles Taylor "Charles Taylor replies" in Flanagan "A Secular Age," 722.
60. Charles Taylor "Charles Taylor replies" in ibid., 723.
61. Gillespie, *The Theological Origins of Modernity*, 4.
62. Ockham famously believed that "only faith gives us access to theological truths. The ways of God are not open to reason, for God has freely chosen to create a world and establish a way of salvation within it apart from any necessary laws that human logic or rationality can uncover." quoted in Dale T. Irvin and Scott Sunquist, *History of the World Christian Movement: Earliest Christianity to 1453* (Orbis Books, 2001), 434.
63. For an account of how Luther was influenced by the *via moderna*, see: Heiko A. Oberman "Luther and the via Moderna: The Philosophical Backdrop of the Reformation Breakthrough," *The Journal of Ecclesiastical History* 54, no. 4 (2003): 641–670; Heiko A. Oberman, *The Reformation: Roots and Ramifications* (Bloomsbury Academic, 2004), 2; See also: John E. Hare, *God and Morality: A Philosophical History* (John Wiley & Sons, 2009), 126.
64. Martin Luther, *Table Talk* (CCEL, 1883), sec. CCCLIII.
65. Roger J. Sullivan, *Immanuel Kant's Moral Theory* (Cambridge University Press, 1989), 6, 262.
66. Habermas, Reder, and Schmidt, *An Awareness of What Is Missing: Faith and Reason in a Post-Secular Age*, 22.
67. Lawrence R. Pasternack, *Routledge Philosophy Guidebook to Kant on Religion within the Boundaries of Mere Reason* (Routledge, 2013), 18.
68. Kant, *Critique of Pure Reason*, B xxx; For an account of Kant's influence on Protestantism, see: Philip Rossi "The Influence of Kant's Philosophy of Religion," *Stanford Encyclopedia of Philosophy*, accessed June 16, 2014, http://plato.stanford.edu/entries/kant-religion/supplement.html.
69. Alister E. McGrath, *Iustitia Dei: A History of the Christian Doctrine of Justification* (Cambridge University Press, 2005), 69.
70. Alister E. McGrath, *Christian Theology: An Introduction* (John Wiley & Sons, 2011), 356.
71. Martin Luther, *Martin Luther, Selections from His Writings* (Doubleday, 1961), 131.
72. Martin Luther "Two Kinds of Righteousness" in ibid., 86.
73. Habermas, *Between Naturalism and Religion*, 242–243.
74. See Jürgen Habermas "The Boundary Between Faith and Knowledge: On the Reception and Contemporary Importance of Kant's Philosophy of Religion," in Habermas, *Between Naturalism and Religion*.
75. Jürgen Habermas "A Postsecular World Society? On the Philosophical Significance of Postsecular Consciousness and the Multicultural World Society".
76. Habermas, Reder, and Schmidt, *An Awareness of What Is Missing*, 18.
77. Thomas Aquinas. Summa Theologica, Part 1, 1:8.

78. For an ambitious account of the theological movement Nouvelle Théologie, see: Hans Boersma, *Nouvelle Théologie and Sacramental Ontology: A Return to Mystery* (OUP Oxford, 2012).
79. Ibid., 90–97.
80. Translation of de Lubac's Surnaturel from: Bryan C. Hollon, *Everything Is Sacred: Spiritual Exegesis in the Political Theology of Henri de Lubac* (Wipf and Stock Publishers, 2009), 86.
81. John Milbank, *The Suspended Middle: Henri de Lubac and the Debate Concerning the Supernatural* (William B. Eerdmans Pub., 2005).
82. Taylor, *A Secular Age*, 773.
83. Ibid., 547.
84. Gilles Deleuze, *Pure Immanence: Essays On A Life* (Zone Books, 2005), 27.
85. Haynes, *Immanent Transcendence: Reconfiguring Materialism in Continental Philosophy*.
86. William E. Connolly, *A World of Becoming* (Duke University Press, 2011), 70.
87. William E. Connolly "Materialities of Experience" in Coole and Frost, *New Materialisms: Ontology, Agency, and Politics*, 198, note 1.
88. Luce Irigaray, *Luce Irigaray: Key Writings* (A&C Black, 2004), 189; Rosi Braidotti, *Metamorphoses: Towards a Materialist Theory of Becoming* (John Wiley & Sons, 2013), 60; Bennett, *Vibrant Matter: A Political Ecology of Things*.
89. Connolly, *Neuropolitics: Thinking, Culture, Speed*, 85; See also: William E. Connolly "The Complexity of Intention," *Critical Inquiry* 37, no. 4 (June 1, 2011): 794.
90. I borrow the term "ethico-political values" from Chantal Mouffe who use the term to denote "specific values that inform the way in which it establishes a particular mode of ordering social relations." Chantal Mouffe "Religion, Politics and Citizenship" in Vries and Sullivan, *Political Theologies: Public Religions in a Post-Secular World*, 321–322.
91. Max Weber "'Objectivity' in social science" in Max Weber, *Max Weber on the Methodology of the Social Sciences* (Free Press, 1949), 58.
92. Max Weber "'Objectivity' in social science" in ibid., 110–111.
93. Jürgen Habermas "Reconciliation Through the Public Use of Reason: Remarks on John Rawls's Political Liberalism," *The Journal of Philosophy* 92, no. 3 (March 1, 1995): 131.
94. Ibid., 130.
95. Connolly, *The Ethos of Pluralization*, 124.
96. Taylor, *Philosophical Arguments*, 61.
97. Charles Taylor "Democratic Exclusion (and Its Remedies?)" in Taylor, *Dilemmas and Connections: Selected Essays*, 143.
98. John Milbank "What Lacks is Feeling" in Calhoun, Eduardo, and VanAntwerpen, *Habermas and Religion*, 331.
99. For an interesting account of the links between Neo-Kantianism and the Weimar republic, see: Frederick Beiser "Weimar Philosophy and the Fate of Neo-Kantianism" in Peter E. Gordon and John P. McCormick, *Weimar Thought: A Contested Legacy* (Princeton University Press, 2013), 119.
100. John Milbank "What Lacks is Feeling" in Calhoun, Eduardo, and VanAntwerpen, *Habermas and Religion*, 332.

Notes

101. Taylor, *Sources of the Self*, x.
102. Robert Stern "Transcendental Arguments," in Edward N. Zalta, *The Stanford Encyclopedia of Philosophy*, Summer 2013, 2013, http://plato.stanford.edu/archives/sum2013/entriesranscendental-arguments/.
103. Charles Taylor "The Validity of Transcendental Arguments" in Taylor, *Philosophical Arguments*, 22.
104. Charles Taylor "The Validity of Transcendental Arguments" in ibid., 25.
105. Charles Taylor "The Validity of Transcendental Arguments" in ibid., 26.
106. Laitinen, *Strong Evaluation without Moral Sources: On Charles Taylor's Philosophical Anthropology and Ethics*, 75–77.
107. Taylor, *Sources of the Self*, 92.
108. Charles Taylor "Iris Murdoch and Moral Philosophy" in Taylor, *Dilemmas and Connections*, 20; See also, Taylor, *A Secular Age*, 438.
109. Abbey, *Charles Taylor*, 211–212.
110. Taylor, *Dilemmas and Connections*, 22.
111. Connolly, *The Ethos of Pluralization*, 15.
112. Ibid., 9.
113. Ibid., 1.
114. Ibid., 16.
115. Connolly, *Why I Am Not a Secularist*, 12, 161.
116. Connolly, *The Ethos of Pluralization*, 188.
117. For an interesting account of Connolly's priority of "becoming" over "being," see: Jeremy Valentine "Time, politics and contingency" in Finlayson, *Democracy and Pluralism*, 203–221.
118. Milbank, *The Word Made Strange: Theology, Language, Culture*, 10–11.
119. Ibid., 112.
120. John Milbank "Only Theology saves Metaphysics: on the Modalities of Terror" in Cunningham and Candler, *Belief and Metaphysics*, 452, note 1.
121. See, Hyman "John Milbank and Nihilism: A Metaphysical (mis) Reading?,", 430–443.
122. Milbank, *Theology and Social Theory*, xvi.
123. John Milbank "The End of Dialogue" in D'Costa, *Christian Uniqueness Reconsidered: The Myth of a Pluralistic Theology of Religions*, 177.
124. John Milbank "The End of Dialogue" in ibid., 189.
125. John Milbank "The End of Dialogue" in ibid.
126. John Milbank "The End of Dialogue" in ibid.
127. John Milbank "The End of Dialogue" in ibid., 177.
128. For an interesting critique of Milbank's account of sociology, see: Hans Joas "Social Theory and the Sacred: A Response to John Milbank," *Ethical Perspectives* 7, no. 4 (2000): 233–243.
129. Connolly, *Identity/Difference*, 160–161.
130. William E. Connolly "An interview with William Connolly" in Chambers and Carver, *William E. Connolly*, 324.
131. Connolly, *Identity/Difference*, 33.
132. Ibid., 159.
133. Charles Taylor "Afterword" in Warner, VanAntwerpen, and Calhoun, *Varieties of Secularism in a Secular Age*, 319.
134. Charles Taylor "Afterword" in ibid.
135. Charles Taylor "Afterword" in ibid., 320.

136. Charles Taylor "The Politics of Recognition" in Taylor, *Multiculturalism*, 33.
137. Charles Taylor "Afterword" in Warner, VanAntwerpen, and Calhoun, *Varieties of Secularism in a Secular Age*, 320.
138. Charles Taylor "Understanding the Other: A Gadamerian View on Conceptual Schemes" in Taylor, *Dilemmas and Connections*, 32–34.
139. Charles Taylor "Understanding the Other" in ibid., 35.
140. Charles Taylor "Understanding the Other" in ibid., 37.
141. Charles Taylor "Understanding the Other" in ibid., 35.
142. Charles Taylor "Understanding the Other" in ibid.
143. Charles Taylor, *Philosophical Papers: Volume 2, Philosophy and the Human Sciences* (Cambridge University Press, 1985), 135–136; Peter Winch "Understanding a Primitive Society," *American Philosophical Quarterly* 1, no. 4 (1964): 307–324; For a critique of Taylor's attempt to overcome incommensurable world-views, see Neil Levy "Charles Taylor on Overcoming Incommensurability," *Philosophy & Social Criticism* 26, no. 5 (September 1, 2000): 47–61.
144. Taylor, *Philosophical Papers*, 147.
145. Ibid., 141–142.
146. Charles Taylor "Understanding the Other" in Taylor, *Dilemmas and Connections*, 36.
147. Charles Taylor "Understanding the Other" in ibid.
148. Charles Taylor "Nationalism and Independence" Canadian Dimension (March 1967):5, quoted in Mark Redhead, *Charles Taylor: Thinking and Living Deep Diversity* (Lanham, Md.: Rowman & Littlefield Pub., 2002), 52.
149. Charles Taylor, *The Pattern of Politics*. (Toronto: McClelland and Stewart, 1971), 124–125; quoted in Smith, *Charles Taylor: Meaning, Morals and Modernity*, 195.
150. Connolly, *Why I Am Not a Secularist*, 32.
151. William E Connolly "A Critique of Pure Politics," *Philosophy & Social Criticism* 23, no. 5 (September 1, 1997): 13.
152. Connolly, *Neuropolitics*, 9.
153. Ibid., 188.
154. John Milbank "The Name of Jesus" in Milbank, *The Word Made Strange*, 153.
155. John Milbank "What Lacks is Feeling. Hume versus Kant and Habermas" in Calhoun, Eduardo, and VanAntwerpen, *Habermas and Religion*, 332.
156. John Milbank "What Lacks is Feeling. Hume versus Kant and Habermas" in ibid.
157. John Milbank "What Lacks is Feeling. Hume versus Kant and Habermas" in ibid., 334.
158. David Hume, *Essays and Treatises on Several Subjects* (A. Millar; and A. Kincaid and A. Donaldson, at Edinburgh, 1758), 460.
159. John Milbank "What Lacks is Feeling. Hume versus Kant and Habermas" in Calhoun, Eduardo, and VanAntwerpen, *Habermas and Religion*, 345–346.
160. John Milbank "What Lacks is Feeling. Hume versus Kant and Habermas" in ibid., 336.
161. John Milbank "What Lacks is Feeling. Hume versus Kant and Habermas" in ibid., 322–346.
162. Connolly, *Neuropolitics*, 25.

190 *Notes*

163. John Milbank "The End of Dialogue" in D'Costa, *Christian Uniqueness Reconsidered*, 181, 187.
164. John Milbank "Liberality versus Liberalism" in Milbank, *The Future of Love: Essays in Political Theology*, 247.
165. John Milbank "Liberality versus Liberalism" in ibid.
166. John Milbank "Postmodern Critical Augustinianism" in ibid., 340.
167. Connolly, *Why I Am Not a Secularist*, 185.
168. Ibid., 9.
169. Taylor's label of "neo-Nietzscheanism" is not aimed to associate those included with fascism, but rather to account for what Taylor sees as Nietzsche's rebellion against "humanism" understood as "a stifling, confining space one has to break out of." The point of the term is to "allow us to recognize that there is an anti-humanism which rebels precisely against the unrelenting concern with life, the proscription of violence, the imposition of equality." This Nietzschean anti-humanism seeks to account for an enhanced conception of life through a negation of life, with a fascination with death and suffering. Taylor here describes this as an 'immanent transcendence'. Taylor, *A Secular Age*, 373, 600.
170. Ibid., 636–637.
171. Ibid., 637.
172. Milbank, *Theology and Social Theory*, 436.
173. Connolly, *Pluralism*, 138.
174. Connolly, *The Ethos of Pluralization*, 93.
175. Ibid., 94.
176. Ibid., 106.
177. Ibid., 178.
178. Ibid., 94.
179. Charles Taylor "The Politics of Recognition" in Taylor, *Multiculturalism*, 72.
180. Taylor, *Sources of the Self*, 27.
181. See for example: John Milbank "Can a Gift Be given? Prolegomena to a Future Trinitarian Metaphysic," *Modern Theology* 11, no. 1 (1995): 119–161; John Milbank "The Ethics of Self-Sacrifice," *First Things*, accessed September 4, 2014, http://www.firstthings.com/article/1999/03/004-the-ethics-of-self-sacrifice.
182. Hubert L. Dreyfus "Taylor's (Anti-) Epistemology" in Abbey, *Charles Taylor*, 2004, 52.
183. René Descartes, *The Philosophical Writings of Descartes: Volume 3, The Correspondence* (Cambridge University Press, 1991), 201.
184. Charles Taylor "Merleau-Ponty and the Epistemological Picture" in Taylor Carman, Mark B.N. Hansen, and Mark Boris Nicola Hansen, *The Cambridge Companion to Merleau-Ponty* (Cambridge University Press, 2005).
185. Charles Taylor "Introduction" in Henry Pietersma, *Merleau-Ponty: Critical Essays* (Center for Advanced Research in Phenomenology, 1989), 1.
186. John. Milbank "The Soul of Reciprocity Part Two: Reciprocity Granted," *Modern Theology* 17, no. 4 (2001): 490.
187. Bennett and Connolly "Contesting Nature/Culture: The Creative Character of Thinking,", 179; Connolly, *A World of Becoming*, 48–51.
188. Bennett and Connolly "Contesting Nature/Culture," 148.
189. Ibid.

190. Ibid.
191. Ibid.
192. Ibid., 152.
193. Ibid., 157; For an account of Connolly's understanding of non-human agency and self-organization, see "Complexity, Agency, and Time" in Connolly, *A World of Becoming*, 17–35.
194. Bennett and Connolly "Contesting Nature/Culture," 157.
195. Charles Taylor "Gadamer on the Human Sciences" in Dostal, *The Cambridge Companion to Gadamer*, 129.
196. Charles Taylor "Gadamer on the Human Sciences" in ibid.
197. Taylor, *A Secular Age*, 171.
198. Nathan Schneider "Orthodox Paradox: An Interview with John Milbank," The Immanent Frame accessed March 27, 2012, http://blogs.ssrc.org/tif/2010/03/17/orthodox-paradox-an-interview-with-john-milbank/.
199. Milbank, *Theology and Social Theory*, 206.
200. Milbank, *Being Reconciled: Ontology and Pardon*, 188.
201. Ibid., 189.
202. Taylor, *Sources of the Self*, 112.
203. Ibid.
204. John Milbank "Culture, Nature, and Mediation « The Immanent Frame," *The Immanent Frame. Secularism, Religion, and the Public Sphere*, accessed January 8, 2013, http://blogs.ssrc.org/tif/2010/12/01/culture-nature-mediation/.
205. Ibid.
206. Ibid.
207. See, Catherine Keller, *The Face of the Deep: A Theology of Becoming* (Routledge, 2003).
208. Connolly, *A World of Becoming*, 107.
209. Connolly, *Neuropolitics*, 3.
210. Milbank "Culture, Nature, and Mediation « The Immanent Frame."
211. For an introduction to the term "world-disclosure," see: Cristina Lafont "Précis of Heidegger, Language, and World-Disclosure," *Inquiry* 45, no. 2 (2002): 185–189.
212. Jürgen Habermas "On Levelling the Genre Distinction between Philosophy and Litterature" in Jürgen Habermas, *The Philosophical Discourse of Modernity* (MIT Press, 1990), 207.
213. William E. Connolly "The 'New Materialism' and the Fragility of Things," *Millennium – Journal of International Studies* 41, no. 3 (June 1, 2013): 400; For a recent account of Connolly's critique of anthropocentrism, see: William E. Connolly and Jairus Victor Grove "The Contemporary Condition: Extinction Events and the Human Sciences," accessed July 5, 2014, http://contemporarycondition.blogspot.co.uk/2014/07/extinction-events-and-human-sciences.html.
214. Connolly "The 'New Materialism' and the Fragility of Things," 400.
215. John Milbank "Faith, Reason, and Imagination" in Milbank, *The Future of Love*, 330.
216. Charles Taylor "The Politics of Recognition" in Taylor, *Multiculturalism*, 73.
217. Taylor, *Sources of the Self*, 95.
218. Connolly, *The Ethos of Pluralization*, 195.
219. Connolly, *Neuropolitics*, 8, 63, 85.

220. Connolly, *The Ethos of Pluralization*, 195.
221. Connolly, *Capitalism and Christianity, American Style*, 121.
222. Glen Lehman "Perspectives on Charles Taylor's Reconciled Society Community, Difference and Nature," *Philosophy & Social Criticism* 32, no. 3 (May 1, 2006): 348.
223. Mark Redhead "Charles Taylor's Nietzschean Predicament A Dilemma More Self-Revealing than Foreboding," *Philosophy & Social Criticism* 27, no. 6 (November 1, 2001): 81–106.
224. Taylor, *Sources of the Self*, 28.
225. Regardless of the misprint/omission in this quote, it is clear that Taylor want to stress that something always has the function of ordering competing goods. Ibid., 95.
226. Ibid., 96.
227. John Milbank "What Lacks Is Feeling: Hume versus Kant and Habermas" in Calhoun, Eduardo, and VanAntwerpen, *Habermas and Religion*, 322.
228. Milbank "What Lacks Is Feeling: Hume versus Kant and Habermas,", 11.
229. Ibid. In the past Milbank has argued that "One should beware of sympathy, because too often we sympathize with what we can make to be like ourselves." see: John Milbank "The End of Dialogue" in D'Costa, *Christian Uniqueness Reconsidered*, 178.
230. Taylor, *A Secular Age*, 694.
231. Ibid., 609.
232. Gavin Hyman "Understanding Secularism by Means of Genealogy" in Brian Black, Gavin Hyman, and Graham M. Smith, *Confronting Secularism in Europe and India: Legitimacy and Disenchantment in Contemporary Times* (Bloomsbury Academic, 2014), 72.
233. John Milbank "Shari'a and the True Basis of Group Rights" in Ahdar and Aroney, *Shari'a in the West*, 139.
234. Charles Taylor "Why we need a radical redefinition of secularism" in Jürgen Habermas et al., *The Power of Religion in the Public Sphere* (Columbia University Press, 2011), 50.
235. John Milbank, *Beyond Secular Order: The Representation of Being and the Representation of the People. Volume 1*, 2014, 253.
236. Ibid., 253–254.
237. Milbank, *Being Reconciled: Ontology and Pardon*, 5; Milbank's depiction of liberal democracy as totalitarian has been severely critiziced. Hans Joas, for example, argues: "whoever calls the Western democracies a more subtle form of totalitarianism, does not know what totalitarianism is." in Hans Joas Joas "Social Theory and the Sacred," 240.
238. Milbank, *The Future of Love*, 342.
239. John Milbank "Postmodern Critical Augustinianism: A Short Summa in Forty Two Responses to Unasked Questions," *Modern Theology* 7, no. 3 (1991): 229.
240. Schneider "Orthodox Paradox: An Interview with John Milbank," The Immanent Frame, *Theology and Social Theory*, 99.
241. John Milbank "Liberality versus Liberalism," in Michael Hoelzl and Graham Ward, *Religion and Political Thought*, (Continuum International Publishing Group, 2006), 253.
242. Milbank, *Theology and Social Theory*, 413.

243. Ibid.
244. Stout, *Democracy and Tradition*, 115.
245. Milbank, *Theology and Social Theory*, 23.
246. Connolly, *Pluralism*, 123–124.
247. Connolly, *Capitalism and Christianity, American Style*, 144.
248. Ibid., 95.
249. Ibid., 94.
250. Taylor, *Sources of the Self*, 517.
251. Ibid., 516–517.
252. William E. Connolly "Catholicism and Philosophy" in Abbey, *Charles Taylor*, 2004, 169.
253. Connolly, *The Augustinian Imperative: A Reflection on the Politics of Morality*, 141–142.
254. Ibid., 142.
255. William E. Connolly "Belief, Spirituality, and Time" in Warner, VanAntwerpen, and Calhoun, *Varieties of Secularism in a Secular Age*, 129.
256. Taylor, *A Secular Age*, 547.
257. Ibid., 607.
258. William E. Connolly "Catholicism and Philosophy – A Nontheistic Appreciation" in Abbey, *Charles Taylor*, 2004, 168–169.
259. William E. Connolly "Catholicism and Philosophy – A Nontheistic Appreciation" in ibid., 169.
260. William E. Connolly "Catholicism and Philosophy – A Nontheistic Appreciation" in ibid.
261. William E. Connolly "Catholicism and Philosophy – A Nontheistic Appreciation" in ibid., 183.
262. William E. Connolly "Catholicism and Philosophy – A Nontheistic Appreciation" in ibid., 166.
263. Charles Taylor "Cross-Purposes: The Liberal-Communitarian Debate" in Nancy L. Rosenblum, *Liberalism and the Moral Life* (Harvard University Press, 1989), 165.
264. William E. Connolly "Catholicism and Philosophy – A Nontheistic Appreciation" in Ruth Abbey, *Charles Taylor* (Cambridge University Press, 2004), 183.
265. By Christendom I intend the cultural hegemony of Christianity as seen as for example in the Middle Ages. In this sense I distinguish between the faith and practice of Christianity, and its cultural and political manifestations.
266. Charles Taylor "Afterword" in Warner, VanAntwerpen, and Calhoun, *Varieties of Secularism in a Secular Age*, 320.
267. John Milbank "The End of Dialogue" in D'Costa, *Christian Uniqueness Reconsidered*, 189.
268. Milbank, *Theology and Social Theory*, 336, 1.
269. Ibid.
270. Ibid., 336.
271. Milbank "Postmodern Critical Augustinianism," 227–228.
272. Taylor, *A Catholic Modernity?: Charles Taylor's Marianist Award Lecture, with Responses by William M. Shea, Rosemary Luling Haughton, George Marsden, Jean Bethke Elshtain*, 16.

273. Taylor "Why We Need a Radical Redefinition of Secularism," in Mendieta and VanAntwerpen, *The Power of Religion in the Public Sphere*, 51.
274. Milbank, "Postmodern Critical Augustinianism," 228.
275. Milbank, *Theology and Social Theory*, 422–423.
276. Ibid., 440.

7 Conclusion

1. Habermas, *Between Naturalism and Religion*, 2.
2. Jürgen Habermas "The Boundary Between Faith and Knowledge" in ibid., 211.
3. Habermas explains this mechanism as follows: "The theory of communicative action detranscendentalises the noumenal realm only to have the idealizing force of context-transcending anticipations settle in the unavoidable pragmatic presuppositions of speech acts, and hence in the heart of ordinary, everyday communicative practice." in Habermas, *Between Facts and Norms*, 19; For a critique of Habermas account of context-transcendence in relation to the notion of situated rationality, see: Amy Allen "Having One's Cake and Eating It Too" in Calhoun, Eduardo, and VanAntwerpen, *Habermas and Religion*.
4. Habermas describes the transcendent power of validity claims as a "thorn in the flesh of social reality" in Cooke, *Language and Reason*, 35.
5. Habermas "A Postsecular World Society? On the Philosophical Significance of Postsecular Consciousness and the Multicultural World Society," 4.
6. Jonathan Z. Smith "Connections" in Smith, *On Teaching Religion*, 54.
7. Hamann argues that "The first purification of reason consisted in the partly misunderstood, partly failed attempt to make reason independent of all tradition and custom and belief in them. The second is even more transcendent and comes to nothing less than independence from experience and its everyday induction [...] The third, highest, and, as it were, empirical purism is therefore concerned with language, the only, first, and last organon and criterion of reason, with no credentials but tradition and usage." Johann George Hamann "Metacritique on the Purism of Reason" in Hamann, *Hamann*, 207.
8. For an interesting account of idealism and materialism in relation to secularization, see: Brown "Idealism, Materialism, Secularism?"
9. Taylor, *A Secular Age*, 213.
10. John Milbank "Transcendence and Materialism" in Creston Davis, John Milbank, and Slavoj Žižek, *Theology and the Political: The New Debate* (Duke University Press, 2005), 393–426.
11. John D. Caputo "The Monstrosity of Christ: Paradox or Dialectic? – A Review," *Notre Dame Philosophical Reviews*, accessed April 17, 2012, http://ndpr.nd.edu/news/24179/?id=17605.
12. See for example: Robert N. McCauley, *Why Religion Is Natural and Science Is Not* (Oxford University Press, 2011); Patrick McNamara, *The Neuroscience of Religious Experience* (Cambridge University Press, 2009); Robert N. Bellah, *Religion in Human Evolution: From the Paleolithic to the Axial Age* (Harvard University Press, 2011); Catherine Malabou, *Plasticity at the Dusk of Writing:*

Dialectic, Destruction, Deconstruction (Columbia University Press, 2013); See also: Adrian Johnston, *Adventures in Transcendental Materialism: Dialogues with Contemporary Thinkers* (Edinburgh University Press, 2014); Crockett and Robbins, *Religion, Politics, and the Earth*.
13. Aaron C. T. Smith, *Thinking about Religion: Extending the Cognitive Science of Religion* (Palgrave Macmillan, 2014), 1.
14. William Edward Arnal and Russell T. McCutcheon, *The Sacred Is the Profane: The Political Nature of Religion* (Oxford University Press, 2012), 183, note 6.
15. For an interesting account of this approach in relation to religious studies, see: Edward Slingerland "Who's Afraid of Reductionism? The Study of Religion in the Age of Cognitive Science," *Journal of the American Academy of Religion* 76, no. 2 (2008): 375–411 This "embodied approach," Slingerhand argues "claims no privileged access to eternal, objective truths, but argues that commonalities of human embodiment in the world can result in a stable body of shared knowledge, verified by proofs based upon common perceptual access," 378.
16. Graham Ward, *Unbelievable: Why We Believe and Why We Don't* (I.B. Tauris, 2014), 221.
17. Markus Dressler and Arvind Mandair, *Secularism and Religion-Making* (Oxford University Press, 2011), 4; For alternative attempts to structure different post-secularisms in clusters of ideas, see: McLennan "The Postsecular Turn" McLennan here labels Connolly as a "Neo-vitalist," and puts Taylor in "the 'religious' end of the spectrum." See also: Beckford "SSSR Presidential Address Public Religions and the Postsecular" Beckford sorts Taylor in the group "Politics, Philosophy, and Theology," and Milbank in the group "A Plague on All Your Houses."
18. Dressler and Mandair, *Secularism and Religion-Making*, 4.
19. Rémi Brague, *The Wisdom of the World: The Human Experience of the Universe in Western Thought* (University of Chicago Press, 2004).
20. Immanuel Kant, *Critique of Practical Reason* (Hackett Publishing, 2002), 203.
21. Brague, *The Wisdom of the World*, 223.
22. Habermas, *Between Naturalism and Religion*, 140.
23. Jürgen Habermas "Discourse Ethics: Notes on Philosophical Justification" in Seyla Benhabib, *The Communicative Ethics Controversy* (MIT Press, 1990), 101.
24. Jürgen Habermas "'The Political' – The Rational Meaning of a Questionable Inheritance of Political Theology" in Habermas et al., *The Power of Religion in the Public Sphere*, 15–33.
25. Donald Wiebe "Religious studies" in John Hinnells, *The Routledge Companion to the Study of Religion* (Routledge, 2009), 121.
26. Russel McCuthcheon "The Study of Religion as an Anthropology of Credibility" in Linell E. Cady and Delwin Brown, *Religious Studies, Theology, and the University: Conflicting Maps, Changing Terrain* (SUNY Press, 2002), 25.
27. Milbank, *Theology and Social Theory*, 54–60; Charles Taylor "Overcoming Epistemology" in Taylor, *Philosophical Arguments*, 1–19; Connolly, *Why I Am Not a Secularist*, 67.
28. Alasdair C. MacIntyre, *Whose Justice? Which Rationality?* (University of Notre Dame Press, 1988), 357.

29. According to Foucault: "Each society has its regime of truth, its general politics of truth: that is the types of discourse which it accepts and makes function as true; the mechanisms and instances which enable one to distinguish true and false statements, the means by which each is sanctioned the techniques and procedures accorded value in the acquisition of truth, the status of those who are charged with saying what counts as true." in Michel Foucault, *Power/Knowledge: Selected Interviews and Other Writings, 1972–1977* (Pantheon Books, 1980), 131.
30. William Desmond, *The Intimate Strangeness of Being: Metaphysics After Dialectic* (CUA Press, 2012), xvii.
31. For an overview of the concept "metaxological," see: Dennis Vanden Auweele "Metaxological 'Yes' and Existential 'No': William Desmond and Atheism," *Sophia* 52, no. 4 (December 1, 2013): 637–655.
32. Taylor, *A Secular Age*, 429, 473; Saba Mahmood "Can Secularism be Otherwise?" in Warner, VanAntwerpen, and Calhoun, *Varieties of Secularism in a Secular Age*, 282–199.
33. John Milbank "The End of Dialogue" in D'Costa, *Christian Uniqueness Reconsidered*.
34. See for example: Connolly, *Capitalism and Christianity, American Style*; Connolly, *The Augustinian Imperative*.
35. Milbank, *Theology and Social Theory*, 207.
36. Ibid., xvi.
37. Taylor, *Philosophical Arguments*, 39.
38. Taylor, *A Secular Age*, 302.
39. William E. Connolly "Method, Problem, Faith" in Ian Shapiro, Rogers M. Smith, and Tarek E. Masoud, *Problems and Methods in the Study of Politics* (Cambridge University Press, 2004), 341.
40. Connolly, *Neuropolitics*, 85.
41. David R. Howarth "Pluralizing methods" in Finlayson, *Democracy and Pluralism*, 2010, 27.
42. William E. Connolly, e-mail message to author, September 12, 2014
43. William E. Connolly "Method, Problem, Faith" in Shapiro, Smith, and Masoud, *Problems and Methods in the Study of Politics*, 342; Connolly, *A World of Becoming*, 74–75.
44. Gavin Hyman "Understanding Secularism by Means of Genealogy" in Black, Hyman, and Smith, *Confronting Secularism in Europe and India*, 72.
45. John Milbank "Shari'a and the True Basis of Group Rights" in Ahdar and Aroney, *Shari'a in the West*, 139.
46. Charles Taylor "Why we need a radical redefinition of secularism" in Habermas et al., *The Power of Religion in the Public Sphere*, 50.
47. Milbank and Surino "Theology and Capitalism: An Interview with John Milbank."
48. William Connolly "Immanence, abundance, democracy" in Lars Tønder and Lasse Thomassen, *Radical Democracy: Politics Between Abundance and Lack* (Manchester University Press, 2005), 239–255.
49. Thomas Nagel, *The View From Nowhere* (Oxford University Press, 1989); Slavoj Žižek, *The Ticklish Subject: The Absent Centre of Political Ontology* (Verso, 1999).
50. Habermas "A Postsecular World Society? On the Philosophical Significance of Postsecular Consciousness and the Multicultural World Society," 4.

Bibliography

Abbey, Ruth. *Charles Taylor*. Acumen, 2000.
———, ed. *Charles Taylor*. Cambridge University Press, 2004.
Adams, Nicholas, George Pattison, and Graham Ward. *The Oxford Handbook of Theology and Modern European Thought*. Oxford University Press, 2013.
Agamben, Giorgio. *The Kingdom and the Glory: For a Theological Genealogy of Economy and Government*. Meridian: Crossing Aesthetics, 2011.
Ahdar, Rex, and Nicholas Aroney. *Shari'a in the West*. Oxford University Press, 2010.
Arnal, William Edward, and Russell T. McCutcheon. *The Sacred Is the Profane: The Political Nature of Religion*. Oxford University Press, 2012.
Asad, Talal. *Formations of the Secular: Christianity, Islam, Modernity*. Stanford University Press, 2003.
———. *Genealogies of Religion. Discipline and Reasons of Power in Christianity and Islam*. Baltimore: The John Hopkins University Press, 1993.
Audi, Robert, and Nicholas Wolterstorff. *Religion in the Public Square: The Place of Religious Convictions in Political Debate*. Rowman & Littlefield Publishers, 2000.
Auweele, Dennis Vanden. "Metaxological 'Yes' and Existential 'No': William Desmond and Atheism". *Sophia* 52, no. 4 (December 1, 2013): 637–55.
Badiou, Alain. *Saint Paul: The Foundation of Universalism*. Stanford University Press, 1997.
Banchoff, Thomas, ed. *Religious Pluralism, Globalization, and World Politics*. Oxford University Press, 2008.
Beckford, James A. "SSSR Presidential Address Public Religions and the Postsecular: Critical Reflections". *Journal for the Scientific Study of Religion* 51, no. 1 (March 1, 2012): 1–19.
Bellah, Robert N. *Religion in Human Evolution: From the Paleolithic to the Axial Age*. Harvard University Press, 2011.
Benhabib, Seyla. *The Communicative Ethics Controversy*. MIT Press, 1990.
Bennett, Jane. *Vibrant Matter: A Political Ecology of Things*. Duke University Press, 2009.
Bennett, Jane, and William E. Connolly. "Contesting Nature/Culture: The Creative Character of Thinking". *The Journal of Nietzsche Studies* 24, no. 1 (2002): 148–63.
Berger, Peter L. *The Desecularization of the World: Resurgent Religion and World Politics*. Wm. B. Eerdmans Publishing, 1999.
Betz, John R. *After Enlightenment: The Post-Secular Vision of J. G. Hamann*. John Wiley & Sons, 2012.
Bhargava, Rajeev. *Secularism and Its Critics*. Oxford University Press, 1998.
Black, Brian, Gavin Hyman, and Graham M. Smith, eds. *Confronting Secularism in Europe and India: Legitimacy and Disenchantment in Contemporary Times*. Bloomsbury Academic, 2014.
Blond, Phillip, ed. *Post-Secular Philosophy: Between Philosophy and Theology*. Routledge, 1998.

———. "Rise of the Red Tories". *Prospect Magazine* 155 (2009). https://www.prospect-magazine.co.uk/magazine/riseoftheredtories/.
Blond, Phillip, and Adrian Pabst. "The Twisted Religion of Blair and Bush – The New York Times". Accessed March 20, 2014. http://www.nytimes.com/2006/03/10/opinion/10iht-edpabst.html?_r=1&.
Blumenberg, Hans. *The Legitimacy of the Modern Age*. MIT Press, 1985.
Boersma, Hans. *Nouvelle Théologie and Sacramental Ontology: A Return to Mystery*. Oxford University Press, Oxford, 2012.
Bolton, Robert. "Plato's Distinction between Being and Becoming". *The Review of Metaphysics* 29, no. 1 (September 1, 1975): 66–95.
Bouchard, Gérard, and Charles Taylor. *Building the Future, a Time for Reconciliation: Abridged Report*. Commission de consultation sur les pratiques d'accomodement reliées aux différences culturelles, 2008.
Braeckman, Antoon. "Habermas and Gauchet on Religion in Postsecular Society. A Critical Assessment". *Continental Philosophy Review* 42, no. 3 (2009): 279–96.
Brague, Rémi. *The Wisdom of the World: The Human Experience of the Universe in Western Thought*. University of Chicago Press, 2004.
Braidotti, Rosi. *Metamorphoses: Towards a Materialist Theory of Becoming*. John Wiley & Sons, 2013.
Brown, Wendy. "Idealism, Materialism, Secularism?" *The Immanent Frame*. Accessed May 16, 2014. http://blogs.ssrc.org/tif/2007/10/22/idealism-materialism-secularism/.
Bryant, Levi, Nick Srnicek, and Graham Harman. *The Speculative Turn: Continental Materialism and Realism*. re.press, 2011.
Bubbio, Paolo Diego, and Paul Redding. *Religion After Kant: God and Culture in the Idealist Era*. Cambridge Scholars Publisher, 2012.
Cady, Linell E., and Delwin Brown. *Religious Studies, Theology, and the University: Conflicting Maps, Changing Terrain*. SUNY Press, 2002.
Calhoun, Craig, Mendieta Eduardo, and Jonathan VanAntwerpen, eds. *Habermas and Religion*. Cambridge: Polity, 2013.
Calhoun, Craig, Mark Juergensmeyer, and Jonathan VanAntwerpen, eds. *Rethinking Secularism*. New York: Oxford University Press, 2011.
———., eds. *Rethinking Secularism*. Oxford University Press, 2011.
Campbell, David, and Morton Schoolman, eds. *The New Pluralism: William Connolly and the Contemporary Global Condition*. Duke University Press Books, 2008.
Candler, Jr., Peter M., and Conor Cunningham. *The Grandeur of Reason: Religion, Tradition and Universalism*. SCM Press, 2010.
Caputo, John D. *On Religion*. London, 2001.
———. "The Monstrosity of Christ: Paradox or Dialectic? – A Review". *Notre Dame Philosophical Reviews*. Accessed April 17, 2012. http://ndpr.nd.edu/news/24179/?id=17605.
Caputo, John D., Gianni Vattimo, and Jeffrey W. Robbins. *After the Death of God*. Columbia University Press, 2009.
Carman, Taylor, Mark B. N. Hansen, and Mark Boris Nicola Hansen. *The Cambridge Companion to Merleau-Ponty*. Cambridge University Press, 2005.
Casanova, José. *Public Religions in the Modern World*. University of Chicago Press, 1994.
Chambers, Samuel A., and Terrell Carver, eds. *William E. Connolly: Democracy, Pluralism and Political Theory*. 1st ed. Routledge, 2007.

Coakley, Sarah. *Faith, Rationality and the Passions*. John Wiley & Sons, 2012.
Cohen, S. Marc. "Aristotle's Metaphysics". In *The Stanford Encyclopedia of Philosophy*, edited by Edward N. Zalta, Summer 2014, 2014. http://plato.stanford.edu/archives/sum2014/entries/aristotle-metaphysics/.
Coles, Romand. *Beyond Gated Politics: Reflections for the Possibility of Democracy*. Minneapolis, MN: Univ of Minnesota Press, 2005.
———. *Rethinking Generosity: Critical Theory and the Politics of Caritas*. Cornell University Press, 1997.
Connolly, William E. "A Critique of Pure Politics". *Philosophy & Social Criticism* 23, no. 5 (September 1, 1997): 1–26.
Connolly, William E. *A World of Becoming*. Duke University Press, 2011.
———. "Beyond Good and Evil: The Ethical Sensibility of Michel Foucault". *Political Theory* 21, no. 3 (August 1, 1993): 365–89.
———. *Capitalism and Christianity, American Style*. Duke University Press, 2008.
———. *Identity\Difference: Democratic Negotiations of Political Paradox, Expanded Edition*. Revised. University of Minnesota Press, 2002.
———. "Metaphysics, Method and Faith". presented at the Problems and Methods in the Study of Politics, Yale University, Department of Political Science, December 6, 2002. http://www.yale.edu/probmeth/Connolly.rtf.
———. *Neuropolitics: Thinking, Culture, Speed*. University of Minnesota Press, 2002.
———. *Pluralism*. Duke University Press, 2005.
———. "Some Theses on Secularism". *Cultural Anthropology* 26, no. 4 (2011): 648–56.
———. "Some Theses on Secularism". *ABC Religion & Ethics (Australian Broadcasting Corporation)*, April 7, 2011. http://www.abc.net.au/religion/articles/2011/04/04/3181942.htm.
———. *The Augustinian Imperative: A Reflection on the Politics of Morality*. Rowman & Littlefield, 2002.
———. "The Complexity of Intention". *Critical Inquiry* 37, no. 4 (June 1, 2011): 791–98.
———. *The Ethos of Pluralization*. University of Minnesota Press, 1995.
———. "The Evangelical-Capitalist Resonance Machine". *Political Theory* 33, no. 6 (December 1, 2005): 869–86.
———. *The Fragility of Things: Self-Organizing Processes, Neoliberal Fantasies, and Democratic Activism*. Duke University Press, 2013.
———. "The 'New Materialism' and the Fragility of Things". *Millennium – Journal of International Studies* 41, no. 3 (June 1, 2013): 399–412.
———. *Why I Am Not a Secularist*. University of Minnesota Press, 1999.
Connolly, William E., and Jairus Victor Grove. "The Contemporary Condition: Extinction Events and the Human Sciences". Accessed July 5, 2014. http://contemporarycondition.blogspot.co.uk/2014/07/extinction-events-and-human-sciences.html.
Coole, Diana, and Samantha Frost, eds. *New Materialisms: Ontology, Agency, and Politics*. Duke University Press, 2010.
Crockett, Clayton. *Radical Political Theology: Religion and Politics After Liberalism*. Columbia University Press, 2011.
Crockett, Clayton, B. Keith Putt, and Jeffrey W. Robbins, eds. *The Future of Continental Philosophy of Religion*. Bloomington: Indiana University Press, 2014.
Crockett, Clayton, and Jeffrey W. Robbins. *Religion, Politics, and the Earth: The New Materialism*. Palgrave Macmillan, 2012.

Cross, Richard. *Duns Scotus*. Oxford University Press, USA, 1999.
——. "'Where Angels Fear to Tread': Duns Scotus and Radical Orthodoxy". *Antonianum* 76, no. 1 (n.d.): 7–41. Accessed November 25, 2012.
Cunningham, Conor, and Peter M. Candler. *Belief and Metaphysics*. SCM Press, 2007.
Dalferth, Ingolf, U. "Post-Secular Society: Christianity and the Dialectics of the Secular". *Journal of the American Academy of Religion* 78, no. 2 (2010): 317.
Davies, Brian, and Eleonore Stump. *The Oxford Handbook of Aquinas*. Oxford University Press, 2012.
Davis, Creston, John Milbank, and Slavoj Žižek. *Theology and the Political: The New Debate*. Duke University Press, 2005.
D'Costa, Gavin. *Christian Uniqueness Reconsidered: The Myth of a Pluralistic Theology of Religions*. Orbis Books, 1990.
D'Costa, Gavin, Malcolm Evans, Tariq Modood, and Julian Rivers. *Religion in a Liberal State*. Cambridge University Press, 2013.
Deleuze, Gilles. *Difference and Repetition*. Continuum International Publishing Group, 2004.
——. *Pure Immanence: Essays on a Life*. Zone Books, 2005.
Deleuze, Gilles, and Félix Guattari. *A Thousand Plateaus*. Continuum, 2004.
De Muckadell, Caroline Schaffalitzky. "On Essentialism and Real Definitions of Religion". *Journal of the American Academy of Religion* 82, no. 2 (2014): 495–520.
Denèfle, Sylvette. *Sociologie de la Secularisation: Être sans-religion en France à la fin du XXe siècle*. Editions L'Harmattan, 1997.
Derrida, Jacques, and Gianni Vattimo. *Religion*. Stanford University Press, 1998.
Descartes, René. *The Philosophical Writings of Descartes: Volume 3, The Correspondence*. Cambridge University Press, 1991.
Desmond, William. *The Intimate Strangeness of Being: Metaphysics After Dialectic*. CUA Press, 2012.
Dolphijn, Rick, and Iris van der Tuin, eds. *New Materialism: Interviews & Cartographies*. Open Humanities Press, 2012.
Dostal, Robert J. *The Cambridge Companion to Gadamer*. Cambridge University Press, 2002.
Dressler, Markus, and Arvind Mandair. *Secularism and Religion-Making*. Oxford University Press, 2011.
Dubuisson, Daniel. *The Western Construction of Religion. Myths, Knowledge, and Ideology*. Baltimore: The John Hopkins University Press, 2007.
Dumont, Stephen D. "Transcendental Being: Scotus and Scotists". *Topoi* 11, no. 2 (1992): 135–48.
Engelhardt, Tristam, and Terry P. Pinkard. *Hegel Reconsidered: Beyond Metaphysics and the Authoritarian State*. Springer, 1994.
Fairweather, A.M, ed. *Nature and Grace: Selections from the Summa Theologica of Thomas Aquinas*. Westminster John Knox Press, 1954.
Finlayson, Alan, ed. *Democracy and Pluralism: The Political Thought of William E. Connolly*. 1st ed. T & F Books UK, 2009.
——., ed. *Democracy and Pluralism: The Political Thought of William E. Connolly*. Taylor & Francis, 2010.
Fitzgerald, Timothy. *Discourse on Civility and Barbarity*. Oxford University Press, 2007.

———. *The Ideology of Religious Studies*. Oxford University Press, 2003.
Flanagan, Kieran. "A Secular Age: An Exercise in Breach-Mending". *New Blackfriars* 91, no. 1036 (2010): 699–721.
Fossum, John Erik. "Deep Diversity versus Constitutional Patriotism Taylor, Habermas and the Canadian Constitutional Crisis". *Ethnicities* 1, no. 2 (June 1, 2001): 179–206.
Foucault, Michel. *Power/Knowledge: Selected Interviews and Other Writings, 1972–1977*. Pantheon Books, 1980.
Franks, Paul W. *All or Nothing: Systematicity, Transcendental Arguments, and Skepticism in German Idealism*. Harvard University Press, 2005.
Funkenstein, Amos. *Theology and the Scientific Imagination: From the Middle Ages to the Seventeenth Century*. Princeton University Press, 1986.
Garsten, Bryan. *Saving Persuasion: A Defense of Rhetoric and Judgment*. Cambridge, Mass.; London: Harvard University Press, 2009.
Gillespie, Michael Allen. *The Theological Origins of Modernity*. University of Chicago Press, 2008.
Gordon, Peter E., and John P. McCormick. *Weimar Thought: A Contested Legacy*. Princeton University Press, 2013.
Gorski, Philip. *The Post-Secular in Question : Religion in Contemporary Society*. New York University Press, 2012.
Gourgouris, Stathis. "Detranscendentalizing the Secular". *Public Culture* 20, no. 3 (September 21, 2008): 437–45.
Gray, John. *Enlightenment's Wake: Politics and Culture at the Close of the Modern Age*. Routledge, 2007.
———. *Two Faces of Liberalism*. Polity Press, 2000.
Gregory, Brad S. *The Unintended Reformation: How a Religious Revolution Secularized Society*. Harvard University Press, 2012.
Groff, Ruth. *Ontology Revisited: Metaphysics in Social and Political Philosophy*. Routledge, 2012.
Habermas, Jürgen. "A Postsecular World Society? On the Philosophical Significance of Postsecular Consciousness and the Multicultural World Society". *Monthly Review*, March 21, 2010. http://mrzine.monthlyreview.org/2010/habermas210310p.html.
———. "A Postsecular World Society? On the Philosophical Significance of Postsecular Consciousness and the Multicultural World Society". *The Immanent Frame*, February 3, 2010. http://blogs.ssrc.org/tif/wp-content/uploads/2010/02/A-Postsecular-World-Society-TIF.pdf.
———. *Between Facts and Norms: Contributions to a Discourse Theory of Law and Democracy*. MIT Press, 1998.
———. Notes on Post-Secular Society *Between Naturalism and Religion: Philosophical Essays*. Polity, 2008.
———. "From Kant to Hegel and Back Again – The Move Towards Detranscendentalization". *European Journal of Philosophy* 7, no. 2 (August 1, 1999): 129–57.
———. *Glauben Und Wissen*. Suhrkamp Verlag, 2001.
———. "Habermas on Faith, Knowledge and 9–11". Paulskirche, Frankfurt, Germany, October 14, 2001. http://www.nettime.org/Lists-Archives/nettime-l-0111/msg00100.html.

———. "Notes on Post-Secular Society". *New Perspectives Quarterly* 25, no. 4 (2008): 17–29.

———. *Postmetaphysical Thinking: Philosophical Essays*. MIT Press, 1994.

———. "Reconciliation Through the Public Use of Reason: Remarks on John Rawls's Political Liberalism". *The Journal of Philosophy* 92, no. 3 (March 1, 1995): 109–31.

———. "Religion in the Public Sphere". *European Journal of Philosophy* 14, no. 1 (2006): 1–25.

———. *The Holberg Prize Seminar 2005, "Religion in the Public Sphere"*. University of Bergen, 2005.

———. *The Philosophical Discourse of Modernity*. MIT Press, 1990.

———. *The Theory of Communicative Action, Vol 1: Reason & the Rationalization of Society*. Beacon Press, 1985.

Habermas, Jürgen, Judith Butler, Charles Taylor, and Cornel West. *The Power of Religion in the Public Sphere*. Columbia University Press, 2011.

Habermas, Jürgen, and Joseph Ratzinger. *The Dialectics of Secularization: On Reason and Religion*. Ignatius Press, 2006.

Habermas, Jürgen, Michael Reder, and Josef Schmidt, S.J. *An Awareness of What Is Missing: Faith and Reason in a Post-Secular Age*. Polity, 2010.

Hamann, Johann Georg. *Hamann: Writings on Philosophy and Language*. Cambridge University Press, 2007.

Hankey, Wayne J., and Douglas Hedley. *Deconstructing Radical Orthodoxy: Postmodern Theology, Rhetoric and Truth*. Ashgate Publishing, Ltd., 2005.

Harding, Sandra. *Objectivity and Diversity: Another Logic of Scientific Research*. University of Chicago Press, 2015.

———. "Secularism, Multiculturalism, and Democracy: Philosophy of Science Issues". Lecture, University of Lethbridge, Canada, September 19, 2013. http://www.lethbridgeliving.com/events/sandra-harding-qsecularism-multiculturalism-and-democracyq.

Harding, Sandra, and Merrill B. Hintikka. *Discovering Reality: Feminist Perspectives on Epistemology, Metaphysics, Methodology, and Philosophy of Science*. Springer, 2003.

Hare, John E. *God and Morality: A Philosophical History*. John Wiley & Sons, 2009.

Harrington, Austin. "Habermas and the 'Post-Secular Society'". *European Journal of Social Theory* 10, no. 4 (November 1, 2007): 543–60.

Haynes, Patrice. *Immanent Transcendence: Reconfiguring Materialism in Continental Philosophy*. Continuum, 2012.

Hekman, Susan. "From Epistemology to Ontology: Gadamer's Hermeneutics and Wittgensteinian Social Science". *Human Studies* 6, no. 1 (December 1, 1983): 205–24.

Herdt, Jennifer A. "The Endless Construction of Charity: On Milbank's Critique of Political Economy". *Journal of Religious Ethics* 32, no. 2 (2004): 301–24.

Hinnells, John. *The Routledge Companion to the Study of Religion*. Routledge, 2009.

Hoelzl, Michael, and Graham Ward. *The New Visibility of Religion: Studies in Religion and Cultural Hermeneutics*. Continuum, 2008.

Hollon, Bryan C. *Everything Is Sacred: Spiritual Exegesis in the Political Theology of Henri de Lubac*. Wipf and Stock Publishers, 2009.

Hume, David. *Essays and Treatises on Several Subjects*. A. Millar; and A. Kincaid and A. Donaldson, at Edinburgh, 1758.

Hyman, Gavin. *A Short History of Atheism*. I.B. Tauris, 2010.
———. "John Milbank and Nihilism: A Metaphysical (mis) Reading?" *Literature and Theology* 14, no. 4 (2000): 430–43.
Irigaray, Luce. *Luce Irigaray: Key Writings*. A&C Black, 2004.
Irvin, Dale T., and Scott Sunquist. *History of the World Christian Movement: Earliest Christianity to 1453*. Orbis Books, 2001.
Joas, Hans. "Social Theory and the Sacred: A Response to John Milbank". *Ethical Perspectives* 7, no. 4 (2000): 233–43.
John Paul II, Pope. "Centesimus Annus, Encyclical Letter", May 1, 1991. http://www.vatican.va/holy_father/john_paul_ii/encyclicals/documents/hf_jp-ii_enc_01051991_centesimus-annus_en.html.
Johnson, Kristen Deede. *Theology, Political Theory, and Pluralism: Beyond Tolerance and Difference*. Cambridge University Press, 2007.
Johnston, Adrian. *Adventures in Transcendental Materialism: Dialogues with Contemporary Thinkers*. Edinburgh University Press, 2014.
Jones, Graham, and Jon Roffe, eds. *Deleuze's Philosophical Lineage*. Edinburgh University Press, 2005.
Kant, Immanuel. *Critique of Practical Reason*. Hackett Publishing, 2002.
———. *Critique of Pure Reason*. Cambridge University Press, 1999.
———. *Critique of the Power of Judgment*. Cambridge University Press, 2000.
Keller, Catherine. *The Face of the Deep: A Theology of Becoming*. Routledge, 2003.
Lafont, Cristina. "Précis of Heidegger, Language, and World-Disclosure". *Inquiry* 45, no. 2 (2002): 185–89.
Laitinen, Arto. *Strong Evaluation without Moral Sources: On Charles Taylor's Philosophical Anthropology and Ethics*. Walter de Gruyter, 2008.
Lash, Nicholas. *The Beginning and the End of "Religion"*. Cambridge University Press, 1996.
Latour, Bruno. "Gifford Lectures: Facing Gaia. Six Lectures on the Political Theology of Nature", February 18, 2013. http://www.ed.ac.uk/about/video/lecture-series/gifford-lectures.
———. *On the Modern Cult of the Factish Gods*. Duke University Press, 2010.
Lehman, Glen. "Perspectives on Charles Taylor's Reconciled Society Community, Difference and Nature". *Philosophy & Social Criticism* 32, no. 3 (May 1, 2006): 347–76.
Levey, Geoffrey Brahm, and Tariq Modood. *Secularism, Religion and Multicultural Citizenship*. Cambridge University Press, 2009.
Levy, Neil. "Charles Taylor on Overcoming Incommensurability". *Philosophy & Social Criticism* 26, no. 5 (September 1, 2000): 47–61.
Lincoln, Bruce. *Religion, Empire, and Torture: The Case of Achaemenian Persia, with a Postscript on Abu Ghraib*. University of Chicago Press, 2010.
Loux, Michael. *Metaphysics: A Contemporary Introduction*. Routledge, 2013.
Lowe, E. J. *An Introduction to the Philosophy of Mind*. Cambridge University Press, 2000.
Löwith, Karl. *Meaning in History: The Theological Implications of the Philosophy of History*. University of Chicago Press, 1957.
Luther, Martin. *Martin Luther, Selections from His Writings*. Doubleday, 1961.
———. *Table Talk*. CCEL, 1883.
MacIntyre, Alasdair C. *Whose Justice? Which Rationality?*. University of Notre Dame Press, 1988.

Maclure, Jocelyn, and Charles Taylor. *Secularism and Freedom of Conscience*. Harvard University Press, 2011.

Malabou, Catherine. *Plasticity at the Dusk of Writing: Dialectic, Destruction, Deconstruction*. Columbia University Press, 2013.

March, Andrew F. "Rethinking Religious Reasons in Public Justification". *American Political Science Review* 107, no. 3 (2013): 523–39.

Mathewes, Charles T. *A Theology of Public Life*. Cambridge University Press, 2007.

McCauley, Robert N. *Why Religion Is Natural and Science Is Not*. Oxford University Press, 2011.

McCutcheon, Russell. *Manufacturing Religion*. New York: Oxford University Press, 1997.

McCutcheon, Russell T. *Manufacturing Religion: The Discourse on Sui Generis Religion and the Politics of Nostalgia*. Oxford University Press, 2003.

McGrath, Alister E. *Christian Theology: An Introduction*. John Wiley & Sons, 2011.

———. *Iustitia Dei: A History of the Christian Doctrine of Justification*. Cambridge University Press, 2005.

McLennan, Gregor. "The Postsecular Turn". *Theory, Culture & Society* 27, no. 4 (July 1, 2010): 3–20.

McNamara, Patrick. *The Neuroscience of Religious Experience*. Cambridge University Press, 2009.

Meillassoux, Quentin, and Ray Brassier. *After Finitude: An Essay on the Necessity of Contingency*. Continuum International Publishing Group, 2010.

Meynell, Robert. *Canadian Idealism and the Philosophy of Freedom: C.B. Macpherson, George Grant, and Charles Taylor*. McGill-Queen's University Press, 2011.

Milbank, John. *Being Reconciled: Ontology and Pardon*. Routledge, 2003.

———. *Beyond Secular Order: The Representation of Being and the Representation of the People. Volume 1*, 2014.

———. "Blue Labour, One-Nation Labour and Postliberalism: A Christian Socialist Reading". Centre of Theology and Philosophy, Nottingham, November 9, 2012. http://theologyphilosophycentre.co.uk/papers/Milbank_BlueLabourOneNationLabourAndPostliberalism.pdf.

———. "Can a Gift Be given? Prolegomena to a Future Trinitarian Metaphysic". *Modern Theology* 11, no. 1 (1995): 119–61.

Milbank, John. "Culture, Nature, and Mediation", The Immanent Frame. *Secularism, Religion, and the Public Sphere*. Accessed January 8, 2013. http://blogs.ssrc.org/tif/2010/12/01/culture-nature-mediation/.

———. "How Democracy Devolves into Tyranny". *ABC Religion & Ethics (Australian Broadcasting Corporation)*. Accessed March 13, 2013. http://www.abc.net.au/religion/articles/2010/07/20/2959228.htm.

Milbank, John. "Liberality versus Liberalism". In *Religion and Political Thought*, edited by Michael Hoelzl and Graham Ward, 225. Continuum International Publishing Group, 2006.

———. "Multiculturalism in Britain and the Political Identity of Europe". *International Journal for the Study of the Christian Church* 9, no. 4 (2009): 268–81.

———. "Postmodern Critical Augustinianism: A Short Summa in Forty Two Responses to Unasked Questions". *Modern Theology* 7, no. 3 (1991): 225–37.

———. "Red Toryism Is the Best Hope of a New Progressive Politics". *The Guardian*, May 22, 2008. http://www.theguardian.com/politics/2008/may/22/2.

———. "Stanton Lecture 1: The Return of Metaphysics in the 21st Century". Item, January 28, 2011. http://www.abc.net.au/religion/articles/2011/01/28/3123584.htm?topic1=home&topic2.

———. "The Ethics of Self-Sacrifice". *First Things*. Accessed September 4, 2014. http://www.firstthings.com/article/1999/03/004-the-ethics-of-self-sacrifice.

———. *The Future of Love: Essays in Political Theology*. Hymns Ancient & Modern Ltd, 2009.

———. "The Gift of Ruling: Secularization and Political Authority". *New Blackfriars* 85, no. 996 (2004): 212–38.

———. *Theology and Social Theory: Beyond Secular Reason*. Wiley-Blackwell, 2006.

Milbank, John. "The Soul of Reciprocity Part Two: Reciprocity Granted". *Modern Theology* 17, no. 4 (2001): 485–507.

Milbank, John. *The Suspended Middle: Henri de Lubac and the Debate Concerning the Supernatural*. William B. Eerdmans Pub., 2005.

———. *The Word Made Strange: Theology, Language, Culture*. Wiley-Blackwell, 1997.

———. "What Lacks Is Feeling: Hume versus Kant and Habermas". *Avello Pulishing Journal* 2, no. 1 (2012).

———. "Without Heaven There Is Only Hell on Earth: 15 Verdicts on Zizek's Response". *Political Theology* 11, no. 1 (2009): 126.

Milbank, John, Catherine Pickstock, and Graham Ward. *Radical Orthodoxy: A New Theology*. Routledge, 2002.

Milbank, John, and Ben Surino. "Theology and Capitalism: An Interview with John Milbank". *The Other Journal*, April 4, 2005. http://theotherjournal.com/2005/04/04/theology-and-capitalism-an-interview-with-john-milbank/.

Milbank, John, Slavoj Žižek, and Creston Davis. *Paul's New Moment: Continental Philosophy and the Future of Christian Theology*. Brazos Press, 2010.

Molendijk, Arie, Justin Beaumont, and Christoph Jedan, eds. *Exploring the Postsecular*. Brill, 2010.

Mouffe, Chantal. *The Democratic Paradox*. Verso, 2000.

Nagel, Thomas. *The View From Nowhere*. Oxford University Press, 1989.

Nynäs, Peter, Mika Lassander, and Terhi Utriainen. *Post-Secular Society*. Transaction Publishers, 2012.

Oberman, Heiko A. "Luther and the via Moderna: The Philosophical Backdrop of the Reformation Breakthrough". *The Journal of Ecclesiastical History* 54, no. 4 (2003): 641–70.

———. *The Reformation: Roots and Ramifications*. Bloomsbury Academic, 2004.

Pabst, Adrian. *Metaphysics: The Creation of Hierarchy*. Wm. B. Eerdmans Publishing Company, 2012.

Paleček, Martin, and Mark Risjord. "Relativism and the Ontological Turn within Anthropology". *Philosophy of the Social Sciences* 43, no. 1 (March 1, 2013): 3–23.

Pasternack, Lawrence R. *Routledge Philosophy Guidebook to Kant on Religion within the Boundaries of Mere Reason*. Routledge, 2013.

Patton, Paul. *Deleuze and the Political*. Routledge, 2002.

Pfau, Thomas. *Minding the Modern: Human Agency, Intellectual Traditions, and Responsible Knowledge*, 2013.

Phillips, D.Z., and Timothy Tessin, eds. *Philosophy of Religion in the 21st Century*. Palgrave Macmillan, 2002.

Pietersma, Henry. *Merleau-Ponty: Critical Essays*. Center for Advanced Research in Phenomenology, 1989.
Pini, Giorgio. "Univocity in Scotus's Quaestiones Super Metaphysicam: The Solution to a Riddle". *Medioevo* 30 (2005): 69–110.
Plato. *Timaeus and Critias*. Oxford University Press, 2008.
Proudfoot, Wayne. *Religious Experience*. University of California Press, 1987.
Rawls, John. *A Theory of Justice*. Harvard University Press, 2009.
——. "Justice as Fairness: Political Not Metaphysical". *Philosophy & Public Affairs* 14, no. 3 (n.d.): 223–51. Accessed May 17, 2012.
——. *Political Liberalism*. Columbia University Press, 2005.
——. "The Idea of an Overlapping Consensus". *Oxford Journal of Legal Studies*, 1987, 1–25.
Redhead, Mark. "Charles Taylor's Nietzschean Predicament A Dilemma More Self-Revealing than Foreboding". *Philosophy & Social Criticism* 27, no. 6 (November 1, 2001): 81–106.
——. *Charles Taylor: Thinking and Living Deep Diversity*. Lanham, Md.: Rowman & Littlefield Pub., 2002.
Robbins, Jeffrey W. "The Problem of Ontotheology: Complicating the Divide Between Philosophy and Theology". *Heythrop Journal* 43, no. 2 (April 2002): 139.
Rorty, Professor Richard, Gianni Vattimo, and Professor Santiago Zabala. *The Future of Religion*. Columbia University Press, 2005.
Rosenblum, Nancy L. *Liberalism and the Moral Life*. Harvard University Press, 1989.
Rossi, Philip. "The Influence of Kant's Philosophy of Religion". *Stanford Encyclopedia of Philosophy*. Accessed June 16, 2014. http://plato.stanford.edu/entries/kant-religion/supplement.html.
Ruether, Rosemary Radford, and Marion Grau. *Interpreting the Postmodern: Responses to "Radical Orthodoxy"*. Continuum International Publishing Group, 2006.
Rupp, George. *Globalization Challenged: Conviction, Conflict, Community*. Columbia University Press, 2013.
Schleiermacher, Friedrich. *Schleiermacher: On Religion: Speeches to Its Cultured Despisers*. Cambridge University Press, 1996.
Schneider, Nathan. "Orthodox Paradox: An Interview with John Milbank", The Immanent Frame. Accessed March 27, 2012. http://blogs.ssrc.org/tif/2010/03/17/orthodox-paradox-an-interview-with-john-milbank/.
Shapiro, Ian, Rogers M. Smith, and Tarek E. Masoud. *Problems and Methods in the Study of Politics*. Cambridge University Press, 2004.
Siedentop, Larry. *Inventing the Individual: The Origins of Western Liberalism*. Penguin Books, 2015.
Sigurdson, Ola. "Beyond Secularism? Towards a Post – secular Political Theology". *Modern Theology* 26, no. 2 (April 1, 2010): 177–96.
Simpson, Christopher Ben. *Religion, Metaphysics, and the Postmodern: William Desmond and John D. Caputo*. Indiana University Press, 2009.
Slingerland, Edward. "Who's Afraid of Reductionism? The Study of Religion in the Age of Cognitive Science". *Journal of the American Academy of Religion* 76, no. 2 (2008): 375–411.
Smith, Aaron C. T. *Thinking about Religion: Extending the Cognitive Science of Religion*. Palgrave Macmillan, 2014.

Smith, Anthony Paul, Pamela Sue Anderson, and Daniel Whistler, eds. *After the Postsecular and the Postmodern: New Essays in Continental Philosophy of Religion*. Cambridge Scholars Publisher, 2011.

Smith, Christian. *Moral, Believing Animals: Human Personhood and Culture*. Oxford University Press, 2003.

Smith, Jonathan Z. *On Teaching Religion: Essays by Jonathan Z. Smith*. Oxford University Press, 2013.

——. *Relating Religion: Essays in the Study of Religion*. University of Chicago Press, 2004.

Smith, Nicholas H. *Charles Taylor: Meaning, Morals and Modernity*. John Wiley & Sons, 2013.

Smith, Steven Douglas. *The Disenchantment of Secular Discourse*. Harvard University Press, 2010.

Stepan, Alfred, and Charles Taylor, eds. *Boundaries of Toleration*. Columbia University Press, 2014.

Stern, Robert. "Transcendental Arguments". In *The Stanford Encyclopedia of Philosophy*, edited by Edward N. Zalta, Summer 2013., 2013. http://plato.stanford.edu/archives/sum2013/entriesranscendental-arguments/.

Stone, Jim. "A Theory of Religion Revised". *Religious Studies* 37, no. 2 (2001): 177–89.

Stout, Jeffrey. *Democracy and Tradition*. Princeton University Press, 2005.

Sullivan, Roger J. *Immanuel Kant's Moral Theory*. Cambridge University Press, 1989.

Taylor, Charles. *A Catholic Modernity?: Charles Taylor's Marianist Award Lecture, with Responses by William M. Shea, Rosemary Luling Haughton, George Marsden, Jean Bethke Elshtain*. Oxford University Press, 1999.

——. *A Secular Age*. Belknap Press, 2007.

——. *Dilemmas and Connections: Selected Essays*. Harvard University Press, 2011.

——. *Hegel*. Cambridge University Press, 1989.

——. *Hegel and Modern Society*. Cambridge University Press, 1977.

——. *Modern Social Imaginaries*. Duke University Press, 2003.

——. *Multiculturalism: Examining the Politics of Recognition*. Edited by Amy Gutmann. Princeton University Press, 1994.

——. *Philosophical Arguments*. Harvard University Press, 1995.

——. *Philosophical Papers: Volume 1, Human Agency and Language*. Cambridge University Press, 1985.

——. *Philosophical Papers: Volume 2, Philosophy and the Human Sciences*. Cambridge University Press, 1985.

——. *Sources of the Self: The Making of the Modern Identity*. Harvard University Press, 1989.

——. *The Ethics of Authenticity*. Harvard University Press, 1991.

——. "The Meaning of 'Post-Secular'". Goethe University, Frankfurt am Main, 2011. http://www.normativeorders.net/de/veranstaltungen/ringvorlesungen/38-veranstaltungen/ringvorlesungen/925-mittwoch-15-juni-2011–18-uhr.

——. *The Pattern of Politics*. Toronto: McClelland and Stewart, 1971.

——. "Two Theories of Modernity". *Hastings Center Report* 25, no. 2 (1995): 24–33. doi:10.2307/3562863.

——. *Varieties of Religion Today: William James Revisited*. Harvard University Press, 2003.

———. "Why We Need a Radical Redefinition of Secularism". In *The Power of Religion in the Public Sphere*, edited by Eduardo Mendieta and Jonathan VanAntwerpen. Columbia University Press, 2011.

The European Court of Human Rights. *French Ban on the Wearing in Public of Clothing Designed to Conceal One's Face Does Not Breach the Convention*. Press Release, July 1, 2014. http://hudoc.echr.coe.int/sites/eng-press/pages/search.aspx?i=003–4809142–5861661#{%22itemid%22:[%22003–4809142–5861661%22]}.

Tocqueville, Alexis de. *Democracy in America*. Library of America, 2004.

Tønder, Lars, and Lasse Thomassen. *Radical Democracy: Politics Between Abundance and Lack*. Manchester University Press, 2005.

Tonner, Philip. *Heidegger, Metaphysics and the Univocity of Being*. Continuum International Publishing Group, 2010.

Vanhoozer, Kevin J. *The Cambridge Companion to Postmodern Theology*. Cambridge University Press, 2003.

Verhey, Allen. *Nature and Altering It*. Wm. B. Eerdmans Publishing, 2010.

Vorster, Nico. "The Secular and the Sacred in the Thinking of John Milbank: A Critical Evaluation". *Journal for the Study of Religions and Ideologies* 11, no. 32 (June 25, 2012): 109–31.

Vries, Hent de. *Religion: Beyond a Concept*. Fordham University Press, 2007.

Vries, Hent de, and Lawrence Eugene Sullivan. *Political Theologies: Public Religions in a Post-Secular World*. Fordham University Press, 2006.

Walzer, Michael. "Drawing the Line: Religion and Politics". *Soziale Welt* 49, no. 3 (January 1, 1998): 295–307.

Ward, Graham. *Unbelievable: Why We Believe and Why We Don't*. I.B.Tauris, 2014.

Warner, Michael, Jonathan VanAntwerpen, and Craig J. Calhoun. *Varieties of Secularism in a Secular Age*. Harvard University Press, 2010.

Weber, Max. *Max Weber on the Methodology of the Social Sciences*. Free Press, 1949.

Wenman, Mark. "William E. Connolly: Pluralism without Transcendence". *The British Journal of Politics & International Relations* 10, no. 2 (May 1, 2008): 156–70.

White, Stephen K. *Sustaining Affirmation: The Strengths of Weak Ontology in Political Theory*. Princeton University Press, 2000.

Williams, Thomas. *The Cambridge Companion to Duns Scotus*. Cambridge University Press, 2003.

Winch, Peter. "Understanding a Primitive Society". *American Philosophical Quarterly* 1, no. 4 (1964): 307–24.

Young, Iris Marion. *Justice and the Politics of Difference*. Princeton University Press, 2011.

Žižek, Slavoj. *Living in the End Times*. Verso, 2011.

———. "Only a Suffering God Can Save Us". Accessed March 17, 2015. http://www.lacan.com/zizshadowplay.html.

———. *The Fragile Absolute Or, Why Is the Christian Legacy Worth Fighting For?*. Verso, 2001.

———. *The Ticklish Subject: The Absent Centre of Political Ontology*. Verso, 1999.

Žižek, Slavoj, John Milbank, and Creston Davis. *The Monstrosity of Christ: Paradox or Dialectic?*. MIT Press, 2009.

Index

Abbey, Ruth, 109
analogia entis, 46
Anselm of Canterbury, 22
Appia, Kwame Anthony, 16
Aquinas, St Thomas, 9, 45, 51, 79, 93, 95, 100, 103
Aristotle, 8, 9, 10, 26, 79, 95, 100, 102
Arnal, William Edward, 141
Asad, Talal, 2, 3, 84
Augustine of Hippo, Saint, 54, 55, 69, 124

Beckford, James, 6
Benedict, *see also* Ratzinger, Joseph
Benedict XVI, Pope, viii, 15, 112
Bennett, Jane, 78, 104
Blumenberg, Hans, 44, 94
Bouchard, Gérard, 37
Bouchard-Taylor Commission, 37–40
Brague, Rémi, 142
Braidotti, Rosi, 104
Bush, George W., 15

Caputo, John, 13, 141
Coles, Romand, x
complexity theory, 68
Comte, Auguste, 23
Connolly, William, 64–90
    agonism, 65, 66, 130, 133
    agonistic respect, 88, 135
    becoming, 78–80
    emergent causality, 68
    identity and difference, 65
    ontopolitical interpretation, 77
corporatism
    Milbank, John, 58
Crockett, Clayton, 7

Dawkins, Richard, 22
de Vries, Hent, 15
Deleuze, Gilles, ix, 56, 64, 76, 82, 84, 96, 97, 98, 103, 104

Derrida, Jacques, 56, 117
Desmond, William, 144
Dubuisson, Daniel, 2

Fitzgerald, Timothy, 2
Foucault, Michel, 3, 54, 64, 69, 76, 82, 109, 117
fundamentalism, iv

Gadamer, Hans-George, 18, 34, 35, 113, 123, 138
Garsten, Bryan, x
Gray, John, 14
great chain of being, 26, 27, 31
Grotius, Hugo, 47

Habermas, Jürgen, iv, v, vi, vii, viii, ix, x, 4, 6, 21, 91, 102, 125, 128, 164
Hamann, Johann Georg, 10, 91, 140
Harding, Sandra, 12
Harrington, Austin, ix
Hegel, George Wilhelm Friedrich, viii, ix, 17, 18
Heidegger, Martin, 9, 18, 51, 125
Heraclitus, 126
Hobbes, Thomas, 47
horizontverschmelzung, 123
Hudson, Wayne, 48
human rights, 15, 36
Hume, David, 115, 128

incommensurability, 123

James, William, 25

Kant, Immanuel, viii, 1, 10, 12, 13, 14, 35, 49, 51, 53, 75, 76, 79, 92, 101, 102, 108, 110, 121, 122
Kuhn, Thomas, 12, 21

Latour, Bruno, 13
Levinas, Emmanuel, 61

Lincoln, Bruce, 15
Lowe, Edward Jonathan, 11
Lubac, Henri de, 103
Luther, Martin, 46, 100, 101, 102

McCutcheon, Russel, 144
MacIntyre, Alasdair, 19, 43, 144
March, Andrew F., x
materialism, 23, 134, 141
   immanent materialism, 64, 104
   new materialism, 78, 79, 104, 133
   non-reductive materialism, 68
   reductive account of materialism, 78
   reductive materialism, 13, 33, 66, 75, 78, 150
   theological materialism, 140
Mathewes, Charles T., 16
Meillassoux, Quentin, 13
Merleau-Ponty, Maurice, 18, 104, 120, 121
metaphysics, 8–14
   analogical metaphysics, 55–56
   immanent metaphysics, 27
   metaxological, 145
micropolitics, 81, 94
Milbank, John, 42–63
   analogical participation, 46, 55, 56, 58, 63
   complex space, 58–60
   corporatism, 60, 61
   harmonious difference, 55
   ontology of violence, 54, 57
   out-narration, 43, 56
   religious group rights, 61–62
Mouffe, Chantal, 65
Murdoch, Iris, 128

Nagel, Thomas, 149
naturalism, iv, v, viii, 18, 80, 129, 134, 146
   immanent naturalism, 67, 68, 81, 89, 96, 134, 146, 147
Nietzsche, Friedrich, 53, 54, 64, 69, 71, 76, 77, 87, 94, 96, 97, 115, 121, 122, 124
nominalism, 46, 50, 93, 94, 95, 101, 103
Nozick, Robert, 135

Ockham, William of, 95, 100, 102, 122
ontological turn, 11
ontology
   ontological turn, ix
   ontopolitics, 69, 77, 109
   ontotheology, 9, 51, 142

Parmenides, 126
Plato, 8, 9, 26, 55, 124, 126
pluralism
   deep pluralism, 66, 73, 85, 118
   liberal pluralism, 16
   organic pluralism, 61
   rhizomatic pluralism, 84, 98, 119
post-humanism, 78, 126, 133
postmetaphysical, vii, viii, ix, xi, 4, 16, 75, 91, 115
post-secularism, 4–8
   Deleuzian post-secularism, 103–105, 149
   French Catholic post-secularism, 103, 104, 149
   protestant post-secularism, 100–102, 104, 149
pure reason, viii, 1, 10, 14, 20, 21, 44, 49, 51, 91, 116
Pyne Addelson, Kathryn, 12

Ratzinger, *see also* Benedict XVI
Ratzinger, Joseph, viii
Rawls, John, iii, vi, x, 16, 21, 36, 37, 69, 83
Red Toryism, 60
religion
   new visibility of, iii
   representational thinking, vii
Rorty, Richard, 13

scientism, iv, v
Scotus, Duns, 9, 10, 44, 46, 48, 51, 52, 95, 96, 97, 99, 101, 102, 103, 122
secular humanism, 118
Shakman Hurd, Elizabeth, 7
Sigurdson, Ola, 6
Smith, James K.A., 7
Smith, Jonathan Z., 14, 91, 140
Smith, Steven D., 6

speculative realism, 13
Spinoza, Baruch, 47, 97, 104
Stout, Jeffrey, 132

Taylor, Charles, 17–41
  buffered self, 95, 122
  immanent frame, 4, 5, 24, 26, 32, 33, 145, 146
  ontic components, 27
  ontological dimension of political thought, 82
  optionality of faith, 23
  overlapping consensus, 37, 36–37
  subtraction stories of secularization, 24, 27
Timaeus, 8
tolerance, i, 14, 30, 60, 61, 63, 65, 66, 88

transcendence
  horizontal transcendence, 147
  immanent transcendence, 67, 80
  mundane transcendence, 81, 134

Vattimo, Gianni, iii, 13
voluntarism, 48, 50

Ward, Graham, 142
Weber, Max, 23, 106
White, Stephen K., 11
Wiebe, Donald, 144
Winch, Peter, 113
Wittgenstein, Ludwig, 18
Wolterstorff, Nicholas, v

Žižek, Slavoj, iii, 5, 12

Printed and bound by CPI Group (UK) Ltd, Croydon, CR0 4YY